The Harvard Entrepreneurs Club
Guide to Starting
Your Own Business

The Harvard Entrepreneurs Club
Guide to Starting
Your Own Business

※ ※ ※ ※

Poonam Sharma

WITH CHAPTERS CONTRIBUTED BY

Ngina Duckett
Anthony Perrault
John Turlais
Steven Chang
Carsten Schwarting
Greg Tseng

**The Harvard Entrepreneurs Club Is a Recognized
Student Organization of Harvard College**

JOHN WILEY & SONS, INC.
New York • Chichester • Weinheim • Brisbane • Singapore • Toronto

Library of Congress Cataloging-in-Publication **Data:**

   The Harvard Entrepreneurs Club guide to starting your own business /
      Poonam Sharma with chapters contributed by Ngina Duckett . . . [et al.].
         p.   cm.
      Includes index.
      ISBN 0-471-32628-3 (pbk. : alk. paper)
      1. New business enterprises—Management.   2. Entrepreneurship.
   3. Success in business.   4. Small business—Management.
   I. Sharma, Poonam, 1977–   . II. Duckett, Ngina.   III. Harvard
   Entrepreneurs Club.
   HD62.5.H3739   1999
   658.4′21—dc21   98-39057

To Renu and Amha P. Sharma:
We've come a long way, Mom and Dad, and I hope I've made
you half as proud as you have made me. But we're just
getting started, right?

Preface

Quite some time ago I began to notice a nationwide trend of college students starting their own businesses. It has been clear for a while that there is a wealth of technical knowledge and enthusiasm coming out of academia. Many successful start-ups in the computer and mass information sectors have been launched by college students and recent graduates, and this is why the phrase "the new Silicon Valley" has been coined to describe the creativity and innovation boom sweeping America's college campuses and taking the corporate world by storm. But I do not attribute the creativity and enthusiasm boom solely to computer wizards and hard-core science majors. On the contrary, it seems pretty clear to me that college students and recent college grads from all walks of academic life (and a broad range of personal interests) have been able to start their own businesses as well.

For over a year, I have had the pleasure of serving as a director of the Harvard Entrepreneurs Club (HEC). In this position, I have been exposed to all manner of entrepreneurship, and I have become keenly aware of the interest students show in the weekly speakers that the club invites to campus. I began to think that this interest was sure to be evidence of a larger trend.

A little research proved to me that there is substantial interest in entrepreneurship all over the country among the college-going population. *Inc.* magazine's March 1998 issue, for example, showcased stories of college students in the process of starting successful businesses. It turns out that there are numerous courses, programs, contests, and clubs that promote entrepreneurship. As interesting and well-intentioned as these programs are, however, they are also usually highly competitive, and do not provide the average college student with a good idea. And there are even fewer outlets for recent college graduates seeking advice on how to get started.

That is when the idea for the *Guide* came to me. In researching other available books and literature, I found that there existed no single manual aimed exclusively at college students and recent grads (i.e., younger people). There are how-to books on starting your own business written for women, minorities, people in Arkansas, people working from home, people on a strict budget, and so on, but no books for the average college kid or recent graduate with a lot of enthusiasm and an innate disposition toward the entrepreneurial spirit. My fellow members of the club board were extremely supportive in this effort, telling me to go ahead and give it a shot. The *Guide* ended up being an exercise in entrepreneurship for me, since I started with an interesting idea, a lot of excitement, and no knowledge whatsoever of the publishing industry. Today, I have arrived at the book you hold in your hands. The process of writing book proposals, outlining chapters, selecting contributors, speaking with publishers and editors, and finally seeing the dream come to fruition has been enormously enlightening, fulfilling, and rewarding.

Entrepreneurship has always been close to home for me. Mom earned her master's degree in economics, and Dad in mechanical engineering. Together they have started businesses ranging from restaurants to real estate, from electrical contracting to assisted living. And there are always more ideas in the house than there are hours in the day. My parents truly are the best examples of entrepreneurship I have found to date, and they make me prouder than they will ever know. Growing up in this environment has been the best exposure to the spirit of entrepreneurship I could ever have asked for. That is where my interest began, and that is where the fuel for this book originated.

Were it not for the encouragement of the executive board of the Harvard Entrepreneurs Club, and of Dean Archie Epps, Susan Cooke, Mike Hamilton at John Wiley & Sons, genuine friends and family who share my joy, and above all, Mom, Dad, and Kavita, this task never would have been accomplished. And of course, eternal thanks to Phillips Exeter, for helping form me intellectually. Taking the time to list everyone whose support has meant so much would fill a book. I thank each and every one of you wholeheartedly. You know who you are.

This book is devoted to the spirit of entrepreneurship. It's not about the money, the power, or the fame. It's about the rush of seeing a dream through from start to finish, and ultimately having no one to thank more for it than yourself.

POONAM SHARMA
Director, HEC
Class of 1999, Economics

Contributors

Ngina Duckett   Chapter 2, "Marketing Your Product"
Class of 2000, Social Studies

Ngina is Vice President of Activities for the Harvard Entrepreneurs Club, and she is founder of Nature's Sweets, which makes all natural pies and pastries.

Anthony Perrault   Chapter 3, "Financing Your Dream"
Class of 1997, Government

Anthony served as president of the Harvard Entrepreneurs Club during his college years. Today, he works for Mercer Management Consulting as a management consultant.

John Turlais   Chapter 4, "The Business Plan"
Class of 1999, Government

John splits his year between attending Harvard in the fall and winter, and playing professional baseball in the spring and summer. After graduation, he hopes to pursue a joint J.D./M.B.A. degree and start his own company.

Steven Chang   Chapter 5, "The Importance of Industry"
Class of 2001, Economics

Steven was valedictorian for James E. Taylor High School, Katy, Texas, 1997.

Carsten Schwarting   Chapter 6, "Protecting Yourself"
Class of 2001, Economics and PreMed

Carsten is Vice President of Publicity for the Harvard Entrepreneurs Club.

Greg Tseng   Chapter 7, "The Faces of Success"
Class of 2001, Physics and Mathematics

Greg is a director of the Harvard Entrepreneurs Club, and has been inducted into the National Gallery of Young Investors.

Contents

꽃꽃꽃꽃

Foreword *by Michael Bloomberg*   xiii

Introduction *by Poonam Sharma*   **1**

    Background and Purpose of the *Guide*   2
    The Harvard Entrepreneurs Club   4
    Reminder: School Regulations   9
    Topics Discussed in the *Guide*   12
    Conclusion   15

1 Think Like an Entrepreneur *by Poonam Sharma*   **16**

    The Qualities of an Entrepreneur   16
    What's the Big Idea?   41
    Myths about the Entrepreneur   47
    Dos and Don'ts   50
    Conclusion   52

2 Marketing Your Product *by Ngina Duckett*   **54**

    What Is a Marketing Strategy?   54
    The Customer: The Center of Your Marketing Strategy   56
    Networking   58
    Marketing Is Dynamic   59
    Steps in the Marketing Strategy   61
    Methods of Marketing   70
    The Marketing Plan: Putting It All Together   76
    Conclusion   80

3 Financing Your Dream *by Anthony Perrault*   **81**

    Venture Capital   83
    Angel Investors   99
    Alternative Financing   104
    Loans   109
    Conclusion   112

4 The Business Plan *by John Turlais*   **113**

   Why a Business Plan Is Necessary   113
   The Goals of a Business Plan   115
   General Tips on Writing a Successful Business Plan   118
   The Business Plan   122
   Conclusion   146

5 The Importance of Industry *by Steven Chang*   **150**

   A Broader Perspective   151
   Competitive Intelligence   158
   Surf's Up: The Industry Climate   167
   Predictability and the Baby Boom   170
   Economics 101   172
   Biz Quiz   174
   Conclusion   174

6 Protecting Yourself *by Carsten Schwarting*   **176**

   Choosing a Legal Structure for Your Business   177
   Copyrights   194
   Patents   195
   Conclusion   197

7 The Faces of Success *by Greg Tseng*   **203**

   Kevin Carlson   204
   Wellie Chao   206
   John Chuang   209
   Ian Eslick   213
   Jacob Farmer   216
   Gregg Favalora   219
   Amar Goel   221
   Krisztina Holly   224
   Mike Itagaki   227
   Joshua Kanter   230
   Conclusion   233

8 The Business Ethic *by Poonam Sharma*   **234**

   What Is a Business Ethic?   234
   Questions You Should Ask Yourself   242
   Conclusion   245

Notes   247

Index   249

Foreword

꘎꘎ ꘎꘎ ꘎꘎ ꘎꘎

Life, as we all know, is unpredictable. Even the best-laid plans fall apart in the face of reality. Better than a rigorous step-by-step strategy, is a vision, an image of goals—but one whose details get filled in step by step as reality is confronted. I speak here from experience; each and every advance I or my company has ever made has been the result of taking small steps we had not previously anticipated.

Presumably you've picked up this book because you want to start your own business, and you're looking for "how to" guidance. Good first step! *The Harvard Entrepreneurs Club Guide to Starting Your Own Business* is a hands-on overview of Entrepreneurship 101. Originally written for college students, the guide has found a much wider audience among aspiring business people determined to make it on their own. The authors, Poonam Sharma and the Harvard Entrepreneurs Club, have drawn a comprehensive outline of the issues and fundamentals of startup entrepreneurship. Here for the budding entrepreneur is information on all the essentials she or he needs to achieve ambitious company creation goals.

The guide is targeted at young entrepreneurs. But this age refers to how experienced one is in getting new ventures going, not one's chronological age. If you're trying to start a business, do not regard yourself as a kid asking permission to get on the playing field with the pros. Think of yourself as a business person who happens to be just slightly more experience deprived than those already there. You have just as much right to be on the playing field as anyone else. You're just a little late in getting started.

Read this book. And let me give you one other piece of advice as you launch your endeavor: Love what you do! I have enjoyed going to the office every morning of my professional life, and have welcomed the opportunities and challenges that each new day has brought. If you love your work, and are willing to put forth the effort it takes (and it takes a lot), and maintain the spirit of entrepreneurship, your venture's got to be a success.

Entrepreneurship is about turning vision into reality. It's about taking an affordable, practical, market-worthy idea all the way from first vague thoughts to company name on a letterhead. It's the process of becoming a member of that elite club: Success on your own!

If you regard this book as your mentor, you'll work your way through some of the early hurdles to be faced in the independent business world. It will make you feel like you got great advice from a trusted friend. *The Guide to Starting Your Own Business* is thought-provoking and insightful. It's a must read.

Best of luck.

MICHAEL BLOOMBERG

August 1998

Introduction

꘠꘠꘠꘠

We are delighted that you have chosen our book as one of your first stepping-stones to success. The *Harvard Entrepreneurs Club Guide to Starting Your Own Business* was conceived in the hopes of sharing and promoting our belief in the possibility of business soon after (or even before) the bachelor's. We will do our best to encourage and educate our readers as to what entrepreneurship is all about.

We are the children of the 1990s. Current college students and recent college grads grew up watching as the yuppies of the '80s realized the folly of their solely money-motivated ways. We have been warned that for women, the glass ceiling in corporate America still exists. We have been conditioned to expect a 90-hour workweek in the first few years out of college—to pay our dues. And at the same time we have been inspired by the story of Bill Gates, a computer geek who dropped out of college and went on to create and conquer the information superhighway. In this age of individualism, we have been encouraged to express ourselves. All of these influences leave us hungry for independence in our lives and control over our futures.

Are you worried about what will happen to you after college? Do you resent the idea of having to work like a dog after college, just because "that's the way it is"? Do you see yourself as a creative person whose ideas and motivation should not go to waste? Or do you simply see a good business opportunity that you want to take advantage of? If you answered yes to any of these questions, then this book is for you. Many college students have good ideas that they just don't try for fear of failing. But the biggest failure, as we see it, is never to have tried. Many recent college grads are dissatisfied in their work, or simply see a good business opportunity but think they are too young to be entrepreneurs. This is exactly the kind of fallacy we want to disprove. Whether you have invented a new software program in your spare time, envisioned a campus pizza delivery service, or identified the need for a job placement agency in your region, your age should not factor into the decision. All you need are the right tools and the right frame of mind—two assets we believe we can provide you with.

We are frustrated by the fact that many bright college students seem to see successful early entrepreneurship as an elusive and unrealistic goal. We don't believe it is ever too early to be a success. A large part of what makes a good entrepreneur is energy and spirit. Many people have that

1

energy and spirit in or shortly after college, and we don't think it should go to waste.

The *Guide* is meant to serve as an introductory survey of the steps involved in the process of successfully starting a business. Targeted specifically at college students and recent grads, the book addresses issues such as financing and business plans in a way you can easily understand, and clearly explains the best options available to you. We aim to encourage you, and lay out the issues you must be prepared to concern yourself with as you strive to be a successful entrepreneur.

Background and Purpose of the *Guide*

There is a growing population of entrepreneurially minded college students who don't want to wait until they are older to start making their dreams a reality. Although precise figures are hard to come by, the article mentions that "rather than partying, many college-goers are settling down to serious business" (p. 20). This increased interest in business and entrepreneurship has been met in part, and is evidenced by, the growing number of courses in entrepreneurship offered at U.S. colleges. In 1997, according to *Inc.* magazine, "an estimated 400 four-year colleges and 600 community colleges offered at least one course in entrepreneurship" (Beck, 1998, p. 52).

Many special programs have also been created through universities and otherwise to encourage the entrepreneurial spirit. For example:

- The University of Iowa recently established and began offering a new Technological Entrepreneurship Certificate. This type of program encourages students, and is an example of where today's youth are or would like to be headed.
- The Washington University Hatchery was founded in 1996 by a professor who wanted to give students the chance to learn from and work with local entrepreneurs as mentors in drafting business plans. The plans are then reviewed and evaluated by an advisory board.
- An initiative by Harvard Student Agencies, called the Let's Grow Contest, encourages students to submit business plans in an annual competition. The winner is awarded $10,000 to be used toward the implementation of his or her plan.
- In 1996 the American Health and Beauty Aids Institute awarded two essay winners from historically black colleges free attendance to its annual Entrepreneurial Leadership Conference.

All of these programs are evidence of the trend, but they do not reach the masses. The important question is, Where is all of this interest in entrepreneurship coming from? The image of the college dropout with a knack for computers who went on to become a computer industry magnate as well as a household name (i.e., Bill Gates) resonates in the minds of college students eager to come up with equally successful ideas. And it's not just the computer geniuses. Students all over the United States, with ideas ranging from delivery services to mail-order pies, from cutting-edge software developments to research outsourcing, want to make their dreams a reality. But they don't know where to start. The foregoing programs are examples of how established forms of encouraging college entrepreneurs necessarily excludes students who simply want to start businesses in their spare time because they recognize a particular niche or a need for a service in their community that has not been addressed.

Purpose

Many students' ideas remain unrealized because the students are put off by the thought of researching the issues of legality, financing, marketing, and so on, which are necessary in any such endeavor. Until now, there has been no sourcebook tailored to the constraints and obstacles facing these young entrepreneurs. The *Guide* is targeted at this audience, and at promoting the entrepreneurial spirit. Its purpose is to bring together all of the necessary information in one comprehensive manual to hopefully show students that their aspirations are possible, realistically manageable, and worth striving toward.

Audience: The *Guide* is not for everyone. We do not hold your hand and walk you through the entire process of a new business start-up. Rather, we explain to you what entrepreneurship involves, laying out some of the entrepreneur's tools and areas of concern, and tell you the stories of 10 successful entrepreneurs.

The *Guide* is meant for highly motivated people with great ideas and good heads on their shoulders, who are capable of balancing two major responsibilities at once. Starting your own business is a major project to undertake at any age. Being an entrepreneur is time-consuming, and you will have little free time, especially if you are also holding down a job. Before deciding to start your own business, consider the following questions, and answer them honestly:

- Can I devote a lot of time to the business without letting my grades or job performance suffer?
- Will I be patient enough to work on the project for months before it takes off?
- Do I have the people skills necessary to establish a successful business?

In order to start a business successfully in college, you must be a go-getter. Are you up for it?

The Harvard Entrepreneurs Club

We thought that since you have entrusted us with the responsibility of your entrepreneurial education, you would like to know a little bit about us: who we are, what we do, and where we believe we as a club are headed.

History

Founded in 1994, the Harvard Entrepreneurs Club (HEC), which can be reached on the web at www.clubhec.org, represents the first effort on Harvard's undergraduate campus to bring the idea of self-employment into the grasp of students here at the college. The *Unofficial Guide to Life at Harvard* (Halliday, 1997) describes the HEC as "an undergraduate organization devoted to exploring issues of entrepreneurship, business management, and the corporate environment. Our aim is to educate students about business by exposing them to entrepreneurs, executives, professionals and professors through a series of seminars, field trips and social events throughout the academic year. Invited speakers address a wide range of interests (venture capital, MBA programs and recruiting) and represent every industry, from beverages to health care to toys" (p. 62).

We have grown substantially from an original core group of a few pioneering students interested in the world of entrepreneurship to the current mailing list of over 300 students. Since its inception, the Harvard Entrepreneurs Club has made its presence known through weekly seminars showcasing CEOs, financiers, and entrepreneurs. From this base, the club has expanded to offer various workshops and informational sessions on such relevant topics as writing a business plan, financing, marketing, and so forth. Aside from this, we have recently added a series of special events that target members of the local community. We have also promoted social functions that bring together the various business-oriented clubs on campus, allowing members to share ideas and perspectives on critical issues pertaining to the world beyond Harvard.

Mission Statement

What follows is the formal statement of purpose for the HEC, as it has evolved over the years.

HEC: *The Voice of Real Business at Harvard*

On a liberal arts campus where economic theory and classes are the closest a motivated and curious student can get to the issues of the real business world, there exists a demand for an organization which can help bridge the gap between the classroom and the boardroom. The Harvard Entrepreneurs Club is devoted to exploring issues of entrepreneurship. Our goal is to act as a resource for students who wish to learn more about business by furnishing links to entrepreneurs, executives, and other professionals through a series of seminars, workshops, field trips, and social events throughout the academic year

The Harvard Entrepreneurs Club attempts to create an opportunity for interested members of the college community at large to share and enhance their understanding of today's business world. We strive to make the best minds and bodies of knowledge available to our members, spanning a broad range of industries and interests. We hope in this way to introduce members to the wealth and breadth of opportunities and avenues which are available for them to explore. We believe that hearing the personal stories of men and women who have succeeded and are succeeding in the business world is crucial to our members' ability to see entrepreneurship as a realistic possibility for themselves. Along those lines, we also try to emphasize the idea of starting your own business. We recognize that companies large and small were started by individuals with an entrepreneurial spirit, and we seek to foster that individualistically entrepreneurial spirit and provide members with the necessary knowledge to pursue their goals. We will work toward accomplishing the goal of reaching our diverse local community through many means: we will be innovative in our projects, creative with our ideas, and above all, informative and substantive in our events. We believe that students from all backgrounds can benefit from the efforts of the HEC, and our challenge will be to dispel the mystery behind business in the real world and make it as accessible as possible to students everywhere.

Executive Board, 1997–1998

Reena N. Rupani	President
Cameron Kinloch	Vice president of seminars
Ngina Duckett	Vice president of activities
Carsten Schwarting	Vice president of publicity
David Park	Vice president of finance
Poonam Sharma	Director
Greg Tseng	Director
Eric Nguyen	Director

Departments

Each department of the HEC encompasses a series of responsibilities and duties. The members of the executive board work with committees of HEC members, to accomplish their goals as stated below.

Seminars: Seminars are the weekly bread-and-butter function of the HEC on campus. We try to maintain variety in the type of speakers we invite, and have been very successful thus far. During our evening meetings, our speakers are free to address any topics they feel may be relevant to our members. Typically, speakers explain a little about the path they took to rise to the level of success they have achieved. They recall some of the obstacles they have faced along the way, and the difficult decisions and trade-offs they have had to make. A question-and-answer session is offered at the end of each seminar, allowing the speakers to make their knowledge and expertise available to attendees in an informal fashion. It is an opportunity for undergraduates to gain access to important executives with whom they otherwise would not have the chance to speak. Students see, through the personal stories of these distinguished speakers, that they, too, can do it.

Activities: We have tried to be innovative in the HEC's efforts to broaden its appeal to a wide audience, and to add variety to hosted events. Toward that end, the activities department has organized field trips to local businesses and offered special workshops on finding financing for your business. In addition, the activities department strives to bring its creativity to bear on the weekly seminars. This is accomplished, for example, by such program enhancements as a guest performance by members of the Harvard-Radcliffe Ballroom Dance Team to supplement a seminar given by the founder of an acoustical consulting firm.

Publicity: Originally, the publicity department was only responsible for the creation and distribution of posters to advertise weekly seminars and events. This was the only vehicle through which the community was privy to information about the HEC and its events. In true entrepreneurial spirit, however, the vice presidents of this department have recently taken publicity to the next level by initiating the design and implementation of a web site. Search the Harvard Home Page at www.harvard.edu, using the keywords "Entrepreneurs Club," for links to HEC pages. Other avenues of publicity include a weekly HEC newsletter, distributed via e-mail to all members. The newsletter provides detailed information on upcoming speakers, panels, workshops, and related points of interest.

Finance: The vice president of finance earns that title above and beyond the title of treasurer for a number of reasons. The Harvard Entrepreneurs Club is about taking initiative and being proactive in what we do. Toward that end, the finance department does more than simply manage the money—this department helps find innovative ways to get the money and to manage it effectively. For example, the department sponsors movie screenings for the college, drafts grant proposals to the university activity office, and supervises the investment of club funds.

Directors: The two elected directors are voting members of the board and are engaged in special projects throughout the year. It is at their discretion which projects the HEC will undertake, and they are expected to be creative and diligent in their efforts to benefit the HEC. They must be self starters who have the ability to aspire toward larger ends. This book is just one of the projects recently undertaken by a director. The position represents an opportunity to use creativity and energy toward a goal with the support and encouragement of the club.

Special Events and Projects

The club has had an exciting year with the help of an extraordinary board in 1997–1998. Here is a sampling of some of the special events and long term projects we have initiated and undertaken:

- *Style '97.* In the fall of 1997, the activities department worked with the directors to coordinate a fashion show to supplement a seminar by two self-employed designers. The theme behind the show was that "fashion is about self-expression of your own style. Being an entrepreneur is about being your own boss. Entrepreneurial fashion designers decide to be their own boss in their own style."

- *HEC web site.* The creation of our own up-to-date web site represents an effort to make our presence known and felt, and to make ourselves available as a resource in the information supermarketplace. We are interested in keeping up with the current state of technology, and have actually begun learning the skills necessary to start a web site almost from scratch. This is proof of the fact that the HEC is dedicated to the idea of hard work and proactive about making our dreams a reality.

- *College liaising.* We feel that our resources can benefit both undergraduate and graduate students, and we wish to encourage all interested people to attend our meetings and be a part of the HEC experience. For this reason, we have begun contacting entrepreneurial organizations on other college and graduate school campuses in order to set up a mutually beneficial network of business-minded students. We feel that by pooling our resources and ideas, we can become an even better source of information and activities for college students everywhere.

- *Business packet.* In an effort to establish meaningful links with respected members of the business community, and to simultaneously enhance our fund-raising efforts, we have recently created a formal HEC business packet. This information folder is our first attempt to directly contact corporations and let them know what we do, in an effort to gain corporate sponsorship. In return for their supportive donations, we offer a wide range of advertising services—on campus, through our newsletter, and on our club web site.

Past Speakers

Here is just a brief sampling of the wide variety of distinguished speakers whom the Harvard Entrepreneurs Club is proud to have attracted to campus:

Speakers from 1997–1998

Louis Kane	CEO and founder, Au Bon Pain
William McDonough	Executive vice president, Boston Federal Reserve Bank
Marvin Traub	Former CEO, president (for 40 years), Bloomingdale's
Jacqueline Morby	Venture capitalist, TA Associates
Angelo Troisi	Senior vice president, entrepreneurial consultant, Lee Hecht Harrison
Thomas Livelli Sr.	Biotech entrepreneur

Speakers from Past Years

Steve Bacque	*Inc.* magazine's 1993 Entrepreneur of the Year
Jill Fadule	Director of Business School Admissions, Harvard Business School
Eliot Feiner	Founder, Boston Chicken; CEO and founder, Brew Moon
Tom First and Tom Scott	Cofounders, Nantucket Allserve (maker of Nantucket Nectars)
Dr. Bob Gaugh	Cofounder, CG & Associates (strategic consulting firm)
Professor Myra Hart	Founding officer, Staples; assistant professor of entrepreneurial management, Harvard Business School
Gary Hirshberg	CEO, cofounder, and president, Stonyfield Farm Yogurt
Erick J. Laine	President and chairman of the board, ALCAS Corp.
Don McLagan	Founder, CEO, and president, Desktop Data, Inc.

Allen Morse — Chairman of the board, Harvard Pilgrim Health Care

Milan Panic — Founder, CEO, president, and Chairman of the Board, ICN Pharmaceuticals; former prime minister (1992–1993), Yugoslavia

Rebecca Mark — CEO, Enron (international energy development company)

Future of the HEC

The recent successes that the Harvard Entrepreneurs Club has enjoyed have served only to increase our enthusiasm for the future. We are excited about all of the plans and projects currently under way, and strive constantly to find new ideas and projects to work with. As we move forward into the twenty-first century, we have a vision of where we would like to be headed. With the support of corporate sponsorships, we hope to expand our range of services and invest in an HEC-based start-up. With the help of our counterparts on other college campuses, we hope to build a national network of business-oriented clubs. With the publicity from this book and our new web site, we hope to begin to expand our area of influence well beyond the confines of these ivy-covered walls. And with the enthusiasm of readers like you, we hope to make a real contribution to student efforts to become entrepreneurs while still in school. We appreciate your faith in the HEC, we support your interest in entrepreneurship, and we encourage your endeavor to strike out on your own and make a name for yourself. There is nothing like the feeling of being your own boss. And much like you, we the Harvard Entrepreneurs Club promise always to seek bigger and better things.

Reminder: School Regulations

When starting a business in college, it is very important to keep in mind that you may be subject to the regulations of your university regarding the right to operate a business, the use of university facilities, and so on. For example, Harvard students are responsible for familiarizing themselves with all of the rules set forth by the college regarding extracurricular activities and businesses. Harvard's *Handbook for Students* (Stewart, 1997) lists specific guidelines for student organizations and clubs. These guidelines pertain to many aspects of starting a business. We include them here to illustrate our point that university policy can be a major factor in your college-based start-up.

General Requirements

There are a number of general requirements under which undergraduate organizations are allowed to operate on Harvard's campus (as adopted by the Committee on College Life). These rules state that organizations must maintain their local autonomy and consult faculty members at the beginning of each term. Members must be students of the university, and all officers must be undergraduates. These organizations may not duplicate the missions of previously existing groups, and they must provide specific documentation for the dean's office. Organizations are required to notify the college of changes in their leadership or constitution. There are many more regulations, and we encourage Harvard students to familiarize themselves with them. The following extracts are from the *Handbook for Students*.

Relations to Harvard University and Radcliffe College

- No organization shall be allowed to appear on a commercially sponsored radio or television program.
- No organization shall in any publication, radio or television broadcast, public performance or otherwise purport to represent the views or opinions of either Harvard University, Radcliffe College, or their student bodies.
- No organization may act so as to endanger the tax-exempt status of either Harvard University or Radcliffe College.
- Until approved, no organization shall be permitted to use the name of "Harvard" or "Radcliffe" or imply through its title or otherwise a connection with the University.
- No organization may be connected with any advertising medium, including the press or other public forum, which makes use of the name of Harvard or Radcliffe.

Solicitation

Solicitation in University buildings and on University property must have prior approval of the proper authority. Permission for each of the following activities must be obtained from the appropriate office:

- Sales of subscriptions.
- All other sales.
- All solicitation must be carried out between the hours of 9:00 A.M. and 9:30 P.M. on weekdays only. Exceptions may be granted by the Office of the Dean of Students.
- Masters may deny permission to carry on the above in their houses.
- Permission of the Dean of Students must be obtained in order to solicit during Registration.

The Use of the Harvard or Radcliffe Name and Logo

The University's Office of Patents, Copyrights and Licensing controls the use of Harvard's name and logo by all commercial companies as well as by Harvard groups and organizations. Students or student organizations interested in using Harvard's name or logo must first receive permission from the Office of the Dean of Students. Those wishing to use the Radcliffe name or logo must also receive permission from the Office of Communications at Radcliffe. Once final approval is secured from the Office of Patents, Copyrights and Licensing, t-shirts, posters, mugs or other approved objects bearing Harvard's name or logo may be produced.

Development

Any organization wishing to raise funds outside the Harvard University Campus whether from an individual or from an organization—must receive prior approval from the Dean of Students. Registered organizations must also obtain permission of the Dean to solicit support from its alumni/ae and may request alumni/ae information for the purpose of development through the Office of the Dean of Students.

Harvard Student Agencies

Harvard Student Agencies (HSA) is an independent corporation managed exclusively by Harvard students. The only University-approved vehicle through which students can operate businesses on the college's campus, HSA offers a tremendous amount of resources and guidance for entrepreneurially minded students. Besides the businesses that it owns and operates, HSA runs an annual business plan competition, the Let's Grow Contest, in which students can gain money and recognition. Their purpose and background are summarized on their web site (http://hsa.net):

> Harvard Student Agencies was born out of Gregory Stone's idea to start a business incorporating the businesses that enterprising students operated out of their dorm rooms, without University supervision. The business formed from the three objectives of: providing employment opportunities to the needy Harvard community, providing valuable services/products to the Harvard community, and providing business experience to students. While fulfilling these objectives, HSA grew into a prosperous business.
>
> Throughout most of its forty-year history, numerous ventures were created to broaden the range of business opportunities available to students. Since HSA's inception it has become the world's largest student-run corporation encompassing eleven agencies and its subsidiary, Let's Go Inc. with over 1,200 student employees. While accomplishing this success, HSA still maintains its founding objective of financing education through student employment and enterprise in its new location at 67 Mount Auburn Street, Cambridge, MA.

While we have done our best to summarize the main campus regulations affecting student-run businesses at Harvard, this section is not meant to serve as a comprehensive account. We advise Harvard students to consult the *Handbook for Students* for more detailed information, and to familiarize themselves with the procedures and rules specifically regarding Harvard Student Agencies, and its relationship to their prospective business. You are urged to contact the appropriate offices and agencies on your campus. Familiarizing yourself with the rules by which you are playing is the best way to make sure that you do everything correctly, right from the start.

Topics Discussed in the *Guide*

This guide represents a very exciting project for us, and is the result of many long hours of blood, sweat, tears, and coffee on the part of the writers of this book. We have exhausted every avenue, consulting hundreds of sources to pull together a highly informative start-up guide. This book is not meant for everyone. We have gone to great lengths to make it user-friendly, and included many anecdotes and examples in order to make it more pleasurable for our readers.

Our intent was to create a guide that lays out all of your options. We wanted to make your transition from mild-mannered college student or college grad to energetic entrepreneur as manageable as possible, by putting all of the basics together into one easy-to-understand manual. Here is a synopsis of what is to come.

Chapter 1: "Think Like an Entrepreneur," by Poonam Sharma

The entrepreneurial spirit is hard to define. It includes optimism, hard work, and a love of business for business' sake, not money's sake. Successful entrepreneurs are not afraid of failure, because they see it as a mere bump in the road. Chapter 1 describes the qualities we have observed in many entrepreneurs so that you may evaluate yourself. The chapter also suggests creative ways to look for business ideas—right in your own backyard. Next, the chapter debunks a few of the common entrepreneurial myths, and explains why they are myths. The chapter concludes with a number of dos and don'ts to keep in mind along the way.

Chapter 2: "Marketing Your Product," by Ngina Duckett

Corporate businesses are those which aim to provide goods and services to other businesses or to the community at large. This requires precise planning and direct research of the particular demographic you intend to target. Campus businesses are those which intend to serve the college community exclusively. This market is more easily targeted but requires an equal amount of research. Chapter 2 explains why your idea may not initially sound as good to customers as it does to you, and why it is important to research the trends in and preferences of your target market. Financing and marketing methods are secondary to the question of whether your product will sell. The consumer is king, so consumer tastes are a major priority. Identifying and targeting these tastes is important. After you have identified your target market, you need to think about marketing methods. The chapter concludes by describing the major components of a marketing plan and how to put your plan together.

Chapter 3: "Financing Your Dream," by Anthony Perrault

Contrary to what Tom Cruise might think, it is not very easy to convince banks to "show you the money." When you are seeking financing, especially as a college student or recent graduate without much in the way of collateral or business expertise, you need to be creative in how you go about looking for money. Chapter 3 describes different sources of financing you can pursue, such as venture capitalists, angel investors, commercial loans, and credit cards, and discusses the pros and cons of each.

Chapter 4: "The Business Plan," by John Turlais

A prerequisite to starting a business today is the writing of a business plan. Far from being only a means by which to raise capital, a well-written business plan serves as a start-up company's blueprint for execution. Within its pages, prospective investors will discover the company's philosophy, plan of action, expected challenges, and hopes for future success. Not ironically, the process of writing a business plan often proves just as revelatory for the young entrepreneur. By researching and outlining the company's market competition, strategies for implementation, and financial predictions, the entrepreneur discovers through the business plan the golden path to vast fortunes and, as the case may be, the potential pitfalls or barriers to entry. Chapter 4 provides you with a step-by-step analysis of each major section of the business plan, helpful hints on writing and researching the various sections, and a sample winning plan. Careful consideration of this material coupled with intense dedication will reward you with a business plan that will both acquire the needed funding for your company and serve as your torch in navigating the business jungle.

Chapter 5: "The Importance of Industry," by Steven Chang

Chapter 5 stresses the importance of research in the industry of your choice before and during the process of launching your start-up. The chapter concerns competition, contacts, and trends. It shows you how to take advantage of the available resources from local libraries, government agencies, and the Internet to have a realistic prediction of how your idea will fit with the industry. Sometimes even the best ideas fail due to poor industry conditions. Keeping abreast of industry trends and being aware of the big picture could mean the success or failure of your business. The chapter explains industry trends and predictability, and concludes with basic information on economics and questions you should ask yourself before you begin conducting industry research.

Chapter 6: "Protecting Yourself," by Carsten Schwarting

Depending on your idea, you may or may not need to think about legal protection. But you do need to consider your business's legal structure. Chapter 6 explains in detail the different ways in which you can legally structure your business, from sole proprietorship to S corporation. It also provides an overview of copyrights and patents, and describes the process of protecting your ideas, including ways that you can save money.

Chapter 7: "The Faces of Success," by Greg Tseng

At this point, your entrepreneur's tool kit is pretty complete. We have supplied you with knowledge on marketing, financing, business plans, industry, and legal issues. Chapter 7 rounds out the *Guide* by presenting the personal stories of students and recent grads who have successfully started their own businesses. The 10 people profiled come from all over the United States. Their businesses range from 3-D display technology to painting services, but the founders have one thing in common: the entrepreneurial spirit. The stories aim to attach real people and real businesses to the ideas and techniques discussed in previous chapters.

Chapter 8: "The Business Ethic," by Poonam Sharma

In the last chapter of the book, we want to leave our readers feeling energized. But it is also important that we leave you thinking realistically. It would be irresponsible of us to baby you—you are young, but not that young. Chapter 8 discusses the key components of a winning business ethic, and encourages an approach to business that is best suited for the college student's lifestyle. There really is no formula for success. Hard work, perseverance, and realistic expectations really do pay off. They are not just catchwords. It takes a confident, realistic, well-prepared individual to deal with the stress of numerous rejections before success actually comes. Setting a timeline for yourself is only half the battle. Some entrepreneurs find instant success, but the majority need to be more patient. The chapter concludes with questions you should ask yourself before you begin your journey on the road to success. Remember, if at first you don't succeed, try, try again.

Conclusion

Now that we have provided you with a brief overview of the topics to be discussed, we hope you enjoy our guide. We bid you a successful trip. Jump in!

Chapter 1

⊰⊱ ⊰⊱ ⊰⊱ ⊰⊱

Think Like an Entrepreneur

A home in the suburbs, 2.5 kids, a dog, two cars, and the expectation of a secure future—this is what Americans dreamed of a generation ago. But we are a different breed with a new American dream: self-employment. Current college students and recent graduates (hereafter referred to as young entrepreneurs) want more than to work for a good company—we want to own the company. There are many of us who want the freedom, independence, and confidence that come with self-employment. The only question that remains is whether we really have what it takes.

The qualities of a successful entrepreneur are hard to isolate and define. It would be impossible to provide a perfect outline. Entrepreneurs come in many different shapes and sizes. This chapter describes some of the qualities we have observed in many successful entrepreneurs. As you read the descriptions, you can evaluate your entrepreneurial potential. But bear in mind, you don't need to have every quality. Entrepreneurs do not fit into a mold. Each has his or her own spirit, and as you read this chapter, it will become clear to you exactly what entrepreneurship involves.

The Qualities of an Entrepreneur

We have observed the following 21 qualities in successful entrepreneurs.

Energy

Can you remember your first lemonade stand? Neither can we. It was years ago. But we see kids going into the business all the time, and we believe that any budding young entrepreneur could learn a lot from their spirit and example. Day in and day out they wait anxiously for customers. When they run out of lemonade, they dash back into the house to stock up. And they refuse to pack up and call it a day until way after dark, no matter how many times Mom calls them in.

The amount of time these kids spend out there is the adult equivalent of about a 12-hour workday, but they don't complain. In fact, they refuse to come inside, because they've got a project that they're excited about, and that gives them endless energy. This is exactly the way you, as a budding entrepreneur, should feel about your idea.

Energy can be defined essentially as the capacity for action. When starting your own business, in the beginning you generally go it alone. And starting while you are in college (or fresh out) is a major undertaking. We applaud you for your motivation, and wish you the best of success, but our task at hand is to prepare you for the task ahead. A serious start-up entrepreneur may need to devote anywhere from 20 to 90 hours a week to his or her project for months before seeing any monetary profit.

Rest assured, however, that success is a pretty direct function of hard work. Your dedication will be rewarded as long as your energy is plentiful enough to fuel your dreams. As an entrepreneur you should have at times what feels like the energy of an entire office staff, since when you decide to start your own business, you *are* the office.

Novelty

Do you remember the Cabbage Patch Kids? How about the charm necklace? And have you noticed the recent bindi craze? What do they all have in common? Their novelty and originality. *Webster's New World Dictionary and Thesaurus* (1996) defines *novelty* as "something popular because it is new." All three of the foregoing examples are slight variations on established products but each was introduced by a clever entrepreneur who had a particular market in mind. Hence, as most members of our generation will remember, virtually every Toys "R" Us in the country had long waiting lists with the names of loving, indulgent parents anxious to spend lots of money on a doll whose only special feature was that it came with an adoption certificate.

Likewise, some business-minded, pop culture–oriented entrepreneur recognized the popularity of the lead singer of the band No Doubt, and decided to capitalize on the adoration of her fans. Anticipating the crazed hordes of identity-seeking, MTV-worshiping, teenage pop singer wannabes, the entrepreneur took a centuries-old Indian cosmetic tradition—the Bindi, a simple dot placed in the middle of the forehead—mass-produced and packaged it, and now sells it at ridiculously high prices. In India you can buy the same bindis for pennies.

The point is that a novel and successful idea can come in one of two forms: either as an entirely new invention, or simply one that is original enough to catch people's attention—even if it isn't entirely novel. A true entrepreneur is able to identify the specific selling points of a product that make it unique, different from what came before, and/or better than whatever else is available.

It has been said that "there is nothing new under the sun except that which has been forgotten." Well, we beg to differ. We say that there is nothing new under the sun except that which remains to be reinvented. Novelty and originality are key components of any successful entrepreneurial game plan.

Time Management

Maybe you love *Seinfeld*. Maybe you also love *The Simpsons*. And maybe you refuse to give them up. We don't believe that means by watching them you're wasting your time. There's a buzzword that is thrown around way too often and inappropriately in the context of college life and time management: *procrastination*. To procrastinate is to put off doing something until later, to delay. But the word has come to bear a very negative connotation over time, as in "to procrastinate is to waste time." And activities like watching television, talking on the phone, or visiting with friends have come to be looked down upon. But that is the wrong way to look at these activities.

When you watch *Seinfeld*, you are devoting a part of the day to relaxation and slowing down. You're not watching *Seinfeld* because you don't want to write a paper, you're watching because you want to—and you have every intention of writing your paper afterward. You *planned* it that way—and planning is what effective time management is really all about. You manage your time effectively enough to have playtime, work time, relaxation time, and even planning time.

Successful entrepreneurs are effective time managers, but not tireless, boring robots. Entrepreneurs are actually some of the most interesting people you will ever meet. Because of their unique ability to balance work and fun in a productive and exciting way, they are actually very well rounded people. They plan their schedules according to what needs to get done, allowing time for fun and relaxation because they recognize it as an essential part of the day. Procrastination, as it has come to be called for lack of a better word, is a very necessary part of everyone's day. As a hardworking person you owe it to yourself to procrastinate when you need to relax. Your drive for success should not take over your ability to enjoy life. Effective time management will prevent this from ever happening to you.

A successful young entrepreneur will attempt to attend three classes, write a short paper, check e-mail and voice mail periodically, and go to dinner with friends, all in the course of one day. Time management is an essential skill. Don't feel guilty for taking the time to enjoy yourself. If you have the time to get your work done and to relax as well, you are way ahead of the game already.

Here's a helpful hint on how better to manage your time. Many college students carry a planner around with them. But these are often bulky, cumbersome items that allow only about three square inches of space in which to write down all of the day's appointments. The problem is that there is no room to include all of the little loose ends that need to be tied up. What we suggest is that you keep a planner somewhere in your dorm room, but also jot down a to-do list each night before bed. It may sound like an infantile act, but it is very difficult to carry around in your head all the appointments and loose ends of a day—especially if you are adding the responsibilities of an entrepreneur to your already heavy load of college work. The to-do list is an excellent memory aid—and it's a lot easier to carry around than a planner.

Readiness for Anything

Change. It scares many people. In fact, most people. But stagnation is much scarier to the true entrepreneur than anything else. A true entrepreneur, like yourself, understands that without change there can be no progress, and progress is an integral part of success. Entrepreneurship is not just about setting a goal and achieving it; it is about the excitement of the process. Entrepreneurs are naturally ready for anything, since they see change as opportunity.

Here is an example you will certainly be familiar with. Anyone who has been alive and conscious (and not living under a rock in the desert) for the past 15 years has seen Madonna go through as many hairstyles and colors as there are people in the free world. She went from a Material Girl to an ambitious blonde, and from a fetish-crazed, porn queen, wanna-be serial nudist to an Argentinean national icon. Around the time when her *Sex* book hit the stores, people everywhere were asking, "How far will she go?" But a better question would have been, "What is her next strategy?"

You see, Madonna is a woman who exemplifies the spirit of readiness for anything—the spirit of an entrepreneur. In the constantly changing pop music world, she has managed to maintain top status for decades. Why? Because she recognized early on that the public would soon grow tired of the same old image of the Material Girl. She was marketing a product: her image. Over time she has simply had the foresight to anticipate changing tastes and modify her product accordingly. In her case, the only difference between Madonna and a typical entrepreneur is that she became so well-known that she actually gained the ability to influence and direct consumers' tastes. The premise, however, is the same: change. Not only does she see change as an opportunity, she takes it one step further—she uses it as a tool. In true entrepreneurial fashion, she has always been ready for anything.

While the daily life of a young entrepreneur may be slightly less glamorous, it will be no less uncertain and full of change. And the key is to be ready for anything by always seeing change as opportunity.

Things almost never go exactly as planned. Those well-known Mentos commercials provide a great example. In one particular scene, a young man who appears to be waiting for an interview realizes that he has been sitting on a freshly painted park bench, and has stained his suit. For lack of a better phrase, he decides to make lemonade from the lemons he has been given, by staining the rest of his suit in the same way, making a pattern of pinstripes.

Plans are not meant to be followed to a tee. True entrepreneurs never rely on circumstances; they rely on themselves to make any given set of circumstances work for them.

Effectiveness at Persuasion
❄ ❄ ❄ ❄

"If you want to get an idea across, wrap it up in a person."
—Ralph Bunche, U.S. diplomat and educator

Do you get extensions on papers or office work whenever you want them? Do you always find a way to convince your mother that you are way too busy to come home and visit? Can you talk your way out of anything? Well, that's great for you as a student or employee, but to be a successful entrepreneur you need to be able to talk your way *into* anything. Persuasion is the art of convincing, and it involves a keen sense of exactly who you are dealing with. In entering the world of self-employment, you leave the comfortable, secure realm of student or employee status behind. You go from a world where people always have time for you (e.g., professors' office hours) to a place where they don't even seem to want to know you. As an apparent nonadult in the eyes of many people, you must be aware that you will have to prove yourself constantly to those who don't believe in business before the B.A. (or even soon after it)—and you will come across many such people.

This is why you need to be effective at persuasion. An entrepreneur usually has a new and untested idea. So he or she must be able to make others see the viability and/or usefulness of that idea. On top of that, however, readers of this book have in common the added condition of youth. There are both advantages and disadvantages of this condition. The disadvantage is a lack of experience, and a constant need to "sell yourself." The advantage is the seemingly boundless energy and the optimism of youth. Use it to your benefit. Being young, you haven't yet been jaded by the harsh and humbling realities of life. So take advantage of your optimism. The stars in your eyes are not a weakness. If used properly, they are an asset.

Be optimistic and eager, and show potential investors that *you* are worth the risk. Being of little experience, and little or no collateral, you are selling *yourself* as well as your *idea*. In order to persuade established businesspeople to take you seriously and give you the help you need, follow these guidelines:

■ *Make a good first impression.* Be businesslike from the moment you first speak with anyone regarding your business. Make a solid impression before your age, experience, or education are mentioned. Highlight your ideas. If you maintain a pleasant and professional phone manner, people will be pleasantly surprised when they meet you and see how young you are.

■ *Maintain a sense of formality.* Although you should not assume that people will try to take advantage of you, you should make it clear that you are intelligent and have considered all the issues relevant to any discussion. Maintaining a certain sense of formality long into any business relationship is a good way to make sure you are taken seriously. And the more seriously you are taken, the more open people will be to your persuasion.

■ *Demonstrate logic.* Always present a clear and logical argument to anyone you are trying to persuade of anything. While people may be apprehensive about your lack of experience, no one can argue with sound logic and a good idea.

■ *Think before you speak.* Although you can say whatever you want to your friends, you can't do that in business. You must always take a moment to consider what your next statement will be—because as the representative of a business, your words will be remembered. And they carry more weight than you might expect. Effective and persuasive businesspeople *never* say anything they do not mean.

■ *Acknowledge the people you're trying to persuade.* A large component of persuasion is getting people on your side. People who find you arrogant or disagreeable will not be open to your skills of persuasion, no matter how convincing you are. A good way to make yourself more likable when dealing with older businesspeople is to be the first one to openly acknowledge their expertise and compliment them. For lack of a better phrase, acting awed and buttering them up never hurt anyone in the negotiation game—when done correctly. It makes people comfortable around you. Acknowledge that the people you are dealing with know a lot—because they do. You can use a statement like "I realize that I am not familiar with all of the different aspects of the beverage industry, but am I correct in assuming that _____?" filling in the blank with an intelligent remark. This gesture will simultaneously show that you are humble, that you respect the person's expertise, and that you have done your homework. Overconfidence in young people is often seen as evidence of naïveté. Thoughtful and direct questions are seen as evidence of critical thinking.

Problem-Solving Skills

Webster's New World Dictionary and Thesaurus (1998) defines *problem* as "a question proposed for solution." An entrepreneur sees a problem as a challenge, not a dilemma. It is a call to action, and a successful entrepreneur will jump right into the search for a creative solution.

Recently, the Harvard Entrepreneurs Club had the pleasure of hearing Louis Kane, CEO and founder of Au Bon Pain, give his personal recollection of the process leading up to the founding of the successful bakery chain. The major selling point of Au Bon Pain was to be its freshly baked bread. Toward that end, Kane and his associates recruited a number of French bakers, flew them to the United States, and put them to work in the newly opened stores. The first problem was that there was no uniformity of bread between the stores, since each baker had a personal baking style. This was a major obstacle for a planned nationwide chain. The second problem was that the bakers had to work long, late shifts in order to prepare bread in time for the breakfast crowds.

To remedy the situation, the company hired some consultants-scientists, who were told to develop a recipe for dough that could be prepared and frozen, and kept for periods of time before being taken out and baked to uniform perfection within 20 minutes as needed. And with this new recipe, Au Bon Pain gained the uniform, hassle-free bread-making ability it needed to become successful. The rest is history.

In the daily life of a young entrepreneur, any number of problems could arise, and it takes a lot of creative problem-solving ability to keep everything running smoothly. Here are some examples of situations you could encounter, and some clever solutions:

■ Imagine that you run a baby-sitting agency from your college, and a sitter calls to cancel her assignment only an hour beforehand because she has an emergency dental appointment. Obviously this is not her fault, but it will reflect poorly on your business and hurt your reputation if you are unable to fulfill a planned assignment. Being the clever entrepreneur that you are, you would have a list of backup sitters for each night of the week, for just such an emergency. And to compensate for the lateness, you would call ahead of time to inform your customer that there will be a slight delay. You would also send along a fruit basket to show how much you value your customers' business—and their kids' health.

■ Assume that you operate a delivery business that picks up food from local restaurants (which do not deliver), and delivers it to dorm rooms for a small fee. Now assume that someone else begins competing with you, by providing the same service in the same region. Clever entrepreneur that you are, you would expand your market by distributing flyers to local apartment buildings and stuffing mailboxes, and by offering a guaranteed delivery time.

■ Here's a scenario where you provide a product instead of performing a service. Say that you carve candles into interesting shapes and designs as a type of personalized gift service. Demand for your product increases as special Valentine's Day orders pile in. The problem is that you have been working on your own and don't know anyone else who can carve candles as nicely as you can. You cannot fill the orders by yourself. Being the clever entrepreneur that you are, you would advertise to local art and sculpture students, train them to carve as well as you do, and hire them on a freelance basis, keeping them as a source of reserve labor for peak seasons.

Risk Taking—in a Calculated Way

If you are (or were) an economics major, then most of the fundamental economic principles are still close to your heart, and the concept of uncertainty is easily recognizable. Loosely defined, *uncertainty* is the quality of being unknown, indefinite, or changeable. This is the normal state of the changing social-economic-cultural-business world in which we live and function. So there is always risk involved in any decisions we make. Standard economics textbooks divide people into three categories: risk-averse, risk-neutral, and risk-loving. A common fallacy that emerges on this point is that entrepreneurs must be risk-loving. But this is simply not the case.

True entrepreneurs do not get a high off of uncertainty, they merely recognize risk and deal with it effectively. Entrepreneurs do not *love* risks, they merely *take* risks, based on informed predictions about likely outcomes. They are "calculated risk takers."

True spontaneity should be a part of your love life, not your work life. The clever entrepreneur is prudent, thoughtful, and prepared. After all of the research, with solid evidence, and having an optimistic outlook while recognizing the inherent element of risk, an entrepreneur starts to make a move. Uncertainty is a fact of life, but it can be diminished with research and preparation.

Ambrose Bierce said, "The gambling known as business looks with austere disfavor upon the business known as gambling." Risk taking in an entrepreneurial sense has often been compared to gambling. And why not? Both involve money, both involve high pressure and high excitement, and both constantly make suckers out of people who fail to weigh their options. Just as most people leave Las Vegas poorer than when they arrived, most new businesses fail within their first year. Starting a new business can seem frighteningly similar (both in losses and in brevity) to gambling in a casino, if you go about it the wrong way. The most common mistakes in both situations are not researching in advance and not knowing how far to go, that is, not showing preparation and restraint.

■ *Preparation.* There is a lot of research necessary to figure out the market potential of a product, the right price to charge for it, and the ideal location to sell it. Many small business owners simply start a business because they like the idea, set a price they would like to be paid, and set up shop wherever it is convenient for them. Because they are not adequately researched, most small businesses fail. Why doesn't anyone make designer rat traps? Because research would show that there is no market for them. A clever entrepreneur needs to be ahead of the game. Be sure to know the rules of the game you are getting into. Understanding the rules of probability is a far better way to succeed in a casino than having a pretty lady blow on the dice. Remember *Rain Man?*

■ *Restraint.* Many gamblers lose money because they simply do not know when to stop. "I'm hot," they say, refusing to stop until they are not. Showing no restraint, they lose out. It is important as an entrepreneur to assess your situation and show the necessary restraint. The decision to expand a business is often both tempting and fatal. Increasing size means taking risk, but without adequately assessing your ability, you have not properly calculated your risk. Bigger is not always better, and only a well-calculated risk is worth taking. Restraint is a crucial tool.

Enjoyment of the Ride

"The chief value of money lies in the fact that one lives in a world in which it is overestimated."

—H. L. Mencken

Clearly Bill Gates had more than just an altruistic motive in mind (to bring civilization into the computer age) when he embarked on his entrepreneurial journey. Money is an incentive. It is not, however, and never should be, your main goal. The process of seeing an idea come alive is more a reward than a chore to an entrepreneur. That process is a journey, and he knows how to enjoy the ride. Bill Gates has clearly reached a level of financial security that is close to if not beyond what he set out to attain, but he's still working. This, more than anything else, should be proof of the fact that a true entrepreneur is someone who enjoys making things happen.

Here is the perfect example of how a true entrepreneur acts. A new idea or project is like a shiny, new toy. The entrepreneur brings it home, shows it to everyone, and thinks constantly about it. As the project grows, so does the excitement, and each step poses a new series of questions and options to be discussed with the family. Discussing the project is a sort of pastime.

As weird and strange as that picture of quality family time and home life may seem to the casual observer, it is exactly that spirit which drives entrepreneurs to success. Entrepreneurs see a project almost as a full-time hobby: something they enjoy, take pride in, and are serious about. It's not just an annoying job that is gladly pushed aside at 5 P.M. Being truly excited about an idea, entrepreneurs do not see the work involved as a burden. Rather, they enjoy the process of making their ideas come alive.

If you are just in it for the money, you may be successful, but you will not be happy. Being an entrepreneur is an enormous time commitment—time spent thinking, planning, and working—and only those who feel the spirit should attempt it. It's kind of like going into the army. If you do it because you feel you should, or because you want the honor you will receive when you return, you are simply in the wrong place. Unless you are truly dedicated to the thrill and joy of serving your country, you shouldn't be anywhere near a recruiting office.

Although starting your own business probably wouldn't be nearly as traumatic as fighting a war, you must sincerely look forward to the thrill of making your ideas become a reality. If not, you do not have the proper mind-set to be an entrepreneur.

Of course, money is a major factor in any decision to start a business—and you should not feel like a greedy capitalist for looking forward to that reward. But keep in mind that your idea will be a constant in your life long before any major profit is, so you had better take the time to find an idea that really excites you.

Negotiation and Compromise

Most of the qualities mentioned so far seem to focus exclusively on you and your needs—or getting what you want. That's okay, because being an entrepreneur is partially about finding creative ways to show the world your great idea and getting what you want. But it is important to realize that as right as you are, and as great as your idea is, not everybody will see it that way, and sometimes they just can't be entirely convinced. There is almost always a middle ground. As a new small business owner, you will need to master two fundamental skills that go hand in hand: negotiation and compromise.

The term *negotiation* often conjures up images of fierce lawyers in expensive suits with constipated looks on their faces, sitting across from each other at a long conference table in a frighteningly silent boardroom, passing around a slip of paper that each lawyer examines, adding or erasing zeros. In reality, as far removed as that scene may seem from your present life, negotiating and compromising skills are essential for you.

Negotiating is simply bargaining with another party in order to come to a mutually beneficial agreement—compromise plays a part in this. The *Wordsmyth English Dictionary-Thesaurus* (1998) defines *compromise* as "a settlement of differences by partial concession of demands by each party."

Although you may be bright and have a great idea, you must be prepared not to be taken seriously by some people. Some people have a difficult time looking past your age long enough to objectively consider your idea. In cases like this, it is important to realize that business is about mutual benefits and trade-offs. Sometimes, making small concessions to business contacts in the beginning of discussions will increase their sense of confidence in you. People will not make a deal that does not benefit them in some way. Once you have developed a relationship with them, then you will have proven yourself, and will be in a more equal position. Negotiation is a skill that involves recognizing the amount of flexibility required of you if you want to make a deal. Being able to accurately judge that level is a skill you will acquire with time.

Things to keep in mind:

■ *Strike a balance between how much you will benefit from working with this contact and how much you are willing to compromise in return.* Maybe supplying your entire first batch of special brownies to the large chain of bakeries for just the cost of ingredients is worth it—in order to develop a solid relationship with such a large potential future customer. But smaller specialty bakeries probably aren't worth the risk, and you should ask for the cost of ingredients plus 25 cents per brownie.

■ *Always be polite, never adversarial.* Regardless of how your business contact acts, you must never lose your cool. During any kind of negotiation, a common tactic people use is to get you angry and flustered so you will make snap decisions. Be careful. Even if you never do business with this particular company, negative word of mouth can be devastating to a new business. If someone is rude to you, simply brush it off. You should not take it personally. As long as you carry yourself well, with manners and intelligent, fair proposals, you cannot go wrong. Your business etiquette and temperament (politeness) will be recognized, rewarded, and remembered.

- *Never jump at the first offer.* When making big decisions or important deals, be gracious, and tell people that you appreciate the offer and will consider it and get back to them. This gives you time to consult other contacts and friends to make sure you have been offered a fair deal. It also prevents you from seeming naive. Taking everything in stride will convince people that you know more than you do.
- *Always give it a shot.* Most of the time, people offer you a little less in order to see how low you are willing to go. This is basic business sense. You should be aware of the tactics people use, and always be willing to give negotiation a try. You have nothing to lose, because rejection can only leave you where you started with the original offer. But always try to get what you can in a deal. This is the business world—remind yourself of that.

There is a lawyer on the popular new television show *Ally McBeal* who is referred to as "the Biscuit." If you have seen the show you will be familiar with his boardroom style. Whenever someone makes him an offer, he wrinkles his brow slightly, puts his elbows on the armrests, purses his lips, joins his fingertips, leans back in his chair, and considers it for a moment. There is often no way to tell what he is thinking, but everyone in the room is hanging on his every word, and he has conveyed the idea that he is making an intelligent, well-thought-out decision. He is not hesitating, he is considering from every angle. Although this may be a little melodramatic, you get the idea. Negotiating is about being careful to make the best deal possible for everyone concerned, and feeling confident in what you have to offer when you are making a deal. All of this is done fairly, in an open and cordial manner. You should always come out of negotiations with a handshake and a smile, and on a positive note.

Exacting and Exhaustive Mentality

In the initial stages of entrepreneurship, you may be acting as the secretary, the lawyer, the marketing director, the sales representative, the delivery crew, the talent, and the CEO. This is a major responsibility, and you deserve much recognition for the formidable task you are undertaking. But you also deserve some advice: Be precise! You must be exacting and exhaustive. If a detail slips through the cracks, then you have no one to blame but yourself. This is the mentality that gets successful people to where they want to be.

When you achieve success as an entrepreneur, you will bask in the light of pride and accomplishment. Likewise, when you fail or make a mistake, you alone will bear the burden of the embarrassment of failure. Entrepreneurs are extremely detail-oriented. Each task you undertake should be carried out seriously and diligently. Each letter drafted should be professional and well written. Each business alliance you form should be strategically beneficial. Research each supplier you use to ensure that he or she can be relied on for consistent quality and efficient business relations. In hiring a staff member, choose each candidate on the basis of genuine usefulness, not your personal relationship. Explore each available avenue in depth. Every possible base should be covered in order to be positive that you are moving in the right direction.

When entering the business world, you should always operate on the assumption that others have been exhaustive in their preparation and extremely detail-oriented. Along those lines, it is very necessary not to take anything for granted, to pay painstaking attention to detail, and to always read the fine print. You must be exhaustive in your efforts to make sure that you are aware of everything that is going on.

A common mistake start-up business owners make is to accept a verbal or good-faith contract, without putting the agreement into writing. This is where the roots of business failure begin to show. People accept verbal contracts without putting everything into detailed writing for a number of reasons. For example:

■ *They do not want to appear distrustful.* When they first enter the business world, many people feel that it will "look bad" if they are overzealous about contracts. They do not want to appear as if they suspect others of foul play. The problem with this mentality is that it prevents people from asking for the agreements in writing. Do not fall into this trap. If the people you are dealing with have nothing to hide, then they will not object to putting the terms of a deal into a contract. And if they do object, then you will know for sure that it is time to worry.

■ *They believe in honesty as a policy.* It is very important that you always conduct business openly and honestly. We believe this is the way people should always act, and we wholeheartedly encourage you to do the same. However, we also wholeheartedly remind you that just because you believe honesty is the best policy, you should not assume that everyone else you deal with conducts business in the same manner. You should operate on the assumption that certain people may not operate on the honesty policy. If you expect the worst, you can only be pleasantly surprised when things work out for the best, or contented when they meet your expectations.

The point here is that you should be extremely detail-oriented and specific about how you conduct your business. We do not advocate a "take no prisoners" mentality. We simply believe that true entrepreneurs are generally harder on themselves than anyone else is. By holding themselves up to a higher level of standards, entrepreneurs set themselves apart, and necessarily perform better than was expected. They are also so concerned with specifics that no slight impropriety escapes them.

Urgency and Restlessness

Presumably at this point, you may already have a product idea. Are you excited about it? If you are, then you know what we mean when we talk about the urgency and restlessness you feel.

"Don't put off until tomorrow what could have been done yesterday," is the motto. A true entrepreneur latches on to an idea and can't wait to see it happen. A certain amount of impatience can be a good thing—it provides the energy necessary to achieve your dreams.

Entrepreneurs are so convinced about the tremendous potential of an idea that sometimes they don't understand why others don't feel the same way. You get to a point where you are so convinced of your idea that you feel it is self-explanatory; accordingly, you expect others to agree with it right away. And it is okay to feel that way, as long as you don't appear pushy. There is a fine line between urgency and overeagerness. You must be careful to advise people of your idea without bombarding them. Usually it is enough to show people how excited you are about it, and let your spirit rub off on them. The urgency you feel to have your idea recognized and the restlessness you feel to get things moving are natural.

Resilience after Failure

Here's a story about two friends. Years ago when Sara had just endured what she perceived to be her biggest failure to date, her best friend, Sam, imparted some kind and passionate words which have managed to ring true and have stayed in her mind ever since. Sara had been walking around sulking and complaining endlessly that she had failed and that nothing would ever get better, when Sam decided she couldn't take it any longer. Sam decided to sit Sara down and have a talk with her. She asked Sara what her problem was and told Sara her complaining was making her sick. Sam said that up until now she had always admired how Sara just went out there and made things happen for herself, and that this failure of hers was really nothing more than a temporary setback. It was like Sara had been riding along on a skateboard down a straight path and was fortunate enough to have had a smooth way until now. This setback was merely a pebble in the road, and her skateboard had simply been shaken by the impact. Sam told Sara that there was no reason to look at it as a failure. She told Sara that people who are meant for success simply find it—despite the setbacks. And her words have stayed with Sara ever since.

There are countless stories of very wealthy people who went broke and then became very wealthy again. Take Donald Trump. In his first book, *The*

Art of the Deal, he explained some of his successful deals and gave readers an insight into his daily work life. After a divorce and a colossal business failure, he wrote his second book, *The Art of the Comeback*, explaining what he had learned. He is the perfect example of how an entrepreneur looks at adversity: as an opportunity to learn a lesson and a chance to make a comeback.

A successful entrepreneur sees himself first and foremost as a person who is destined for success. When a particular business move fails, a lesson is learned and a new plan is drafted. You didn't fail, your plan did. Keeping this frame of mind is what helps you to see yourself as a successful person, and seeing yourself as an inherently successful person is an asset. You need to believe that your being successful is the natural state of things, and that failure is simply an isolated incident or an aberration. Separating yourself from your actions is the type of mentality that will help you to be resilient after failure. When something doesn't work out right, it simply presents another lesson to learn and another problem to solve. This is how entrepreneurs grow. If the bad times didn't exist, you wouldn't recognize the good times when they come. Resilience after failure is the result of a positive point of view and a genuine belief in your destiny for success.

Initiative

A lot of people with great ideas never actually make them happen. The reason is that they lack the capability to take that first step—to take the initiative. How do you do it? Well, much like the rest of being an entrepreneur, there is no formula for how to take the initiative. There is, however, a way to make that first step easier for yourself.

Whenever there is a formidable task in front of you, say a 25-page paper, you probably sit down and write an outline of the paper for yourself. It makes you more relaxed, it puts things into perspective and it helps you to visualize the process of arriving at your final goal of a polished, well-written, substantial 25-page paper. The technique you use to prepare yourself for a paper can be applied to any major task, such as starting your own business. The difference is that you need also to visualize it in your head instead of simply writing it down on paper. And the benefit is that laying out the steps mentally and on paper makes it easier for you to picture completing the entire project. Since the first step is simply one piece of the larger plan, it seems like that much less substantial a task.

It's like that first date, and the good-night kiss question. You know he's gonna drive you home. You know he's gonna walk you to the door. You know you will say something like, "Gee, *blank*, I had a really nice time." You know he will politely agree. You know he will ask if you would like to go out again sometime. You know you will accept. And you know there will be an awkward pause: The moment of truth has arrived. After an entire evening of conversation and flirting, this component should seem like a simple little part of the evening, right? Well, most people attach a lot of importance to this moment. And building it up in your mind makes it seem like more than it is. Will you take destiny into your hands and kiss him? We hope so. And we hope that the same kind of mental planning will prepare you to see that first step into business as an equally important move—one that has its place and does not warrant so much hesitation.

The point is that initiative is the ability to simply go out there and get things started. A useful tool to encourage yourself to make that first move is to lay out the larger plan and convince yourself of how small a piece the first step is. Instead of feeling the stress of thinking, "Today I am going to start a business," you can feel the ease of thinking, "Today I will find out what the cheapest way to advertise my massage business is." You get the idea.

Alertness

Successful airplane pilots are always on the ball. This means they are alert and attentive to whatever is going on around them. The wind speed, the visibility, the distance, the altitude, the weather forecast, and the directions from ground control are all crystal clear in the mind of a pilot at any point during a flight. Why? Because although the pilot is essentially the "boss" of the flight crew on the aircraft, he or she does not rely on anyone else for the essential knowledge. A responsible pilot could comfortably fly the plane without anyone else on board or any help from ground control.

Being alert to the details is equally as important as having a firm grasp on the larger picture. As the entrepreneur of a new company, you are also at the head of your ship, and should hold yourself equally responsible for its highs and lows. The details are your business and your responsibility. One major reason is that you may be the only employee of your new business, and therefore be performing the tasks of the CEO, the CFO, the analyst, and the secretary, all at once. In that case you must make sure you know every aspect of your business, and every detail that may be relevant. Being alert and keeping abreast of any slight changes in business conditions could make or break your firm. Of course, even when your company expands and you become a leader instead of a one-man show, you still need to be alert to everything that affects your business. Mike Bloomberg is the head of the largest financial commodities market news provider in the world, and still arrives to work before most of his employees each morning. He doesn't want to miss a beat, and it is that spirit which keeps him alert and moving forward. Try to be like Mike.

Leadership Style

> *"My mother said to me 'If you become a soldier, you'll be a general; if you become a monk, you'll end up as the Pope.' Instead I became a painter and wound up as Picasso."*
>
> —Pablo Picasso

It is said that 95 percent of the people in this world are followers, and only 5 percent are capable of being leaders, so you only have to make it into the top 5 percent to become a leader, you don't necessarily have to be number one. Assuming that many of you who are reading this book are (or consider yourselves to be) overachievers, you may fit into that 5 percent. So you presumably have the potential to lead. But the question that remains is whether you actually have the charisma, style, and mannerisms that will make you an effective leader.

What is the difference between a businessperson and an entrepreneur? Both want to make money. Both want to see their ideas come to life. Both want to be in charge. But the difference lies in how they view their roles, and that is reflected in how the world views them. While businesspeople see themselves as representatives of a business, entrepreneurs see themselves as the crux of the business. Start-up entrepreneurs must see themselves as being the business, in order to be effective leaders. If they don't buy the idea, they certainly can't sell it. So they become their own best piece of advertising. And in presenting such a compelling self-image, they cause others to want to follow them. Their excitement about the idea is magnetic, and their enthusiasm draws others into following the idea as well.

Entrepreneurs are often referred to as born leaders or natural leaders. Early on, entrepreneurs have a way of making others want to follow. If you have been encouraged by peers, counselors, bosses, or friends to become an entrepreneur or to take on leadership positions, don't take their support so lightly. People have a way of recognizing leadership potential in you sometimes before you even see it in yourself. Their instinctive support of your leadership abilities is the biggest compliment you could get. If you are encouraged by peers to run for board positions in extracurricular organizations, you should take their encouragement to heart, and let it help build your leadership confidence. The fact that they want you to represent them speaks volumes about how much they respect your opinion and your ability to deal with tough situations.

If you seem to have the predisposition for leadership inside you, but don't know exactly how to call upon it, realize first and foremost that there is no one right way to lead. Your reputation is very important, however, so you should have an idea of the sort of image you wish to portray in order to attract and maintain the confidence that people have in you. Consider the following leadership tactics that people have been known to use:

- *Team leadership.* Create the feeling of a winning team. Make it clear that each and every person involved is an integral part of the project. When you give people the feeling that they are working with you, not for you, you generally keep happy employees. Avoid pulling rank, except in extreme situations. Everyone knows that you are the boss and have the final say, but they do not appreciate hearing it. If you set yourself up to be seen as the coach of the team, people are comfortable coming to you for advice, because they are sure that they will receive genuine help, not condescension and rank pulling.

- *Example leadership.* When you are in a position of leadership, there is no question that your every move is noticed and remembered. You may want to take advantage of that by setting the example of the kind of mind-set you want others to have in your business. Many bosses use this tactic to be able to show, not tell, what needs to be done, so they don't appear authoritarian. Those who work under you are obviously interested in making a good impression, but you should be, too. Seeming too preachy or anal retentive will only lose you popularity. If you set a positive, honest example, your employees will have a clear picture of the kind of behavior expected of them. For example, if you are wrong, be the first to admit it. This way, not only will others feel comfortable coming forward for help when they mess up, but they will also see you as a person and respect your admission of fault as a leadership strength and a sign of fairness, not as a weakness or a sign of incompetence.

- *Available/accessible leadership.* Some people feel that in order to inspire respect in people, they must keep a certain distance and nonaccessibility from their employees. On the other hand, we feel that it is much more appropriate to make yourself accessible and available to them, within reasonable limits. As their leader, you are not their personal counselor, and should not be available to help with all their personal problems, but you should treat them as people and ask them how everything is going. Make it clear that they are welcome to stop by and ask your advice or chat whenever they need to.

Being accessible makes people feel comfortable around you, since they see you as a person. Maintain a certain level of dignity, and do not discuss too many personal affairs, but be friendly. Your history of impressive accomplishments coupled with the fact that you are friendly will make you seem even more awesome in their eyes. And that is when they will truly respect you. As a robot, you gain reverence, not respect. As a person who has distinguished himself or herself but is still real, you gain lasting respect and loyalty.

■ *Aikido leadership*. There is a Japanese form of defensive martial art, known as aikido, "the way of harmonizing with energy," which has an underlying philosophy of dealing with issues of power. Recently, this philosophy has taken the corporate leadership world by storm, and many executives are being sent to take aikido classes in order to learn how to become more effective leaders. These skeptical executives are taught to examine their underlying assumptions about power and its role in leadership. The goal of such seminars is to teach leaders to recognize most business issues as struggles for power, and to train them to flow with the energy of an opponent, not to attempt to block it. The idea is that you can find positive alternatives to conflict by diverting the energy and force of an opponent's movement into a different direction in order to lead that opponent, instead of fighting. The ensuing dance of power that executives experience through the physical art of aikido is then applied to everyday conflicts.

The value of aikido leadership is that it does not attempt to calm people down when they disagree with you. It does not belittle them or trivialize their concerns; it merely prepares you, the leader, for an opponent's force by training you to redirect that force into a mutually beneficial solution. The basic idea can be applied to your everyday life as a young entrepreneur. When dealing with business contacts, suppliers, or employees, you must never trivialize their concerns. Take them under consideration and try to make suggestions for better alternatives to an unsettling situation, so that you are leading them in a new direction while recognizing their concerns.

■ *"Give credit where credit is due" leadership.* It seems that a major issue many people have with their bosses is that their hard work goes unnoticed. Don't let this be a downfall of your leadership. Make sure to recognize and honor the achievements of your employees and to give everyone a piece of the limelight when it is due. Show them that you are proud of them, and that you enjoy giving them the recognition they deserve, both privately and in front of their coworkers. You would be surprised how much happier workers are when they feel they are noticed. Shining the limelight on someone else takes nothing away from the prominence of your leadership; in fact, it increases your popularity.

Keep in mind that these leadership styles do not necessarily conflict, nor are they necessarily mutually exclusive. You must strike the proper balance in order to deal effectively with your employees and coworkers— each situation and/or person may call for a slightly different tactic. As an effective leader, you should be able to recognize what is most appropriate. The common qualities of successful leaders are that they motivate, encourage, and plant positive purpose. And remember, leadership is not just about directing and controlling, it is about inspiring.

―― ✄✄✄✄ ――

"The final test of a leader is that he leaves behind him In other men the conviction and the will to carry on."

―Walter Lippman

Stress Management

Stress is defined as a force that strains or deforms—in other words, mental or physical tension. It is important to remember that stress is a fact of life. You can't hide from it. And you shouldn't want to. But you shouldn't fear it either. The important thing is how you decide to deal with it. And yes, it *is* a decision. Do not internalize the stress. Manage it.

Here's a scenario. You have promised a hundred widgets to a customer by Friday, and it is Monday It takes an hour to make a widget, one of your employees ran off to Vegas with her boyfriend last night, and the other one has a paper due on Friday which he says he needs to work on all week. As if all of that wasn't enough, you have run out of cash in your bank account, and you need to buy supplies. So how do you deal with it? How do you feel about it? Will you hyperventilate? Can you find a solution?

We are not going to lay out the solution. It should be pretty obvious to you that you would have planned ahead to have backup workers, and that you will ask for a deposit from your customer to cover the cost of materials. But the issue here is not how you solve a stressful situation, but how you deal with the situation emotionally.

In general, an entrepreneur looks at business as fun, and at stress as a bad thing. The idea of solving problems is a challenge, not a burden. While stress is a natural physical reaction to uncertainty and changing circumstances, the successful entrepreneur does not let it sink in. Adverse circumstances are beyond your control. But creative solutions are your responsibility. Issues of business should not keep you awake at night. You are young and do not have a family to support, so take advantage of your freedom and keep things in perspective. If you are starting a business so young, you probably plan to be an entrepreneur well into the future. In that case, the way in which you train yourself to deal with stress right now will have long lasting effects on your future success and health.

So if you have done your best, then by the end of each day, you should be able to sleep comfortably. They say that if you lie down with dogs, you will wake up with fleas. Along the same lines, if you take your concerns to bed with you, you will wake up with a neck so stiff you won't be able to turn your head.

So try never to go to bed stressed. Here are a few constructive ways to work it off:

■ *Come up with a creative new plan for how to deal with the situation.* Sometimes just putting it down on paper is enough to calm you down. Knowing that you have not been left without recourse often helps to assure you that you can and will overcome the issue.

■ *Exercise.* The best way to make sure that emotional stress does not have adverse effects on your body is to physically work out the stress. An hour of exercise daily is recommended for people with a lot of responsibility.

■ *Do something else.* When all is said and done, sometimes you have done all that you can to solve a situation but you still can't seem to get it taken care of. If the fact that you have done your best is not enough to help you sleep at night, you may want to consider some other diversion before the night is over. Go out with friends. Watch a movie. Have a nice dinner with that someone special. It helps get work off your mind. Remember that you are young, and it is not the end of the world.

In the words of the character Whitley Gilbert, from the popular *Cosby Show* spin-off *A Different World,* "Relax, relate, release!"

Persistence

❄❄❄❄

"Nothing in this world can take the place of persistence. Talent will not; nothing is more common than unsuccessful people with talent. Genius will not; unrewarded genius is almost a proverb. Education will not; the world is full of educated derelicts. Persistence and determination alone are omnipotent. The slogan 'press on' has solved and always will solve the problems of the human race."

—Calvin Coolidge

Let's look back in time a little bit. You are seven years old and it is bedtime. So your loving parents decide that they will take story time as an opportunity to teach you a little lesson in life. And which story do they choose? *The Little Engine That Could.* Although their intentions may have been correct, they could have chosen a more appropriate story. Instead of the little engine in the story huffing and puffing up the hill chanting, "I think I can, I think I can, . . . " it should have been chanting, "I know I will, I know I will. . . . " You see, your parents were trying to teach you about persistence. They wanted you to grow up to be the kind of person who would keep trying to achieve your goals, despite the odds. But they didn't take it far enough.

What distinguishes the kid with the summer job making photocopies in a law firm from the kid who convinced a lawyer to hire him or her as a summer deposition reviewer is the latter's persistence. Lots of things are handed to us in this lifetime. You will get into a college. You will get a job. But will you get the one you really want? Or will you tell yourself that you are under-qualified and not bother trying? You would be surprised how many nice people are willing to help you out or give you a chance once they actually see your enthusiasm. Along the same lines, as an entrepreneur, you must keep trying. If they won't meet with you, ask for a 15-minute phone appointment. If they won't hire you right away, offer to work for free for two weeks so they know what they are paying for if they decide to hire you afterward. If they don't want to make a deal with you, get a partner and approach them again with a new presentation. If they don't want to listen at first, try again. Do not become a nuisance, but also do not give up too soon.

We are not advocating that you wage a war against people who don't agree with you, using terrorist tactics to frighten them into compliance. We are simply saying that sometimes, even though your ideas and credentials speak for themselves, they may need to be repeated before they are entirely noticed. It is up to you as an entrepreneur to create a following for your idea, and to get people's attention. Don't be pushy or arrogant, be honest and enthusiastic. And always, always, give it a second try.

Idealism Coupled with Confidence

> "If you are not an idealist by the time you are twenty, you don't have a heart, but if you are still an idealist at thirty, you don't have a head."
>
> —Randolph Bourne

If you are an idealist, you act and think based on a conception of things being the way you think they should be. Basically, you act as if you live in an ideal world. In an ideal world, people would be convinced of everything you have to say. In that case, you would be confident enough to make your presentation of ideas to anyone who might be of help. This sense of idealism coupled with confidence is what entrepreneurs strive to maintain.

As we age, we see more of the world, and are humbled by the realities of life. But you are still young. So as we mentioned before, take advantage of that. Aim high and believe in yourself. Allow yourself the luxury of confidence. If you are confident and reasonably idealistic, your spirit will take you farther than you would probably expect.

To quote the famous Reverend Robert Schullen, "What plans would you hang on your drawing board if you knew you could not fail?" Ask yourself that question, and put together a wish list. Then be idealistic and confident enough to try them. Hold on to the feeling you had at the moment when you received your diploma and graduated high school. Let that spirit be your guide.

They say that if you reach for the heavens you will at least land among the stars. Do that, and maybe you will even land in the heavens where you belong.

Reflectiveness

❀ ❀ ❀ ❀

"Reflection ensures safety, but rashness is followed by regrets."
—Burtin Stevenson

The idea of reflection conjures up images of an old man leaning on the railing of a dock at the waterfront and looking out over the water contemplating whether he should have eloped with that girl in France all those years ago. And although reflection may be an appropriate word for that moment, it has many more uses than just the sentimental.

Reflecting in a business sense consists of thinking back on past experiences and creating new ideas by combining old lessons. It is important to be able to learn from every experience you endure, and to be capable of getting something positive out of it. Look back on the most trying experiences you have had, the most disappointing lessons you have learned, and the hardest failures you have been through. Now be honest with yourself, and ask yourself whether you really reflected on these experiences as you should have. Did you think long and hard about what went wrong and what was the greater meaning of the experience in your life? Or did you simply curse misfortune and put it out of your mind? Remember, you are only being honest with yourself. The inability to learn the right lesson is a major obstacle to your personal growth.

The best decision in business is not always the easiest. And it is even harder to make the best decision when you lack the necessary maturity. The maturity to be able to learn valuable lessons of life by reflecting on past experiences is a very necessary asset in the life of an entrepreneur. When you decide to start your own business, you generally go it alone. And it is therefore extremely important to be able to recognize your own mistakes and teach yourself your own lessons, because there is no power structure in place to help you learn. The point is that you must constantly be evaluating and reevaluating your past moves and future plans in order to be a dynamic entrepreneur.

Say that early on in your business career you started a business partnership with a friend which proved to be unsuccessful. After one year you realized this partner was completely inept and that consequently your business was suffering. So you parted ways and moved on, never looking back. You had learned your lesson, which was never to do business with a friend. But that wasn't the whole lesson. Ten years later you have an employee whose continued lack of people skills has put your customers off of the company. You like him, and do not want to fire him, so you keep him on the job, but after six months you realize that he has cost your company more money than he was worth. If you had been reflecting on your past failures correctly, you would have realized that the first lesson you learned should have had two parts, not just one. Never do business with a friend, and never allow friendship to factor into a business decision. The second part of the lesson would have prepared you to fire the employee in time to protect your company. Your friendship would not have factored into the decision.

It is important to try to learn as much as you can from each experience you have in the business world—to reflect on everything and make sure the lesson you walk away with goes deeper than just the surface.

Imagination

There are some things you just can't learn. Imagination is one of those abilities which is so personal that it cannot be taught, and it knows no bounds. In the life of an entrepreneur, imagination is an extremely important vehicle for the creation of a plan of action. The major difference between someone who enters a nine-to-five job right after college and an entrepreneur is the latter's imagination. Entrepreneurs see the larger picture, and they want to be a part of it—to make a real impact. Their imagination allows them to come up with ideas about how to make things happen. They see possibilities and opportunities where others see nothing. They see business ideas and underserved markets where others see nothing. They see life as a wide open field of chances to create something new, and that is why they start new businesses.

Entrepreneurs do not want to fill in a formula or fit into a mold, they want to create a new dimension, and their imaginations give them the power to do so. Imagination is the sense with which an entrepreneur can creatively consider any problem in a different light than most people. Textbooks are of no help when vital business functions are required and deadlines need to be met.

There is a concept called imagineering, referring to the mixing of the abilities to imagine and engineer aspects of a business. Successful entrepreneurs can combine their natural imagination skills with the business engineering skills acquired in school or through experience.

Talent for Thinking Strategically

Entrepreneurs must be mentally one step ahead of anyone else in the room. What that means is that they should have the ability to progressively search for and refine the perfect game plan, given the circumstances under which they are operating. To strategize is to shape and reshape as circumstances change and the validity of your assumptions is tested, proved, and disproved.

It is difficult to explain what strategy is all about. Basically, it means identifying short- and long-term remedies for financial and structural crises that come up in daily life. Strategy involves the following components:

- ■ *Define the imperfections of your organization.* You should be able to examine your business from an outsider's point of view to identify areas that have been arranged imperfectly. Can you make production more cost-efficient? Could you speed up your delivery process? Is there a market your advertisements are not reaching?
- ■ *Isolate the strengths and weaknesses of your project.* Examine your power structure, your boss-employee relationships, your choice of suppliers, and so forth. Decide how well the different parts of your power structure work, and how well they support each other.
- ■ *Target your energy toward those areas which most need restructuring.* Research new ideas and ways of running your business.
- ■ *Propose various solutions for the problems facing your project.* Analyze each possible solution, and test its predicted success before implementing it.

Now that we have discussed the 21 qualities that characterize the successful entrepreneur, you may be a little confused. But while these qualities would describe the ideal entrepreneur, you do not necessarily need to exhibit every one of them. They are meant to serve as an inspiration and a guide for thinking in an ideal world. They do, however, serve one other purpose. Those of you who have been paying close attention would have been disturbed by the large number of qualities listed in this chapter, and would have asked yourselves why we felt the need to list so many different qualities. First of all, it seemed limiting to try to isolate five simple qualities. But beyond that, those of you who were thinking about the larger picture will already have noticed that the first letters of each of the 21 qualities form an anagram that spells ENTREPRENEURIAL SPIRIT.

Energy

Novelty

Time management

Readiness for anything

Effectiveness at persuasion

Problem-solving skills

Risk taking—in a calculated way

Enjoyment of the ride

Negotiation and compromise

Exacting and exhaustive mentality

Urgency and restlessness

Resilience after failure

Initiative

Alertness

Leadership style

Stress management

Persistence

Idealism coupled with confidence

Reflectiveness

Imagination

Talent for thinking strategically

Above all else, it is important that a successful entrepreneur have a sense of the larger picture and a true feeling of the entrepreneurial spirit. The entrepreneurial spirit is about feeling the excitement of a new idea— of seeing a project through from start to finish, and everything in between. It is a love of the process of seeing a dream become a successful enterprise, and a willingness to put in all the necessary time and effort along the way. The love of the game is a rush you feel the moment the right idea first springs into your mind. Visualizing the possibilities, planning the strategy, dreaming of the recognition and fulfillment the project will bring—this is the entrepreneurial spirit. And if this seems comical, this book is not for you.

What's the Big Idea?

"There is one thing stronger than all the armies in the world, and that is an idea whose time has come."

—Victor Hugo

The idea as we know it is a strange beast indeed. We know it when we get it, we can explain it to each other, and we are always capable of putting it to good use when we get one . . . but how do we define it? The term *idea* is defined as a thought that can lead to action, but we don't believe that a simple definition will do it justice. An idea is like a gift of opportunity—it is, in a word, a possibility.

We feel it is much more useful to examine the idea by showing you how to find one. In order to prepare your entrepreneur's tool kit, you need a number of different items, but the most important one is the idea—it will inspire the others into action.

The thing about a bright idea is that you can't just decide to get one. There are, however, a few ways to make yourself more likely to get one. It is kind of like falling in love. You can't decide to do it. And once love (or the idea) comes to you, it is nearly impossible to deny. And you definitely know it when you see it, but there is no formula for love. There are, however, a few things you can do to make a meaningful relationship more likely: Take care of yourself, be friendly and outgoing, be open and non-cynical, be patient and don't obsess over it, be childlike enough to trust it when it comes, take chances when the odds are in your favor, and try to be in the right place at the right time. If you are lucky and happen to chance upon an idea of real personal interest, then it can actually be a lot like falling in love—at times almost better. Your idea will inspire you, excite you, intoxicate you, and begin to take control of your thoughts.

But we digress. Romanticizing is fun when you have your idea, but first you must get your hands on that treasure. Although there is no formula for getting an idea, there are a few strategic tactics you can use. In this section, we will describe these tactics, show you how to become idea-prone, and lay out the three idea categories into which your gem will eventually fit.

Tactics

There are basically two strategic ways to visualize your hunt for the perfect idea. These can be compared by their titles: the inside-out tactic or the outside-in tactic.

1. *Inside-out tactic.* Any business involves a certain type of skill. Many entrepreneurs are entrepreneurs by trade, meaning that they merely started out in, say, the construction industry, gained substantial expertise, and started their own firm in construction. Along the same lines, as a college student, you may be majoring in, say, computer science. As a skilled programmer, you can develop your own idea by creating a product based on your expertise. This is the inside-out approach, because you simply pull together all of the skills you have, and search for a problem to which you can apply those skills. You come up with an idea you can market and sell in the real world, bringing your skill from the inside out.

2. *Outside-in tactic.* In contrast to the above situation, you may be a college student with a good head on your shoulders—a self-starter with high ambitions and a desire to start your own business. That's a perfectly legitimate situation, as long as you recognize that it will take a little more creativity on your part to come up with an idea. The outside-in approach is about looking at the larger picture, evaluating the market in which you wish to operate, isolating a neglected problem or need in your community, designing a creative and profitable way to solve that problem, and locating the appropriate resources, talent, and/or skills to get it started.

Being Idea-Prone

Some people walk through life blissfully unaware of the opportunities around them, and others recognize the need for solutions to everyday problems as ideas for entrepreneurship. While there is no isolated and proven recipe for concocting the perfect idea, there are some ingredients we believe will help the average person become more idea-prone. And when you are open to ideas, they are more likely to come to you. The following is a list of ways to make yourself idea-prone:

1. *Expose yourself.* Expose yourself to everything (not everyone, silly), and be open to learning about the different things occurring around you. When you broaden your horizons, you get a better sense of what people are about, you meet and talk to new people, and you find out what they want and what they need. By exposing yourself we mean that you should literally get out there and mingle with your market. Living on a college campus, we often get caught up in our own social groups and fail to take advantage of the incredible diversity around us. By exposing yourself to those you would not otherwise get to know, you broaden your frame of reference beyond the narrow confines of the people you always hang out with. And by meeting people who are different from you, you have the unique advantage of being able to view the situation from an outside perspective. The point is, do not limit your interactions . . . you are also limiting your range of ideas. Make the world your classroom, and you will soon realize the benefits of an open mind—it is more likely to attract interesting ideas.

   Another important way to expose yourself to new ideas is to read, read, read. Often during our college years, we complain that we feel we are living in a bubble—we feel isolated from the outside world. We have time to party all weekend, but somehow can't find a moment to pick up a copy of the *New York Times*. For our own good, we must fight the tendency to lose contact with the outside world by constantly trying to keep up with current events. Along the same lines, if you want to expose yourself to the aspects of life that will in-spire you with worthwhile ideas, a good place to start is at the fore-front of world events. Reading newspapers and magazines is a good way to be aware of events around you. This opens up the opportu-nity to recognize trends and make predictions about consumer pref-erences, which will help you to come up with profitable ideas.

2. *Be a kid again.* Try to remember what it was like to be excited and in-trigued by everything you saw. Question things, and search for cre-ative answers. Be playful and imaginative in approaching problems, and don't be so quick to let things slide—question them. When the child in you complains that there should be an ice cream flavor that combines peanut butter and strawberries, follow that thought through and see if it is possible. Other people might feel exactly the same way. Try keeping quiet and letting your inner child do some of the talking for once. You might be surprised by all the interesting stuff the kid in you has to say. Don't dismiss that input.

3. *Keep a wish list of the things you believe should be different.* For example, why doesn't a certain pizza place deliver? Or why don't they make those dresses in solid colors? Or why doesn't lipstick smell as good as the cherry-flavored lip gloss we wore in junior high school?

   Your wish list could be in the form of a notebook of ideas, or a list on a napkin in your wallet, or even a bunch of small pieces of paper in a shoebox under your bed. Keep it going, and add to it whenever the spirit moves you. Then you can go back later and see if a creative solution or idea hits you.

4. *Remember that your needs are everybody's needs.* As a possible college en-trepreneur, you have the benefit of being surrounded by a market you live in and understand firsthand. So who better than you to identify its needs? Quite often, the idea for a product or service that would be perfect for a particular market is right under your nose.

   Take, for example, the perpetually smoking character played by Janeane Garofalo in the movie *Romy and Michelle's High School Reunion.* As the movie goes, she was a chain-smoker in high school. In one of the early scenes, she is portrayed ducking behind the school be-tween classes to smoke a quick cigarette. The problem is that the bell always rings before she finishes her cigarette, so she ends up wasting half a cigarette each time. She complains that someone should make a cigarette you could smoke to the end between classes. Lo and behold, as we discover later in the reunion scene, she has gone to business school and developed the formula for a quick-burning paper that allows cigarettes to burn faster, and has made millions of dollars off the market she represents. She is the perfect example of how to recognize the opportunities that are (literally) right under your nose.

The point is that the idea you undertake does not necessarily have to be a billion-dollar computer chip empire. If you already have that kind of an idea, more power to you. But if you don't, you can still be an entrepreneur. If you begin to view yourself as your target customer, you will probably begin to generate creative and profitable ideas for products and services in no time.

Now that we have explained to you some of the tactics for concocting ideas, as well as some of the specific ways to keep yourself idea-prone, you are prepared to begin your search for the perfect idea.

What Is Your Idea Type?

As you move closer to the point of finding your idea for a new business, you should be thinking about some of the different categories into which your idea will fall. There are essentially three idea categories: service, product, or technical innovation.

1. *Service.* To provide a helpful service is perhaps the easiest idea to come across. Using yourself as a target consumer, you simply find a service that can cost effectively fulfill a need. The hardest part is simply coming up with the service idea. After that, you simply need to put together the manpower, of which there is certainly no shortage on a college campus.

   Think about all of the inconveniences that pervade your daily life. Is there no dorm cleaning service that keeps rooms sanitary? Start a cleaning service where you contract to provide weekly bathroom cleaning services for lazy undergrads. Are there no college-based dating services on the Internet that cater specifically to computer science majors who want to meet other computer science majors? Set up a web-based dating service called Computer Passion. Do you find it impossible to find a TF who will take the time to look through your paper to edit and comment critically? Well then, set up a network of seniors and graduate students who will edit papers, and charge a minimal fee for finding customers. There are a million good money-making service ideas all around you, and they can be the result of simply removing an inconvenience you deal with yourself.

   Loosely defined, to perform a service is to provide some intangible assistance that benefits someone. If you want to perform a service, you should look for ways to make people's lives easier, and pick things they are likely to be willing to pay for. The advantage of providing a service is that you can find a lot of cheap labor in your peers, and the disadvantage is that others can enter your market and profit from your idea simply by putting together some manpower and performing the same service.

2. *Product.* This type of business idea hinges on the creation of an item that does not already exist. Typically, you must envision and create a tangible good that people will believe is worth their money. Some examples include large throw pillows with college names on them, credit card–sized campus bus schedules, or your own new line of clothing. Sometimes it is useful to take advantage of seasonal preferences, by predicting peak school spirit times (i.e., homecoming weekend) to sell popcorn sculptures in the shape of your school mascot, dyed to match your school colors. While campus sentiment is a nice thing to capitalize on because of the predictability, you can also consider larger trends. For example, as winter approaches, you might consider hiring local knitting clubs to make mittens in bulk, and selling them when appropriate. By adding something as simple as a money pouch to something as conventional as a mitten, you will have created an entirely new product.

A product is a creation that can add to people's lives in some positive way. Whether it fulfills a need or a desire, a new product is always beneficial and original. The advantage of a product-based business is that you are creating a niche, and the rights to your idea will be exclusively yours. The disadvantage is that the initial costs of creating and testing a product can be substantial.

3. *Technological Innovation.* Basically, it's like going from chicken soup to Tylenol. Or from coffee to cappuccino. Or from a regular modem to a superpowered twice-as-fast modem. Get it? A technological innovation is an improvement on a current method or product, or a cure for cancer.

In general, the technological innovation type of idea seems to be the realm of the technically inclined. And what we mean by that is not that you have to be a computer/biochemistry/physics wizard in order to come up with an innovation. It simply means that a certain level of expertise is required—in any field. The advantage of a technological innovation is that as the creator, you have all the necessary expertise to avoid structural mistakes and to defend and properly market your idea. The disadvantage is that many people who come up with innovations believe that the idea is enough, and they fail to properly prepare to compete against and act as business-minded entrepreneurs. Steer clear of that trap!

As mentioned earlier, finding your perfect idea can be like falling in love—as frustrating, as exciting, as fleeting, as scary, as difficult, and as rewarding. Once you find it, hold on and give it your all. At least then, you can never say you didn't try, and you won't have to wonder "What if?" Be idea-prone and let your imagination run wild the ideas will start coming to you before you know it.

Whether you are an outsider looking in or an insider trying to apply your expertise to the larger picture, or whether you are providing a service, a product, or an innovation, you need to make sure you cover all the bases. Once you have your idea, you must play devil's advocate with it. Is your idea viable? Who are the competitors? If you provide it, will it be bought? A good entrepreneur isolates all of the potential shortcomings of a project, in order to be able to address them intelligently when necessary.

Myths about the Entrepreneur

The word *entrepreneur* does not typically come up in people's everyday conversation. It seems that there are a lot of false ideas out there about what it means to be an entrepreneur. Many people mistakenly believe that entrepreneurs must be over 30 years old, that they are always men, or that they are capable of squeezing 25 hours out of each workday, and of leaping tall buildings in a single bound. Here we will try to lay out some of the common fallacies about entrepreneurs, and to dispel these counterproductive myths.

Myth 1: Age Matters

Many people mistakenly believe that only middle-aged people with a lot of experience can be true entrepreneurs. This is the first myth that should be forgotten right away. This entire book is dedicated to the idea that you can do it now, while your are young. All you need is a good idea, a lot of enthusiasm, and a serious amount of energy to dedicate to solid preparation and planning. There is something to be said for experience, but we do not advocate that you jump headfirst into the business world. On the contrary we encourage you to think long and hard about your idea, to plan conscientiously for possible pitfalls, to conduct an exhaustive research into competitors and demographics, and then to make your move. The amount of preparation you will do will constitute a vast amount of relevant experience in itself.

Myth 2: Since Most New Businesses Fail, Yours Will Not Beat the Odds

The statistics are real—most new businesses started in this country in any given year do fail. But that statistic doesn't tell you much about the specific characteristics and shortcomings of the businesses that failed, does it? The truth is that many of the new businesses started each year are the product of ill-conceived (and untested) ideas, or of inadequate research and strategic planning. Many mom-and-pop stores are started close to home with no real concern for key business issues like location, marketing, and competition. People who start these types of businesses are more concerned with being self-employed than with watching a business idea grow and come alive. But you are already ahead of the game. In buying this book, you have shown your commitment to doing your homework before jumping into anything. Any successful entrepreneur will plan ahead and cover all the bases. You can beat the odds, as long as you are willing to do the work. It takes a lot more than just elbow grease.

Myth 3: Men Make Better Entrepreneurs

For those of you to whom this myth seems obviously stupid, we applaud your being in tune with modern thinking. But for those women who are allowing themselves to be held back by a myth as silly as this one, allow us to lay out the facts for you. In recent years, women have been starting new businesses in record numbers all over the United States. This trend is attributed in small part to the idea that women are rejecting the corporate lifestyle in favor of the freedom of self-employment. It has also been partially attributed to the idea that the glass ceiling is still in place in corporate America, and many women have therefore decided to make it on their own. Another reason may be that women are simply feeling more confident to go out there on their own than in decades past.

Whatever the reason, the trend shows no signs of slowing down. And the numbers don't lie. The growing number of female entrepreneurs shows that women can and do see entrepreneurship as a realistic option for themselves. Follow their lead, because the only thing holding you back now is yourself.

Myth 4: Every Entrepreneur Is a Superhuman

There is a general sense of awe inspired among the masses when they hear of an entrepreneur. The idea is that this person is a major force in the direction of the industry, and that he or she has single-handedly created, run, and managed a multimillion-dollar company from the start. This fallacy must be corrected, lest it discourage many bright people with great ideas from even attempting to pursue their dreams.

An entrepreneur is clearly more motivated than your average person, and very dynamic and exciting to be around. But the myth that entrepreneurs can and do everything is exactly that—a myth. They simply have the drive to start things from scratch, and to work until the wee hours of the morning if need be. But that doesn't mean they will never ask for help. Having a partner is not something to be ashamed of. Entrepreneurs get a lot of work done in the course of a day, and certainly do not waste any time, but that doesn't mean they can save the world, nor do they believe they can. They simply do their best.

Myth 5: Entrepreneurs Are All Children of Bill Gates

Besides the fact that Bill Gates has only one child, there are many other reasons you can bet that most entrepreneurs are not the children of billionaires and CEOs. First of all, there aren't that many billionaires in the world. And even among the children of billionaires, there aren't many who are entrepreneurs—they simply take over the family business. Why start from scratch when you have it all already?

Another issue is the desire to succeed. It is pretty simple to see why ordinary people strive for greatness—they want to be extraordinary, achieve something major, and distinguish themselves from the rest. There is a major gain to success for people who come from humble beginnings. Others will admire their perseverance. The point is that the majority of entrepreneurs are ordinary people who want to be extraordinary. No doubt a few connections will help the billionaire's child to get a meeting or two, but in the larger scheme of things, no one will back an idea that isn't worth it. So where you come from really doesn't matter—more important is where you are going.

Myth 6: A Good Idea Is All It Takes

As much as we would love to be able to tell you that finding your idea is half the battle, we just can't knowingly mislead you. The right idea is about 10 percent of the game. But being an entrepreneur is about a lot more than that. Many people have planned incorrectly and been known to run a perfectly good idea into the ground.

Take the idea of opening up an Indian restaurant in your college town. Maybe you know there is a large Indian population, and maybe you make a mean masala, but your business still goes bankrupt within a year. Why? Because you failed to recognize that while the students wanted good Indian food, they weren't willing to pay $30 for a meal in your fancy restaurant. You should have opened a fast-food place instead, keeping your original Indian food idea, but aiming it more specifically at your target market. A good idea is not all it takes, it is just the beginning.

There are many obstacles to your becoming a successful entrepreneur, but the biggest one is your own apprehension. Keep in mind that these impediments to your success are myths, and convince yourself that the only thing holding you back is you. There is so much wasted entrepreneurial potential in this world—don't let yours fall prey to something as simple as a myth.

Dos and Don'ts

While it would be impossible for us to give you a comprehensive list of what you should and shouldn't do in the shark-infested waters of the business world, it would be irresponsible not to offer any advice at all. You know by now what the qualities of an entrepreneur are, you know how to look for an idea, and you know which myths to put out of your mind. But most of the advice we have given up until now has focused on ways of thinking. Now we feel we should give you a few simple pointers on ways of acting. Remember that none of this is written in stone—but in our experience, following these guidelines will help you significantly.

Do Use Every Connection You Have
Don't Believe That Connections Are All It Takes

We don't believe there is anything wrong with allowing friends or family to help put you in touch with people you need to know. If it only goes up to a point, then no crime has been committed. If you don't take advantage of every connection you have, it is the equivalent of not taking advantage of every opportunity you have. That would be insane and extremely impractical. As long as you understand what a connection means and how far it will go, you will be fine playing the name game (i.e., name-dropping). A connection is merely a way of getting your foot in the door—it doesn't mean you will be asked to stay. In the business world, it is often difficult to get people to hear you out. If a connection gets you that meeting you wanted with a major supplier, then consider yourself blessed, not sanctified. Connections get meetings, not deals. No intelligent business executive is going to give you a deal or a partnership based on a connection (other than family, which doesn't count as a connection). At best, people will hear you out, and if your idea shows real potential, they may then decide to work with you. But the burden of convincing them is on you. Go to it.

Do Select a Partner Based on Skills
Don't Select a Partner Based on Friendship

While business partners may later make friends, friends should never become business partners. If you have known someone in a social context, shared personal stories, had fun times, and helped each other out, then a lot of expectation arises from the relationship. At base, it is an emotionally dependent relationship, where you expect to respect each other's feelings. At base, however, the business relationship is one of mutual responsibility and convenience. The problem arises because friends play on each other's emotions, and sometimes expect not to be held completely accountable for their actions. Why would you knowingly leave yourself open to such a conflict of interest? Unless your friend is the best partner you can objectively find, you should steer clear of a business-friendship relationship. Tempers begin to flare, and before long the best of friends can become the fiercest of enemies. Try to choose a partner based on his or her skill set, dedication, and seriousness about the business.

Do Be Friendly with Everyone
Don't Let Friendship Factor into Decisions

Once you have found a business partner or partners, it becomes important to maintain a friendly working relationship. You have to deal with these people on a constant basis, and tension can make even the simplest meeting a chore. So right from the start, you should go out of your way to establish a friendly atmosphere.

However, don't take this too far, because you risk falling into the same predicament just described: If you are overly friendly, people expect you to bend the rules of basic business fairness for them. And you shouldn't feel obliged to make anything other than the soundest business decisions. The future of your business depends on it. That is why you shouldn't let friendships made on the job factor into business decisions. All the business world cares about is the bottom line, and you can't afford to let emotions and friendship factor in. You are not being cold or callous—this is the business world.

Do Be Honest, Trustworthy, and True to Your Word
Don't Make Verbal Contracts

Sometimes in business, you get involved with people who like to consider themselves to be from the old school of thought, believing that their word or handshake is as weighty as a contract. And most of the time, these people are true to their word. You must be the same way if you want to gain the respect of these and any other businesspeople. Your word should be something they know they can count on. But while you should be trustworthy, you shouldn't necessarily trust everyone. In general we like to believe that people mean what they say and want to stick to their word, but when push comes to shove, people sometimes answer to a higher, greener power. That is why you should never accept a verbal contract. Be honest with people and always stand by your word, and show them that you trust them in general. But when it comes down to it, get everything in writing. No one will consider you a fool for it—people will actually admire you for your business smarts and wish they had thought that way at your age. If they have no ill intentions, they will have no problems signing a contract. And even if they do so only to humor you, the bottom line is that you will get it in writing.

Do Be Persistent and Determined
Don't Absolutely Refuse to Give Up

Dedicating yourself to success at any cost may end up costing you your business. When we advocate persistence we are totally serious—up to a point. It is a major character flaw to keep running headfirst into the same wall, refusing to give up until you crack open your skull. After a while it begins to sink in that no one can break down a wall without some help. Knowing when to call it quits is an important quality. And although it is always tough to decide to stop trying, you must be willing and able to do so when necessary. Many overachievers have major problems with defeat, and therefore cannot bring themselves to stop something they started— but that is why their companies fail. Don't be a statistic. Don't be a victim of your own ambition. Don't refuse to give up.

Do Ask for Advice and Constructive Criticism
Don't Take It Personally

If you have half a grasp of reality, you realize that other people have good advice for you. Along the course of your entrepreneurial adventure, you must be willing to actively seek constructive criticism at every turn. By buying this book, you have sought help in getting started, which is great. But along the way you should always be asking for advice and criticism from others who see things from a more objective point of view. You must remember that you are often too invested and involved in your project to make an impartial judgment.

Once you get the constructive criticism you were asking for, you must be willing to accept it and learn from it. Take it as a criticism of a particular plan or strategy, not of you. Taking constructive criticism personally is a weakness and a sign of immaturity. Overachievers will tell you that the hardest thing to deal with is criticism. One of the major things that drives them to great lengths to achieve perfection is often a fear of criticism. That is why they (and you, if you are one of them) need to learn to see criticism as advice, not as a personal attack. Don't take it personally.

Conclusion

Hopefully, this chapter has gotten you thinking along the lines of the type of personality it takes to become a successful entrepreneur. At the same time, you should have started to identify the traits in yourself that will help or hurt you in business. The right frame of mind is the first and perhaps most important piece in your entrepreneur's tool kit. Once you recognize your assets and dispell any myths that may be holding you back, you will be ready to get started.

The process of finding your idea may take time. Once you have isolated what you want to achieve, you can begin to formulate your game plan. The next few chapters will add to your tool kit, by laying out the necessary steps involved in the successful marketing, financing, and presentation of your business.

Chapter 2

❧❧❧❧

Marketing Your Product

What exactly is marketing? Philip Kotler (1997) in *Marketing Management* gives a concise definition of *marketing* as "a process by which individuals . . . obtain what they need and want through creating, offering and exchanging products of value with others" (p. 9). In this chapter, we plan to break down the steps and explain the methods of marketing in a way you can really work with.

There are two types of people involved in this exchange: the marketer (you) and the prospect (the potential customer). The difference between the two is that the marketer actively seeks the exchange while the prospect might take part in it. The marketer wants to make the transaction happen because you the marketer need the prospect's money in order to have a profitable business, but the prospect does not necessarily need your product, because there are plenty of other vendors. Thus, the burden is on you to prove to prospects that it is worth their while to spend their hard-earned money on your product or service instead of on someone else's. In order to do this, you have to not only create a product with unique customer benefits, but also be able to effectively communicate this special value so that consumers are compelled to buy from you. It is only when someone purchases your product or service that he or she becomes your customer. Transforming prospects into customers is the essence not only of marketing, but in some sense also of your business. It does not matter how ingenious your product is. Without customers your business is at most an awesome idea. Profits sustain and revitalize your business and they are derived from customer sales. Thus, customers are the life source of your business.

What Is a Marketing Strategy?

A marketing strategy consists of five steps that enable you to build a customer base:

1. Researching the market
2. Segmenting the market
3. Communicating your unique selling proposition (USP)
4. Building long-lasting relationships with your customers
5. Developing a distribution plan

In this section we will explain the what, why, and how of each of these five steps. Later in the chapter we will explore each step in depth.

Researching the Market

What? Conducting market research means gathering information in order to understand customer preferences for products and services. Are your customers city or country dwellers? How old are they? What gender?

Why? The only products that will sell are ones that satisfy customer needs and wants. Market research is the key to discovering these consumer desires and creating a profitable product.

How? Use primary and secondary research tools. Primary tools are surveys, focus groups, and personal interviews. Secondary tools are online databases, libraries, and newspapers and magazines.

Segmenting the Market

What? Markets are not homogeneous, they are segmented. Let's take the cookie market for example. There are those customers who like soft home-baked cookies and those who like crunchy cookies. There are junkies who are tired of all the fat-free imitations, and health food freaks who only want all-natural. Segmenting the market means identifying the different customer groups and selecting one to focus on, so that you are meeting the standards and satisfying the needs of that one group.

Why? Instead of doing a mediocre job trying to please everyone, you use segmenting to focus your energy and provide the highest-quality product or service to a particular group. High quality is what keeps customers coming back again and again.

How? There are two crucial criteria in choosing your market segment: (1) identification of unfulfilled wants or needs, and (2) your ability to do an excellent job satisfying them.

Communicating Your Unique Selling Proposition (USP)

What? Your unique selling proposition (USP) is the special or unique benefit your product or service offers customers.

Why? The USP is the abracadabra of marketing. The USP is the magic word that will turn prospects into customers. It gives people a reason to buy from you instead of from someone else.

How? There are countless methods to communicate how special you are. This chapter will focus on the most up-to-date and effective ones.

Building Long-lasting Relationships with Your Customers

What? Building relationships with your customers means creating not just customers but loyal customers.

Why? Customer loyalty is the critical factor that separates business failures from business successes. In addition, keeping a loyal customer costs five times less than creating a new one.

How? Maintain ongoing personal communication with customers in order to ensure their satisfaction. Ask for their feedback on products.

Developing a Distribution Plan

What? A distribution plan identifies where you are going to sell your product or service. Are you going to have street stores or cyberstores where you sell over the net?

Why? People can be running wild in the streets for your product or service, but if they do not know where to go and, worse, you do not know how to get it to them, then clearly the outcome will be no sales, no revenue, no profit.

How? Identify your competitors' distribution styles, the larger distribution trends, and so on, and choose the most profitable way to distribute.

The Customer: The Center of Your Marketing Strategy

Picture yourself in the hottest luxury car around. With a full tank of gas, you are cruising through a beautiful part of the countryside. There are open fields full of colorful wildflowers, and in the background are beautiful, majestic mountains. There is not a cloud in the sky, and the road is all yours—there is not a soul around (not even the sheriff to catch you speeding). Your destination: heaven on earth. But there is just one problem: You have never traveled through this area before. To make it worse, there are many forks in the road, and it is difficult to tell if you have gotten anywhere because the scenery looks the same no matter how far you drive. What are you going to do? Reach for the map and compass. You have already used the map and compass in order to determine the best route to get you to your destination, and you will refer to these tools during your trip to make sure you do not take a wrong turn. The compass and map constitute your frame of reference: They help you find the best path, giving you an idea of how far you have come, where you are, and how much farther you need to go. They tell you whether you are headed in the right direction or lost.

Likewise, when you are cruising along to reach your marketing goals, such as a certain percentage increase in sales, you need something to help guide you there. The customer is your frame of reference on the tricky road of marketing. Regularly refer to the customer when planning and implementing your marketing strategy. Operating with a customer frame of reference or customer focus means making an ongoing effort to understand and satisfy customer needs and preferences.

Traditionally, businesses focused on themselves instead of the customer. Because business owners were preoccupied with product and profit, the customer was lost in the sauce. Not until recently has the customer moved to the center of marketing and business. Why this change? Because businesses are beginning to understand that the customer is the source of their survival and growth. Buzzwords such as *customer loyalty* and *relationship marketing* are playing key roles in shaping the successful marketing strategies of today. Here's what those words mean.

- *Customer loyalty.* Loyal customers are not only interested in their own satisfaction. In a sense, they are also interested in yours—they want to see you do well. They are your cheerleaders. They will brag about you to friends and family, pay a little more for your product or service, and continue to purchase from you.
- *Relationship marketing.* Various marketing techniques strive to maintain a personal and long-term relationship with customers. One of the primary goals of relationship marketing is to inspire customer loyalty.

The difference between the customer (outward) and business (inward) orientation is captured by replacing Lauterborn's (1993) Four C's, from the text *Integrated Marketing Communications*, with the more traditional Four P's: (1) customer needs and wants instead of the product, (2) customer communication instead of promotion, (3) customer cost instead of price, and (4) customer convenience instead of place.

Customer Needs and Wants Instead of the Product

Let's say you have a great idea for a product and are convinced it will sell. Sorry to burst your bubble, but no matter how brilliantly conceived a product is, if consumers do not want or need it, it will not sell. In order to create a product that satisfies your customers' needs and wants, you have to get to know your customer. How? Use available data such as opinion polls and market studies, or create your own with interviews and surveys.

Customer Communication Instead of Promotion

The main way to get the word out about a business and its product used to be promotion: talking *to* customers. Now, it is all about communication—

talking *with* customers. It's a two-way street: The business and customers exchange ideas. When the marketer engages in this dialogue, it is crucial to listen to what the customer has to say.

Customer Cost Instead of Price

The customer determines the price tag, not you. In order to price your product or service, you have to consider more than just profit. You have to take into account what the customer is willing and able to pay. If you price your product inappropriately for your target customers, you risk losing them.

Customer Convenience Instead of Place

Today, convenience is one of the most important customer preferences. People like stores such as Kmart because they can drive to one place and pick up ballpoint pens, houseplants, and makeup all at once. When deciding where you are going to sell your product, your first priority ought to be customer convenience. Reducing costs is a legitimate concern, but if you choose a business location only because it is a low-rent area, you've made a bad move—most customers won't budge to buy from you because your low rent is not making their life any easier.

One reason cyberstores (web sites that allow customers to order products online) are becoming popular is that they are the epitome of convenience: Customers can shop from the comfort of their own home.

Networking

If a mountain is in your path, don't be so quick to put on your hiking boots. Ask the old woman sitting under the tree if there is an easier way.

The National Foundation for Women Business Owners (1998) reports that from 1987 to 1996, the number of American companies owned by women increased by 78 percent. These businesses are not small-time mom-and-pop shops either. They are lucrative, fast-growing start-ups with employment and sales that grew by 183 percent and 236 percent respectively. The reason for their phenomenal growth is networking.

A network is the contact information shared by a group of people. A business network can consist of former coworkers, media contacts, business centers, and mentors. Networking can help you get the financing you need or just some sound business advice. But advice goes a long way. More experienced entrepreneurs who have already been through the maze of marketing decisions can help you save time and money. As an entrepreneur and marketer, you are aware that time and energy are even more valuable than money because they are the source of your profit. You want to use time and energy in the most efficient and productive way possible—and reinventing the wheel is not the way. Don't repeat failed ventures, and don't take 10 months to learn something you could have learned in a 10-minute phone conversation.

In order to build a network, you simply keep in contact with people through your experience in the business world. For example, if you cash out of a company (sell a young start-up for a lot of money), don't throw away the phone numbers and e-mails associated with the venture. Keep the contacts because they may come in handy later. If you do not have a network in place and feel you have no one to turn to, do not despair. The following mentoring programs can match you with a more experienced entrepreneur:

- *Small Business Development Centers.* These offer free counseling and training programs. There are 970 centers nationwide, 48 of which are on college campuses. Contact: 703-271-8700 or www.asbdc-us.org.
- *The Initiative for a Competitive Inner City.* This organization encourages entrepreneurship in urban areas. Free mentoring services are available, and it is affiliated with the Harvard Business School. Contact: 617-292-2363 or www.icic.org.
- *National Association of Women Business Owners* (NAWBO). This organization matches women entrepreneurs with other women who have had experience running a company. Contact: 800-55-NAWBO or www.nawbo.org.
- *The Economist.* This monthly magazine is a great source for contacts and networking information.
- *The Financial Times.* This London daily is another widely read and informative publication.

Marketing Is Dynamic

Just like fashion trends, the best marketing strategies are constantly changing. You understand that only the best businesses enjoy long-lasting success, but how do you know what the best marketing strategy is if it is always changing?

Like a person who always dresses in style, a successful marketer must always be hip. As explained in this section, a successful marketer always knows about the latest trends concerning consumers, competitors, business, and communication. But unlike the sharp dresser, if the marketer is not up-to-date, he or she doesn't just get a bad reputation, but also risks the livelihood of his or her business.

Consumer Trends

Consumer trends mainly consist of changes in lifestyles and values. The marketer is interested in these trends because they affect where and how consumers spend their money. To understand consumer lifestyles, investigate indicators such as crime rates and the state of the economy. If the crime rate is up, maybe customers will not frequent evening hot spots as often. If unemployment is down and the Dow Jones is skyrocketing, consumers might be more willing to spend a few extra dollars on luxury items.

The Gap is launching a campaign to capitalize on one of the most famous aspects of New Yorkers' lifestyle: being in a rush. According to the president of Gap Inc., New Yorkers (especially Manhattanites) are busy—too busy to get to the closest Gap store. So, Gap to Go has made various clothes available by fax: Shoppers fill in the size and style on order forms which they then fax to the store. Within hours, the order arrives at the customer's doorstep for a $10 delivery fee and $3 handling charge.

The customer of today is sophisticated and efficient. Consequently, two important customer values are quality and convenience. A product will not sell itself just because it is cheap. Customers are looking for durable, well-made goods. At the same time, as 50 to 60 work hours a week have become the norm, consumers want to save time and highly value convenient ways to shop.

Competitor Trends

> *To increase your market share in today's market place, no matter what your business is, you have to take customers away from the competition.*
>
> —Britt Beemers (1997, p. 151)

Beemers (1997) argues that there are fewer and fewer undecided customers in the marketplace—they are either yours or someone else's. For this reason it is crucial that you always keep up with your competitors' marketing strategies. What kind of technology are they using? How are they distributing their products? Have they introduced any new products or services recently? Keep your marketing strategy flexible in order to be able to launch a successful counterattack against your competitors. (Chapter 5 provides more information on keeping abreast of the competition.)

Business Trends

How do you keep up with how businesses do business? Read. Newspapers, magazines, and journals are highly recommended because they provide current information on a monthly, weekly, or even a daily basis. The following are good sources of information on business trends:

- Inc.
- Small Business Report
- Nations Business
- Business Week
- Forbes
- Entrepreneur
- Fortune
- Wall Street Journal
- New York Times

One major change that has altered the internal structure of business has been the shift from hierarchy to teamwork. The traditional business structure is very hierarchical: Orders are handed down from the top to the bottom rungs, where employees must "just do what the boss said." Questioning authority and sharing ideas are discouraged. But now this ancient pyramid structure is being replaced by a more level playing field as business adopts a team culture.

How does this change affect marketing? The team culture goes beyond the company itself and permeates its relationship with customers, as businesses attempt marketing *with* not *at* the customer. This engenders communication instead of promotion.

Communication Trends

If you haven't noticed, we are in the midst of a communication revolution. Laptops and portable PCs have enhanced the net's ability to electronically link people with one another. On some college campuses even though campus phone calls are free, e-mail is one of the most widely used forms of communication. Why are these new technologies so popular ? They are fast and productive. Businesses have picked up by going online and providing not just a toll-free phone number, but also a web address. Desktop marketing—using your personal computer to design and execute marketing strategies—is widespread. Databases created and stored by computer software systems help companies recall the purchases and pet peeves of any customer with the stroke of a key.

Steps in the Marketing Strategy

Earlier in this chapter we gave you the what, why, and how of the five steps of marketing strategy. Let's look at each step in depth now.

Step 1: Research the Market

The purpose of researching the market is to gather information in order to understand customer preferences for products and services. You will need two types of marketing research: primary and secondary. Primary research gives you an up-close and personal view of your potential customer, and secondary research provides guidance and perspective.

Look before You Leap: Marketing research is most useful when you first plan and define goals. Do you just want to explore and get a feel for the market, or are you trying to solve a specific problem? What will you measure? How? Why? Once you have answered these questions you are ready to embark on your quest to know the customer. Your information on the whole should play a major role in shaping important business decisions.

Start with Secondary Research: Secondary research entails gathering and interpreting ready-to-use data. It should be done before primary research because with little effort, you can get large amounts of information that can play a crucial role in guiding primary research, which tends to be much more time-consuming and/or costly. Some sources for secondary research are as follows:

- Demographic studies
- Marketing research studies
- Newspaper and magazine articles
- Opinion polls

Money is only green paper if we do not know what to do with it. Likewise, we've got the sources, but so what? Let's take a look at the demographics. If you are interested in, for instance, selling women's clothing, you would probably want to know the age range of females in an area. How many females are there? What is their income? Are they single or married?

Secondary information can be stored in two forms: print or online. Newspapers, magazines, microfilm, and CD-ROMs are all considered printed material. Helpful CD-ROM databases are as follows:

- *Moody's*
- *Business Newsbank*
- *General Business File*
- *Standard and Poor's Register*

Online information is in the form of computer databases. The benefits are that it is faster and it's free if your library computer system is hooked up to the net. There are many different kinds databases (see Chapter 5).

Move On to Primary Research: Secondary information has its limitations. Statistics and studies are useful only to a certain extent. A customer is a human being, and if you really want to understand him or her, you cannot rely solely on data. Primary research humanizes the customer, as it involves collecting information directly from potential customers. Three very common sources of primary research are interviews, focus groups, and customer surveys.

Now, you are probably wondering, How do I find the right people to interview and fill out my surveys? What you need is a list of prospects for your product or service. The best list is made up of those people you wish were your customers—the people you have identified as your prospects. Researching from a bad list is like asking a goldfish about the landscape of the Sahara desert—you probably wouldn't get very good information.

There are thousands of quality lists compiled in many different ways, ranging from attendees of trade shows to voter registrations. You can buy or rent them from list vendors, who can be found in the telephone book under "Mailing Lists." There are even list compilers who can create a customized list of prospects for your company. Once you compile a list and contact prospects, you can begin gathering information, using such tactics as interviews and questionnaires.

INTERVIEWS Interviews include personal interviews, focus groups, and telephone interviews.

■ *Personal interviews.* A face-to-face encounter fosters in-depth discussions that will allow you to address complex issues. Remember, getting a pat on the back tells you you're going in the right direction, but you also need criticism to tell you when you are not on the right path. A downside to personal interviews is that there is an interview bias: Interviewees may be afraid of expressing their true feelings for fear of insulting you.

■ *Focus groups.* You can interview more than one customer at the same time.

■ *Telephone interviews.* A personal interview can easily be conducted over the phone. The interview bias is reduced, because people tend to be less shy about telling a stranger what is really on their mind.

QUESTIONNAIRES Since prospects can respond to questionnaires anonymously, the interview bias is not a problem. Questionnaires should be concise and easy to complete. The principles of a good questionnaire are that the questions should be worded simply, address marketing problems and/or issues, and should not conflict with each other. Before you start handing it out, test your questionnaire by asking prospects about the quality of the questionnaire.

Remember, your goal is to learn what your potential customers think by getting them to talk. People tend to be less inhibited when they are relaxed, so don't be afraid to use informal ways to mingle with prospects, such as in casual conversations or at parties.

Step 2: Segment the Market

Segmenting the market means grouping similar customers together. There are many ways to group customers: demographics, geographics, taste, experience, income, gender, or customer needs. Use one or several of these ways to choose the market segment(s) you would like to be your prospects. In this way, you can focus your energy and do a better job of satisfying your customers.

Because of the demand for customized products and services, marketers are increasingly turning to needs-based segmentation. Market segments are defined by customer needs and are like personality types: the no-frills customer versus the one who prefers intense service. Unlike segments solely based on factors such as income and geographic location, needs-based segments enable the marketer to meet individual expectations.

A *Niche of Your Own*: Your product or service should not only fulfill customer needs, but do it well. If you want to be successful, your product should be very high quality, not mediocre. If you have found where your expertise and customer needs intersect, you have found your niche. You just struck gold, baby, so start digging now. If you find a market segment that you feel has a lot of potential, but you lack the know-how to meet their needs, don't despair. Think about establishing a partnership or outsourcing where you can hire advertisement or distributing agencies. Your niche gives you a foothold in the market: a strong and loyal customer base that gives you the foundation to expand.

Microsoft identifies consumers who use online services and entertainment as a growing and profitable market segment. Their latest move was to bring the power of the Internet to the consumer through the TV set.

In Microsoft's 1997 Annual Report, the company describes plans to tap this market segment by bringing the power of the Internet (via a fast, easy to use delivery system) to the TV set. (1997 Annual Report, p. 18)

Pricing: Attracting your target market will depend to a large extent on what price tag you put on your product or service. The price conveys your image as a business and attracts a certain kind of customer. When it comes to price, all customers are somewhere in between the two extremes of big spender and bargain hunter. Where does your customer fall on this spectrum? Saks Fifth Avenue appeals to the big spenders. If Saks slashed prices in half, they would probably lose customers because their cus tomers find value—and status—in the high prices. The bargain hunter keeps a lookout for discounts, and if Kmart upped prices, the bargain hunter would be on the streets in a flash, looking for low prices. Determining which group you appeal to is key in your pricing strategy.

The best price will give you the most dollars for your entrepreneurial labor. Although the trend is high quality and low price, you do not want to fall into the trap of charging a price so low that you undervalue your own work. In addition, a cheaper product does not automatically mean increased sales. Keep in mind that quality, status, and convenience are key factors that also enhance products and services. Your best price is one that allows you to make a profit and be competitive with other companies.

Step 3: Communicate Your Unique Selling Proposition (USP)

A USP is the special benefit that you provide the customer. It is the magic touch that will transform a prospect into your customer. The following are some examples of USPs:

- Skytel's USP is the fact that they are the first nationwide paging service that guarantees you'll get all of your messages.
- Telecom's USP is savings on long-distance calls: Dial 10-10-321. Save up to 50 percent.
- Little Bear Organic Foods's USP is that their tortilla chips are made with organic white corn and no hydrogenated oils.

Your USP will cast a spell if you keep in mind these two pointers:

1. Good USPs address customer values such as knowing what's going on at all times, saving money, or being healthy.
2. Your USP should be a short, clear statement that gets to the point.

Part of the Picture: You've been working hard at packing all of this information into your head, so we're going to take you on a short trip. You are on a beautiful beach in the Caribbean. You are enjoying a leisurely walk, the sun is bright and warm, and the sea spray is refreshing. Unfortunately, because you are an entrepreneur it's hard to get away from business, and you encounter your USP in 3-D block letters written in the sand in front of you. You stop, and take 10 giant steps backward. Do you see it any differ- ently? Of course you do. Your USP is part of something larger—your image. Your USP along with a name, trademark, and symbol constitute who you are to the customer. Taking a few steps back can help you get a better perspective on how the customer sees you.

Company names often describe the personality of a business. For instance, FreeLoader, which sold for $38 million eight months after its birth, was the perfect name for a company that sold offline Internet browsers. Why? Because the word *freeloader* suggests something wild and different. The company was young and hip . . . and the owners had goatees. A cool name like Freeloader (and uncool ones also) can be legally protected by a trademark so that no one else can use it. Trademarks can also include any symbols and descriptive words. (See Chapter 6 to learn more about protecting yourself in business.)

ABC's recent advertising campaign used the color yellow and catchy slogans. In an effort to compete against cable television and to improve ratings, the TV network painted garbage cans, coffee cups, and food carts yellow and peppered them with phrases like "Hello? It's free," or "You're breathing. We're breathing. Let's get together." The bright yellow and playful comments were part of the effort to depict ABC TV as a fun and happenin' network, and to grab people's attention.

Okay, let's assume you have a fly image. How do you get customers to take notice? Later in this chapter you'll learn cutting-edge marketing methods that will help you communicate your USP.

Consumers Are Shedding Their Numbers and Declaring Themselves Individuals: Consumers want to be treated as individuals. Not only do they want products and services to be tailored to their individual needs, but they want you to communicate with them on a personal level. Mass marketing is not very personal because its tactic is to broadcast advertisements to anyone within earshot. On the other hand, direct marketing (also known as relationship marketing or micromarketing) is becoming increasingly popular, because it makes it possible for businesses to tailor their messages to a more specific group of individuals, thereby laying the foundation for a long-lasting and personal relationship with each customer.

The shift away from mass marketing is fueled by the desire not only to reach the individual, but also to cut costs: businesses are moving away from paid advertising while mass media (television and radio) costs have increased.

Media Is Interactive: What makes media interactive is that it

- Is easily accessible
- Engages the customer
- Encourages dialogue between the business and the customer

Where's the Beef? During a time where people want more information but have less time, people want useful facts, not fluff. One major reason the Sprint Corporation failed to generate excitement about its communications network in June 1998 at Times Square is that even with all the hype and the flashy multimedia display, Sprint failed to explain the details. People needed to know exactly how Sprint would provide the communications network that would allow people to talk on the phone, surf the net, receive video images, and get data access with a single connection.

The following are characteristics of cutting-edge marketing methods:

■ Targeted at specific market segments
■ Low-cost
■ Personal and tailored to the individual
■ Interactive
■ Chock-full of information

The five marketing methods discussed later in this chapter conform to the above profile. These methods will help you fine-tune your USP.

Step 4: Build Long-lasting Relationships with Your Customers

We have some bad news for you if you are set on being the sole boss of your company. If you want to be successful, you will always have a partner—the customer. Your customer is your partner because you can't do it alone—without customers there are no sales or profits. Just like you would with any legal business partner, discuss your ideas with the customers and consult them before making crucial business decisions. How? Primary and secondary research are an ongoing job for the marketer. Check the stats, regularly conduct interviews and circulate customer feedback surveys. Here are some questions to keep in mind:

■ *Are my employees knowledgeable?*
■ *Does the company web site provide enough information?*
■ *Is ordering through the company web site fast and easy?*
■ *Are my employees helpful?*
■ *Is it easy to find the products and services customers are looking for?*
■ *How would I rate product quality?*
■ *Are my prices competitive?*
■ *Is my location convenient?*
■ *What would make the customers' experience with us better?*

Remember the concept of dialogue. On surveys, ask customers if they would like a response from you. If so, request that they leave contact information. After you have gone through all the trouble to get customers, keep them. If you were building a house, would you be very successful if every time you added some new material to the structure, the foundation caved in? Likewise, building a strong customer base is not about just acquiring new customers, but rather adding new customers while maintaining the ones you already have.

Treat Her Like a Lady—Treat Her Like a Customer: Building a lasting relationship with a customer is no different from building lasting relationships with a family member or a friend. Let's say that you have a girlfriend whom you intend to marry. If times get hard, you will be there for her. If you two have an argument, you discuss your feelings and try to understand her point of view. You cheer her on. You share your laughter and tears. You never stand her up. If you want to develop a long-lasting relationship with a customer, you have to act the same way: courteous, confident, reliable, supportive, caring, understanding, and communicative.

The Database: The Key to Building Relationships with Customers

FIRST GUY: Hey, Rich! What's up? How's the family? How was the trip up to Martha's Vineyard?

SECOND GUY: Oh, great! We really had a good time. The weather was great.

FIRST GUY: I know your wife, Carol, must have had a really good time with all that ocean. Were you able to get some biking in?

SECOND GUY: We biked the whole island. . . . Say, what was your name again?

Rich just made a big social blunder, and probably lost a potentially good friend. The lesson: Make an extra effort to know people by name. This is a skill you need not only in social circles but also in the business world.

Know your customer by name. How? Just as you can purchase (or rent) lists of prospects and customers with their contact information from list vendors, you can create a computerized customer database to store and organize contact information. The database can represent and sort your customers in a variety of ways, such as opinions, preferences, or buying patterns. With this information, you can establish sales follow-up systems such as warranties, customer support, repair, and post-sales questionnaires. This kind of ongoing contact helps you create loyal customers.

Not only do you want your database to include information on how to contact your customer, but you also want it to include a customer profile that can be shaped around a variety of tools: customer surveys, complaints, product returns, or a casual conversation. There are a variety of database management software programs that can sort customer information in different ways. For instance, customers can be sorted by frequency or recentness of purchase, income, demographics, age, or sex.

There are plenty of database management software programs available. In the June 1998 issue of *Small Business Computing and Communications*, Pat Carey suggests that for the real do-it-yourselfer (which is you if you are an entrepreneur), Lotus Approach, Micros Access, and Corel Paradox are the best.

Step 5: Develop a Distribution Plan

Distribution is simply the way in which you answer the question of where you choose to sell your product. How do you make that choice? Locate the profits. For example, Coca-Cola Bottling Consolidated noticed that cold drinks sold in vending machines and by fountain equipment were less susceptible to "pricing pressures and thus produc[ed] higher margins" (Coca-Cola Annual Report 1994, p. 11). Consequently, they significantly increased the number of vending machines in places such as hotels, factories, schools, and offices. A lot of Starbucks customers purchase drinks from Starbucks coffeehouses (Starbucks Annual Report 1997, p. 20, p. 23). However, in 1997, the company began to distribute a new product via supermarkets: coffee ice cream. Starbucks introduced six unique coffee ice cream flavors, expanded its market for ice cream by 32 percent and is currently considered the number one ice cream maker in the United States.

Convenience is another key issue to keep in mind when thinking about the best location. Customers want to get what they want quickly and easily.

A distribution channel is the path of the product from you to the customer. There are two types of distribution channels: indirect and direct.

Indirect Distribution Channels: An indirect distribution channel simply means that between you and the customer, there is an intermediary who is responsible for getting the product to the customer—a middleman. Distributors specialize in distribution. They know what they are doing, and they know how to make a product move. Distribution may be a burden on a company, and if the benefits outweigh the costs of paying outsiders to do the dirty work, then go for it. In 1995 Nantucket Nectars sold their two distribution companies and hired outside distributors because the outsiders really knew how to deliver the juice. Those cool cats who founded Freeloader created a distribution partnership. *Hotwired* magazine distributed Freeloader's software, and in exchange Freeloader sold versions that automatically subscribed their customers to *Hotwired*. Besides doling out your goodies, intermediaries can provide many more useful services, such as conducting market research, sharing business risk, and providing customer service.

Unfortunately, unless you have a Freeloader-*Hotwired* connection going on, middlemen incur costs that come out of either customers' savings or your profits. However, manufacturing agents may be able to solve the cost problem. They specialize in selling many different types of products and are paid on commission so the cost is kept at a minimum. In *Guerrilla Marketing*, Jay Levinson and Seth Goodin (1993) argue that marketing agents are great assets because they expand the work and sales force without your having to hire many employees.

Direct Marketing Channels: A direct marketing channel means your business distributes the product. These channels have several benefits.

- It is conducive to just-in-time inventory systems where you order the product from suppliers (or make the product yourself) when you receive consumer payments instead of having a preordered inventory. The result is that you can cut down on inventory costs and offer a greater variety of products.
- You can cut out the cost you pay to distributors since there is no need for them. You, not the distributors, are sending the product directly to the customers.
- Mail-order and online catalogs are also popular forms of direct distribution channels.

Indirect or Direct? Before you decide whether to do direct or indirect distribution, do three things.

1. Find out what distribution channels exist in your industry.
2. Understand the trends that are developing in distribution channels.
3. Know which channels are most profitable for you.

Methods of Marketing

There are five methods of marketing: (1) direct marketing, (2) word of mouth, (3) the press release, (4) guerrilla marketing, and (5) making your customer feel special.

Method 1: Direct Marketing

Direct marketing was explained earlier, but we are going to repeat it for you: It means that you communicate with customers in a direct, personal, and ongoing fashion. A crucial component of direct marketing is computer databases that allow you to identify and differentiate one customer from the other.

Spiderman's Weapon Is Also Yours: The Web and Online Marketing: The Internet is increasingly becoming an integral part of marketing, as more and more company web sites are popping up on the net. They are considered the epitome of interactive media, because the customer can reach you at any time from any location, actively seek out information, and ask you questions via your e-mail address posted on the home page.

Web sites can offer a variety of services, from providing automated customer information to purchasing products over the net. For instance, Delta is offering online services tailored to the "busy entrepreneur" that allow customers to book meetings online. Another web site is part of the "Women on Their Way" program, which addresses issues female road warriors face such as safety and staying fit while traveling. If you want to book a flight, do it on the net.

An increasing number of small businesses are going online and setting up web sites that enable customers to purchase products online by clicking on an item and filling out the order form and credit card information.

As with any store, it is important to protect your e-commerce systems from breaking and entering by hackers. If you decide to sell online through credit cards, be sure that credit card numbers are well encrypted and stored in secure databases.

Web sites are inexpensive because supply has outpaced demand. Not only are they cheap to buy, but they stay cheap even when you are serving a growing customer base. Contrast this with direct mail, where for each additional customer you have to pay for another envelope and more postage.

Keeping costs low is good, but never at the expense of your business. If you are ignorant about web sites and even with a lot of effort you can only create a mediocre one, your time is better spent doing something else. Hire someone who knows what he or she is doing to design your web site. If you can't find that someone in your employee pool, you can outsource the work to companies that set up web sites, such as CyberSource, IBM, and iCat.

But if you want to give web site creation a try, Microsoft BackOffice Small Business Server is very user-friendly. It helps you to easily keep your web site up-to-date and send brochures and newsletters via e-mail.

Telephone, Telephone: Using the telephone as a medium for marketing is called telemarketing. Outbound telemarketing is when you call customers in order to make sales or gather customer information. If you decide to sell over the phone, you are not only a marketer, but a salesperson. You are like a door-to-door salesperson except that you are sitting at your desk. Many door-to-door salespeople have broken noses. Why? Because while they are happily giving their sales pitch, doors slam shut right on their faces. Likewise many telemarketers are cut off by a click and a dial tone. What's the message? Being a good salesperson is a natural gift, and not everyone has the gift.

Norm Brodsky, a retired entrepreneur whose businesses have been featured several times in *Inc.*, describes what makes a good salesperson in the June 1998 issue of *Inc.* (Brodsky, 1998, p. 41).

- Gift for connecting with people
- Ability to handle rejection
- Ability to provide service to customers
- Entrepreneurial spirit

If outbound telemarketing isn't your style, there is inbound, which might be more fun. Inbound telemarketing is when customers call you because you posted a toll-free number on your web site. Getting calls always makes you feel good.

Forget what your parents told you and spend more time on the phone rather than less. Did your customers have a good day? Did they catch the Bulls game? Establish a friendly rapport and come away with new information about each customer.

Direct Mail: Direct mail allows you to use mail in order to directly communicate with your customer. You may use direct mail to notify your customers about special offers, request that they fill out a response card, or sell your product or service. (Newsletters and brochures are often sent via regular mail, also known as snail mail; however, an increasing number are now sent to customers via e-mail.) You can get names and addresses of prospective customers from a list broker.

Unfortunately, many people who receive direct mail use it to practice their Michael Jordan shots into the trash basket. Direct mail is often considered junk mail. How do you ensure that the mail you send is not junk? Personalize, personalize, personalize.

- Hand-address the envelope and make sure you spell the names—even the really long or tricky ones—correctly.
- If you don't have too many letters, sign each one.
- Get out the database, and in the body of the letter convey the sense that you understand customers' individual needs.
- Always provide your customer with a way to contact you immediately via e-mail or a toll-free number.

Mailings may seem like slow torture, but although e-mail is faster, snail mail will always be more personal. For some reason paper is just more warm and friendly. When we think of real love letters, we think of waiting for the postman to deliver a missive written on perfumed stationery. And people love to curl up with a good book, not a computer screen.

Method 2: Word of Mouth

"Hi! Are you the girl who bakes the sweet potato pies? My friend Giselle is roommates with Aisha whose boyfriend Mike ordered one, and he said they were really good. I would love to buy one from you."

Word of mouth means that a satisfied customer tells acquaintances, friends, and family how good your product or service is. Word of mouth is considered one of the most powerful forms of marketing because it has more influence over people's purchasing decisions than does advertising. In addition, Michael E. Caffery, author of *Let Your Customers Do the Talking*, claims that 80 percent of people use recommendations from "a family member, friend or business professional" (Caffery, 1997). If word of mouth is this effective, it should be an integral part of any marketing program.

How Do You Get Customers to Say Good Things about Your Product and/or Service? Word of mouth can go three ways: (1) the customer mentions your product to a friend but says only bad things, (2) the customer doesn't say anything at all, or (3) the customer praises your product and takes every opportunity to mention it not only to acquaintances and friends but even possibly to strangers. When a customer says bad things about your product, you lose sales. When a customer doesn't say anything, your sales stay the same. When a customer says good things about you, sales increase. It is obvious that you want your customers to brag about how good you are, but you are probably wondering, How can I have any influence over what someone else says? Here's how.

How to Get Customers to Say Bad Things about Your Product and/or Service   Cause your customers a big inconvenience or make them extremely dissatisfied. For example:

- An airline delays hundreds of passengers for several hours because of technical difficulties.
- At a restaurant, a customer finds a cockroach in the food.
- An appliance store advertises next-day delivery, but customers do not receive the goods until days after orders are placed.

How to Get Customers Not to Say Anything   Be mediocre. A customer will not say anything about your product or service if it is just okay. People like exciting discussion material.

HOW TO GET CUSTOMERS SO EXCITED ABOUT WHAT YOU HAVE TO OFFER THAT THEY MENTION IT TO FRIENDS, FAMILY, ACQUAINTANCES, AND EVEN STRANGERS Be exceptional. For example:

■ Have good prices or a high-quality product. Sometimes this can be enough to impress customers.

■ Support a noteworthy nonprofit organization or cause. Stoneybrook Farms Yogurt donates 10 percent of all profits toward saving the environment. You do not always have to give money. If you are in the food or restaurant business, you can provide the food for a special event.

■ Give free gifts for a limited time.

■ Hold fun contests.

Method 3: The Press Release

A press release consists of one or two pages that describe your business, product, or service. A press release sent to magazines or newspapers reaches potential customers in the form of an article. What is so special about a press release is that it is like an ad, in that you get space in a magazine or newspaper, but the beauty of it is that you don't have to pay a dime. A full-page newspaper ad can cost up to $80,000, but with a press release, you don't have to pay for space, design, typesetting, or layout.

There are two major types of magazines: consumer magazines and trade magazines. Consumer magazines are the ones you see at the newsstand or read at Barnes and Noble. The readership consists of consumers. Trade magazines cater to people who are knowledgeable in a specific field or industry. Although there are far fewer trade magazines per industry than consumer ones, and they reach a relatively small audience, trade magazines are important because the people who read them have deep and wide networks.

Who Does It Concern? Press releases are not just sent to a magazine or newspaper, but to a person—the editor. Ms. Editor is probably very busy at work—she may even have a headache the day she gets your press release in the mail. She receives lots and lots of press releases all the time and dumps a lot of them. During the bustle of a typical workday, what will make her slow down, thoughtfully read yours again, and use it in the paper? Two things: an interesting idea that is well conveyed, and a professional level of writing.

Don't let her even think about yawning. Make your press release interesting. Here's how:

■ Understand what market you are writing for and tailor the news to that audience.

- Editors are always looking for something new or exciting in order to spice up their publications. Your idea is awesome. Make sure the language you use conveys it.
- Make sure you convey your USP loud and clear.

Break out the blue suit—be professional. Here's how:

- Guard against typos and inaccuracies
- Include complete contact information.
- Write in newspaper style.
- Be factual yet descriptive. Avoid using a lot of adverbs and adjectives.
- Be cool. Don't bug the editor by calling everyday to ask, "Did you get it?"

Method 4: Guerrilla Marketing

The term *guerrilla marketing* was coined in the 1980s and refers to marketing driven by one idea: to get the biggest bang for your buck. The way you stretch your advertising budget is to attract attention. Ask a guerrilla marketer how to market your product and you'll get an answer something like this:

1. Do some wild comedy improve on a busy sidewalk wearing glasses with a Groucho Marx nose, and hand out some literature about your business.
2. Don't just put the name of your business on your company van, paint it in a loud color that everyone will notice—just make sure your name is readable. Maybe even let cans drag from the back fender.
3. Put on a cool costume and hand out free samples of your product.

Method 5: Making Your Customer Feel Special

Remember in grade school when the teacher gave you a gold star if you did your homework well? Those shiny stickers made you happy because they made you feel special—not everyone can get a gold star. Making your customer feel special as a marketing technique is like handing out gold stars. It isn't just a coincidence that many credit cards with special offers and rates are called gold cards.

A good criterion for membership in your company's "cool customer club" is how much business a particular customer gives you. If you reward frequent or long-term shoppers, these preferred customers will strengthen and expand your customer base.

Having a marketing strategy means devising a plan that covers all the bases, so pursuing one marketing method exclusively is not strategic. If it fails, you're in deep yogurt. Implement a few methods, so that if one isn't so hot, you will have others that will do the job. Besides, variety is the spice of life.

The Marketing Plan: Putting It All Together

A marketing plan simply puts your marketing strategy into writing so that it becomes a tangible, concrete, and more useful frame of reference. In addition, your marketing plan includes a mission statement, benchmarks, and time frames.

Although a marketing plan is often a segment of a business plan, it is different in key ways. For instance, your marketing plan is a customized strategy that addresses your unique needs, whereas your business plan is a standard document that is usually presented to venture capitalists and others in order to gain investment and funding.

Creating a marketing plan is the last crucial step that will make your marketing strategy effective. Why? The purpose of a strategy is to help you best achieve a goal or reach an end from a starting point. If you do not know where you stand now, or where you want be in the future, you cannot know the steps in between. These steps are your marketing strategy.

Components of a Marketing Plan

A marketing plan can be divided into four sections that answer specific questions. First, the mission statement answers the question "What is my purpose?" Second, the situation analysis answers the question "Where am I now?" In this part of the plan you discuss your product, market, regulations, and competition. Third, the marketing objectives answers the question "Where do I want to be in the future?" Here you identify your marketing goals. Fourth, the overall strategy answers the question "How will I get there?" In this final section you identify and explain your communication tactics, pricing, distribution, and potential problems and solutions.

Mission Statement: Yes, it's that document that redefined Jerry McGuire's life: the statement of purpose. A mission statement is key to a successful marketing plan, and a successful business. It gives your business a sense of purpose and a guiding light in the labyrinth of marketing decisions you will have to face every day. It also provides a concise reference point.

Your mission statement need not be as long as Jerry's—a few lines is all you need. A mission statement does not even have to be labeled as such. Just make sure that somewhere you have jotted down some words that capture the personality and aspirations of your business.

The following are mission statements of The Body Shop and Starbucks, respectively:

- To dedicate our business to the pursuit of social and environmental change.
- To creatively balance the financial needs of our stakeholders: employees, customers, franchisees, suppliers and shareholders.
- To courageously ensure than our business is ecologically sustainable: meeting the needs of the present without compromising the future.
- To passionately campaign for the protection of the environment, human and civil rights, and against animal testing within the cosmetics and toiletries industries.
- To tirelessly work to narrow the gap between principle and practice, whilst making fun, passion and care part of our daily lives (Body Shop, 1997, p. 43).

We realize more than ever, that what we're trying to do has never been done before. We know we got this far by being passionate: by knowing what's special about roasting and brewing coffee, about gathering at a coffeehouse, and most of all, about each and every person who holds a cup of Starbucks coffee. . . . We want to try things no one's thought of and go beyond what is expected. In 26 years we've become a successful company by never forgetting the small and personal things. We've gotten this far by taking the road less traveled, and we're just getting started.

Starbucks has designed a place to think, talk, to imagine . . . an extension of everyone's front porch. It's a rich and comforting place that provides a sense of community. . . . Where do we go from here? In 1997, we set out to explore what our stores can look and feel like in the future. We wanted to design stores that reflect our love of coffee while rewarding our customers with surprise, stories, ceremony and richness. (Starbucks, 1997, pp. 2, 3, Annual Report)

Situation Analysis: The situation analysis consists of the following components.

BRIEFLY DESCRIBES YOUR PRODUCT AND/OR SERVICE What are the key features of your product and/or service? What is your USP? How is your product and/or service purchased—in bulk or unit, or with other products and/or services? Identify your target market(s). Who are you selling to? Are you targeting young women with children, or bachelors? The middle class or the affluent? If you are selling more than one product or service, identify your target market for each.

IDENTIFIES MARKET POTENTIAL Which prospects do you think you could target in the future? Are there any profitable market niches you could do well in?

IDENTIFIES RULES AND REGULATIONS   What rules and regulations have a significant impact on your business and/or product? Do you need a license? Are you aware of them?

Identifies and Understands Your Competition   It is crucial that you always know who you are competing against and what your competition is up to. By knowing your competitors' marketing strategies, you can devise a marketing strategy that can counterattack theirs. For instance, if your competition has just set up a web site that offers a slew of additional services and free information, you may want to consider doing the same thing—only better. This isn't copycat, it is a lion's game and your business is at stake.

The following are some questions to consider:

- Who are your competitors?
- What is competition based on—price and promotion, or more quality and wider selection?
- What technology are they using?
- Have they introduced any new products?
- What services are they offering?

Marketing Objectives: Marketing objectives or goals refer to target increases in sales, profits, and market share. These goals ought to be measurable, and set within a time frame, or else they are virtually useless. If you cannot tell when you've reached your goal or how long it took you, you might as well be blindfolded and walking a tight rope—you'll never survive. Instead of "We aim to increase market share some time soon," a much more practical and useful marketing goal would be "We aim to increase market share by 10 percent in the next year," or "We aim to increase sales from $100,000 to $170,000 in the next two years."

It is important to set not only long-term objectives, but also short-term ones. Short-term objectives are like stepping-stones: They guide your path, helping you to reach your final destination. How much do you want sales to increase in six months? In a year? In three years? (Always list objectives for different products and services separately.)

Overall Strategy: The overall strategy consists of the following components.

COMMUNICATION TACTICS   The first tactic is to identify your communication goals. Remember, the purpose of communication goals is to help you reach your larger marketing objectives. Here are a few examples:

- Penetrate specialized markets.
- Sell more to present customers.
- Create a new product line or service.
- Sell at a different location
- Increase sales of one product or service and phase out another.
- Increase the number of loyal customers and instate more sales follow-up systems.

Besides identifying communication goals, you need to determine the methods of communication you are going to use based on your marketing objectives. These methods include web sites, press releases, brochures, direct mail, telemarketing, and so forth. Further, you need to determine your total marketing budget and how much money you intend to allocate to each communication method, determine how long each method will take to implement, and decide when you want each method to be completed. For each job, make sure that one person is responsible.

PRICING   To find the best selling price, you have to know what kind of customer are you catering to—the bargain hunter or the status seeker? If positive perceptions increase with higher prices, it's safe to set your price above the competition's. However, if you wanted to be hunted by coupon-clipping bargain hunters, you better set your prices a little lower than the norm.

Finding the best price involves not only keeping an eye on the competition but also looking out for your business. Your price should be in line with your costs and help you reach your marketing goals, not your competition's. When setting prices always know what the other guy is doing, but also keep your eyes on your prize.

Once you have taken these considerations into account, slap a price tag on your product or service. If you are offering a service, will you be paid on commission? What percentage cut will you get? If you intend to charge by the hour, describe the hourly fees for each service.

DISTRIBUTION   Distribution addresses the following questions:

- If you sell your product direct to the consumer in stores, what hours will your stores be open?
- Where will your stores be located?
- Will you offer mail order, or will customers be able to order your product over the web, or both?

POTENTIAL PROBLEMS AND SOLUTIONS   The goal here is to think of significant problems now, instead of later when they happen. Being thus prepared always saves time and money. There is no way to foresee every problem, but you should definitely identify major ones that would seriously prevent your business from running smoothly.

Do customers face any risks when purchasing your product or service (such as those associated with airlines, amusement parks, etc.)? Have you thought of ways to eliminate or reduce these risks? Does your business have any sources of serious liability (such as cars and trucks)? Will you need insurance to address these liabilities?

Conclusion

No matter how fast technology can pump your information, products, or services across the world, people are people and they will always need a personal touch. Successful businesses not only are up-to-date, but also meet this basic human need. Through all those wires, screens, and buttons, make sure that after every transaction you leave your customer with a warm smile and a solid handshake.

Marketing is about understanding and communicating with the individual, not with the masses. The marketer is no longer the one with the biggest mouth and the most promotion power, but rather the one called upon to listen and be willing and able to exchange ideas with the individual.

Remember that there is no bottled magic marketing formula. Each business has its own marketing strategy, and it is through careful planning and creativity that you will find the one that works for you. Developing a marketing strategy is an ongoing process. As customers, business, technology, and communication change, so must you change the way you market.

Although the marketing road is bumpy and winding, it is one of the most exciting aspects about starting a business. So enjoy the ride and have fun.

Chapter 3

─────────────── ❧ ❧ ❧ ❧ ───────────────

Financing Your Dream

How you finance your start-up is as important as the product you provide and your strategy for growth. Having enough of the right type of capital will determine how you invest for growth and the rate of growth and margins your company must achieve in order to pay back investors and creditors. Steven Burrill, former head of the High Technology Group of Ernst & Young and coauthor of the firm's *Guide to Venture Capital*, states: "An entrepreneur's initial major failing is not recognizing that the way they finance at their earliest stages drives their strategies. They like to think that they first figure out what business they're going to be in and then go about financing it. In fact, your strategy is driven by where you get your funding" (Mandell, 1989, p. 20). Experts also cite that the most common error entrepreneurs make is not raising enough money. Entrepreneurs frequently underestimate their company's cash "burn rate" and end up scrambling for more capital as their businesses struggle to make payroll or to pay suppliers. Unfortunately, though nothing may be wrong with the start-up, these careless miscalculations make the entrepreneur appear incompetent. As a result, investors and bankers are less likely to provide him with the capital to save the company and/or to continue the start-up's growth trajectory. This is the point when many entrepreneurs lose control of their company, or the business is sold or liquidated.

Fortunately, in today's economy, if you can make accurate projections (a challenge in itself) and convince an investor to commit some initial capital, you should have no problem raising the rest of the cash to meet your company's needs. The venture capital community is awash in funding. The *Wall Street Journal* reports that $11.4 billion was invested in nearly 2,000 deals in 1997, almost three times as much as in 1992 (Selz, 1998). Moreover, pension funds, insurers, and other large investors continue to pour money into existing and new venture capital funds, indicating that the private equity market should continue to grow for some time to come.

As a result, *Inc.* magazine reports that the tables have turned in favor of entrepreneurs (Jill Andresky Fraser, "How to Finance Anything," *Inc.* magazine, February, 1998, p. 36). It used to be the case that start-ups would struggle to find seed funding, working the private equity and debt markets to no avail. Today, venture capitalists complain that there aren't enough opportunities to invest. "Too much money chasing after too few good deals" is a common complaint echoing throughout the venture capital community. Though venture capitalists (VCs) invested nearly $12 billion in 1997, tens of billions still sit in the coffers, waiting for the appropriate investment opportunities.

Instead of begging venture capitalists and giving up large percentages of their companies, many entrepreneurs are now turning the VCs down and retaining most of their equity. After receiving $15 million in start-up funding, Jerome Duluk Jr. of Raycer Graphics reports that he had to refuse potential backers and ask current investors to give him less money (Selz, 1998). Several years prior, Duluk ran a company that folded when funding dried up—he won't have that problem this time. At a recent presentation to the Harvard Entrepreneurs Club, the CEO of a biomedical foods start-up also reported having to turn investors away during his quest to raise capital. "There is a ton of money—so much liquidity throughout the market place that there is now private-equity money available for companies at every stage of development," states Mendy Kwestel of Grant Thronton LLP (Fraser, 1998, p. 37). Many VCs are now concentrating on niche markets, funding ventures that, under normal circumstances, would have been left in the cold. Bill Vogelgesang of Brown, Gibbons, Lang, and Company states: "We see deals—and are doing deals—now that could never have gotten done five or six years ago" (p. 37).

The investment fever sweeping the private equity markets has also seized credit and lending institutions. The recent wave of bank mergers and acquisitions has applied pressure on banks to reinvent themselves or face closing down. As a result, entrepreneurs are finding bankers increasingly receptive and innovative in their efforts to satisfy the financial needs of young businesses. Between 1995 and 1996, the number of microloans (business loans of less than $100,000) increased by 26 percent to $15.8 billion (p. 40). Because of a flood of loan approvals, *Inc.* magazine reports that start-ups are now enjoying the benefits of layered financing, a luxury usually reserved for larger companies (Jill Andresky Fraser, "How to Finance Anything," *Inc.* Magazine, 2/98, p. 37). Layered financing occurs when a small company reduces the investment risk to potential lenders by securing a commitment from a private equity partner. Confident in the entrepreneur's probability of success, the bank approves a loan. The entrepreneur then uses the loan to reduce the amount of money needed from the venture capitalist, simultaneously decreasing the amount of equity that must be relinquished to the VC.

In addition to the traditional markets, opportunities abound for entrepreneurs to take advantage of alternative forms of financing. Many nonbank banks (e.g., large credit card companies and brokerage houses) appeal to small business owners by offering substantial lines of credit. For example, American Express Small Business Services extends unsecured credit lines ranging from $5,000 to $50,000, equipment loans and leases, and flexible payment terms. Many entrepreneurs are also using the abundant availability of personal credit cards to finance their small businesses. In 1997, the Survey of Small and Mid-Sized Business, by Arthur Andersen's Enterprise Group and National Small Business United, reported that 34 percent of respondents used credit cards to finance their companies, up from 17 percent in 1993 (Hise, 1998, p. 50). Though using personal credit cards to fund a business frequently violates the terms of credit card agreements, credit cards have become an increasingly popular form of financing.

Today's booming economy has flooded the private equity and debt markets with excess cash, and alternative financing has become abundantly available. However, financing a start-up company remains a difficult, complex, and time-consuming task. Raising capital still presents tremendous challenges, and many businesses fail because they simply run out of money.

In this chapter, we will lay out all of the formal financing options available to you both now and in the later stages of business development. However, we encourage you to actively seek out capital through many means. Chapter 7 showcases the stories of people who have already successfully started their own businesses while still in (or shortly after) college, and their examples should serve as inspiring proof of the diversity of options available. Kevin Carlson's partner invests in the company, and Ian Eslick has successfully acquired $11 million of venture capital. Krisztina Holly did not need capital; instead she and her partners licensed their first invention in order to have capital for developing their software products. John Chuang got capital for his business from his first contract for services. These examples show how students can gain funding from any number of different sources.

If you're serious about raising capital for your company, this book represents only the beginning of a long journey involving lots of research and hard work. Many books have been written on each type of financing. We encourage you to seek out as much literature as possible. Beginning the fund-raising process well informed will be critical to successfully financing your company.

Venture Capital

Broadly defined, the term *venture capital* refers to money invested by individuals or venture capital companies in small, high-risk businesses. In return, venture capitalists receive equity ownership (ownership of a portion) in the companies in which they invest, usually in the form of stock. Venture capital can come from many sources. Friends and family members, angel investors, and venture capital companies can all qualify as venture capitalists. Banks and most lending institutions are not considered venture capitalists (VCs) because they typically do not accept equity participation in the companies to which they lend money. Moreover, venture capitalists often take a more active role in the management of their investments, holding board seats and working closely with entrepreneurs and their management teams. A venture capitalist becomes the entrepreneur's partner, assisting him or her to the greatest degree possible to ensure that the company achieves its growth targets and that the entrepreneur reaps some of the financial rewards. Venture capitalists usually have expertise in the industry and markets in which they invest. They utilize their knowledge and business contacts to give their companies a competitive advantage.

Venture capital companies typically come in two forms, leveraged and equity. Leveraged VCs borrow money from the government or private sources. Because they borrow their capital, leveraged venture capitalists can only offer start-ups loans or convertible debentures. With a loan, the small business makes payments back to the venture capital company which uses the interest charges to pay the interest on its own debt. With a convertible debenture, the venture capitalist makes a loan and retains the option to purchase shares in the company at a future date. Most leveraged venture capital companies are licensed by the Small Business Administration (SBA) and are called small business investment companies (SBICs). Equity venture capital companies do not borrow their capital. Instead, they purchase shares in small businesses with capital from their stockholders, repaying the stockholders when they sell those shares at the exit. This is the most common form of venture capital and the type usually referred to when someone uses the term *venture capital*.

Venture capital companies can also be divided between those that are managed by wealthy individuals or families and those that are professionally managed institutions. Wealthy individual investors are usually referred to as "angels," a special class of investors that will be discussed in the next section. Institutional venture capital firms are set up as corporations or partnerships and managed by professional investors much like any other financial company. Some venture capital institutions are public companies; however, the vast majority remain private. Larger funds (over $10 million in assets) may be partially leveraged; however, the majority are equity-oriented. Smaller funds tend to be leveraged SBICs that issue high-interest loans. For the purposes of this discussion, assume that the term *venture capitalist* refers to a private, professionally managed, equity-oriented firm, the most common form of VC.

The Venture Capitalist's Goal

Venture capitalists are investors. Their goal is to maximize the return on their investment (ROI) and increase the wealth of their shareholders. Many come from investment banks and consulting firms and a large number hold M.B.A.s from prestigious universities. The primary difference between venture capitalists and institutional investors is that VCs invest in private, high-growth businesses, whereas institutional investors typically invest in larger, publicly traded companies. By their nature, young companies have a much greater chance of failing (some studies claim that 80 percent of start-ups fail in their first five years). The reasons for their high failure rate seem obvious: Small businesses have less capital. They compete against larger, well-established companies. They frequently rely on a few important customers. Their products are new and untested in the marketplace. Because start-ups have such a small chance of succeeding, venture capitalists incur a large amount of risk when they invest in a young company. Moreover, venture capital investments are less liquid than investments in stocks or mutual funds. Venture capitalists cannot simply sell their equity in a public market. In order to "cash out" of an investment, a VC must wait until a larger company purchases the start-up, the business sells stock to the public through an initial public offering (IPO) on the stock market, or the company is in a financial position to repurchase the venture capitalist's equity.

In order to offset the high risk and illiquid nature of their investments, venture capitalists expect a greater reward (i.e., higher ROI) than the typical investor. They measure their return on investment through an internal rate of return (IRR), otherwise known as a compounded annual growth rate (CAGR). These terms measure the year-over-year rate of growth of their investment. For example, a return on investment of two times in five years (doubling your money every five years) yields an internal rate of return of 15 percent. In other words, if the venture capitalist invested the equivalent amount of money in a mutual fund that appreciated 15 percent each year, in five years the investment would have doubled. While most people would be delighted to double their net worth every five years, if a venture capitalist invested in a company that only returned 15 percent a year, he or she would consider this an unsuccessful investment.

We use a five-year time horizon because most venture capitalists think in terms of five-year investments. In other words, after five years, they expect to exit the investment through an IPO, by selling their stake to another company, or by selling their stock back to the start-up. Some investments may require more or less time before they can be properly "harvested," but five years seems to be the average. If venture capitalists are not satisfied with a 15 percent internal rate of return, then what level of return are they seeking? In the *Venture Capital Handbook*, David Gladstone (1988) remarks, "These people (venture capitalists) expect very high, exorbitant, unreasonable returns" (p. 22). A return of five times on an investment in five years (a 38 percent annual growth rate) will begin to catch the venture capitalist's attention. After five years your company should generate revenues of at least $10 million with pretax profit margins of 15 to 20 percent. Of course, in today's high-tech marketplace many of these rules are changing. Many web-based companies don't generate revenue or profits for their first three to five years. However, by securing high "hit rates" or subscription numbers, web entrepreneurs can convince investors that the company has a great deal of future potential value. For example, in 1997 Yahoo! generated only $67 million in revenue with negligible profits; however, its market capitalization hovers around $5 billion. Today's economy values many high-tech companies far above price-earnings (P/E) ratios, allowing venture capitalists and entrepreneurs to reap large rewards before achieving "financial" success. Yahoo! Though the measures of success will vary by industry, one rule remains the same: Venture capitalists expect the value of their investment to increase dramatically over the period of their investment. Table 3.1 illustrates the annual return on investment a company must generate in order to increase the VC's investment by a specific multiple. These calculations can be performed on most financial calculators by using the CAGR function.

Why do venture capitalists require such a rapid appreciation in the value of their investments? After all, wouldn't they be successful with a 25 percent ROI? While the firm as a whole may be successful with a 25 percent ROI, on an individual basis, the venture capitalist must aim for investments that will achieve much higher returns. The venture capitalist never expects to lose money on an investment, but the truth of the matter is that many investments will return only mediocre results. Realistically, of 10 investments, 5 to 8 of those will probably return 15 percent or less or never recognize any gains at all. The venture capitalist makes money on

Table 3.1 Return on Investment Needed to Increase Venture Capitalist's Investment

Increase in Value of Investment	Compounded Annual Return on Investment
2 times in 5 years	15%
3 times in 5 years	25%
5 times in 5 years	38%
7 times in 5 years	48%
10 times in 5 years	58%

the one or two blockbuster hits that return hundreds or thousands of percent on the initial investment. In order to ensure that their portfolios consist of several companies that will actually return these results, venture capitalists must invest in many companies that fit the high-return profile.

Every entrepreneur seeking VC funding should understand the mentality of the venture capitalist. Most entrepreneurs launch and manage businesses for many reasons besides the return on investment. However, when approaching venture capitalists, you must prove that your company will grow in a manner that will generate significant returns to your shareholders. Your other personal reasons for being in the business do not matter. Your proposal and business plan must prove that your company can sustain a high growth rate and that, in approximately five years, you will take measures that allow venture capitalists to exit their investment.

Stages of Development

The amount of equity and return on investment venture capitalists expect depends a great deal on your company's stage of development. The more mature and stable your business, the less risk the venture capitalists take when they invest. In general, venture capitalists recognize five stages of development:

1. Seed
2. First round or "start-up"
3. Second round
4. Third round or expansion financing
5. Fourth round or growth stage

Seed: Sometimes venture capitalists come across promising ideas that require a small investment to develop a prototype, business plan, or market study. At this stage, the entrepreneur frequently has not even formed a company or hired a management team. In today's fast-paced, high-tech markets, venture capitalists search for great ideas sooner, and the entrepreneur who has a successful history with other start-ups can receive a significant amount of capital. Venture capitalists perceive seed financing as the riskiest type of investment. Very few new ideas have the potential to make money, and as a result, the venture capitalist will require a significant equity stake in the company and will expect a return on investment of up to 80 percent.

First Round or "Start-Up": Today, many venture capitalists invest in start-ups, recently formed companies that usually have a working prototype, a management team, and a business plan. With a hot economy and a flood of capital, venture capitalists scramble to find companies with great potential, eager to get in early to realize tremendous gains. Approximately one-third of VC investments occur at this stage, up from 10 percent several years ago (Gladstone, p. 8). However, frequently, start-up businesses have not yet generated any revenue and are several years away from breaking even or generating a positive cash flow. While great ideas are a dime a dozen, venture capitalists recognize that companies generate value through execution. Therefore, start-up financing remains a highly risky proposition to venture capitalists, who generally only invest in companies with the potential to generate returns greater than 50 percent. The entrepreneur uses the capital to take the product to market and gear up for expansion.

Second Round: By this stage of development, most companies begin to generate revenue and have proven that their product can survive in the market. Venture capitalists view these investments much more favorably than seed and start-up ventures, and as a result, the entrepreneur has a good shot at obtaining equity financing. However, because the company has probably not reached cash flow break-even, the entrepreneur has yet to prove that the business can generate a profit. Therefore, the venture capitalist will still expect a very high ROI, often above 40 percent.

Third Round or Expansion Financing: By this point, the young company has probably exhausted its capital reserves in order to get the business up and running. Now, the entrepreneur seeks additional funding to expand the business and begin a rapid growth trajectory. Fortunately, venture capitalists eagerly seek out and fund companies at this stage of development, and the entrepreneur should have little difficulty negotiating a reasonable price for more capital. Companies seeking third-round financing are close to breaking even or are already generating a small profit. Once your business reaches this stage you will have to give up little equity for additional funding.

Fourth Round or Growth Stage: Once your company is breaking even or generating a profit, you can turn your attention to rapid growth and expansion. Provided that a large enough market exists for your product, venture capitalists will bang down the doors to finance your business at this stage of its development. If you're generating a profit, why do you need to continue seeking more venture capital? Chances are that your business still doesn't generate enough positive cash flow to finance the type of large-scale investments necessary to grow into a company ready for an IPO. Moreover, if competitors have begun developing or marketing a similar product, then you may have to rapidly attain critical mass in order to remain competitive. At this point, size begins to matter. By this stage, you may also be able to balance your debt-to-equity ratio by attaining a loan from a local bank, reducing the amount of venture capital you require and the amount of equity you must cede to the VC. Since you've already proven the viability of your business, the venture capitalist will also expect a lower return on investment.

You must determine the stage of development of your business in order to set reasonable expectations for yourself and the venture capitalist. Table 3.2 illustrates the development category and the ROI most venture capitalists will expect your business to generate. The more mature your company, the easier and cheaper it will be to raise capital. The earlier the venture capitalists invest, the more risk they assume and, consequently, the higher ROI and more equity they will demand in return. As an entrepreneur, it should be your goal to move your business through each stage of development using as little venture capital and retaining as much equity as possible. If you can develop a prototype by raising money from friends and family (bootstrap financing), don't raise venture capital until you have tapped out alternative resources. However, do not become so greedy that you concentrate on owning as much of the company as possible. Your goal is to rapidly grow the company and generate wealth for you and your investors. You will fail to raise the necessary capital to achieve these goals if you become concerned about retaining your equity position.

What Is the Venture Capitalist Looking For?

We've discovered that obtaining venture capital involves convincing the venture capitalist that investing in your company will yield superior returns on investment. Unfortunately, proving that your company presents an excellent investment opportunity is not as simple as projecting financial growth. Persuading venture capitalists to part with their money requires that you present the critical elements of your business that will allow it to grow in a manner that significantly increases the value of the VC's investment. This process involves submitting a proposal, meeting the venture capitalist, giving him or her a tour of your facilities, and introducing the VC

Table 3.2   Return on Investment Expected by Venture Capitalists for Each Stage of Development

Stage of Development	Annual Rate of Return
Seed	80%
Start-up and first round	40% to 60%
Second round	30% to 40%
Third round	20% to 30%
Fourth round	20% to 25%

to your management team. During each stage of the process you should be selling the venture capitalist on your company, showcasing your business in a manner that highlights the uniqueness of your situation and convinces the VC that your company will succeed.

During the evaluation of your company, the venture capitalist will look for the following:

■ A competent management team that can execute the business plan
■ A unique product or service with a viable market
■ A real opportunity for substantial growth
■ An exit strategy that allows the venture capitalist to cash out of the investment

The venture capitalist will also observe you closely in order to understand your personality and sense of business ethics. You must possess honesty, integrity, and a deep commitment to the success of your company. Con artists and criminals constantly proposition venture capitalists, and more than one VC has lost a substantial amount of money to a disingenuous entrepreneur. You must expose your business and personal life to the critical eye of venture capitalists, allowing them to gain a complete picture of the nature of their investment. The success of a young business depends a great deal upon the leadership of the entrepreneur and his or her management team. In most public companies, the board of directors (which represents the shareholders) selects the CEO and other important executives, ensuring that the management team represents their interests. At least initially, the venture capitalist does not choose the entrepreneur who leads your company, nor can the VC rely on a board of directors to elect you to that position. Therefore, the responsibility falls upon you to convince the venture capitalist that you possess the appropriate character and personality to lead your business. Now, let us discuss the more substantive characteristics listed at the beginning of this paragraph.

Competent Management: Most venture capitalists believe that the management team is the most critical determinant of the success or failure of a business. VCs live by the adage "You can have a good idea and poor management and lose every time." Frequently, they find that the converse can be true: A mediocre or poor idea can often turn into a good investment under a competent management team. The secret of success lies in the effective execution of the business plan. Regardless of who generates the idea, the management team converts that idea into a business by targeting a market, aligning suppliers, hiring employees, and coordinating the critical elements that allow the company to produce a profit. Another saying paraphrases Edison's famous words: "Entrepreneurship is 1 percent inspiration and 99 percent perspiration." After you've provided the 1 percent of inspiration, the success of your business will depend upon the quality of the 99 percent of your perspiration. The venture capitalist wants to ensure that your management team can produce the results you promise.

Management experience and industry knowledge will be critical factors for you and your management team to possess. If you lack certain skills, it will be important for you to seek out and hire people who complement your deficiencies. Marc Andreessen, Senior Vice President of Technology and CTO at Netscape Communications, presents a perfect example. Though a brilliant programmer, Andreessen recognized that he lacked the management experience necessary to run a successful business. Therefore he hired James Barksdale, who had a strong management background, as his CEO before launching Netscape. The partnership worked out brilliantly. Andreessen provided the technical expertise and Barksdale leveraged his years of management experience to help Netscape grow into the dominant competitor in web browsers. You will most likely discover that you lack specific knowledge and skills critical to the success of your company. Try to fill those gaps before you seek venture capital financing, or express how you plan to meet the management needs of the company soon after acquiring additional funding. If you require the assistance of the venture capitalist to locate management, be sure to communicate this in your proposal. Finally, be sure to articulate precisely how the knowledge and experience of your management team will translate into a successful business. Provide resumes, references, and explanations of each person's unique talent and contribution. Express why this combination of individuals is ideally suited to managing your company.

A Unique Product or Service: The venture capitalist will want to know what makes your company's situation unique. Do you possess a technology that no one else has discovered, a different manufacturing system that makes your product superior to your competitors', or have you devised a more efficient means of distribution? In your proposal and during your interactions with the venture capitalist, you must continually stress the elements of your business design that give your company a competitive advantage and allow it to capture value in the market. Beyond demonstrating the viability of your business, having a unique offering will help your proposal stand out from the crowd and get noticed. Venture capitalists do not like investing in me-too businesses. It's very difficult to prove that your company can generate value from an idea that's already been played out in the marketplace.

This does not mean that you must have a revolutionary product to obtain financing. In fact, venture capitalists shy away from offerings that are so revolutionary that they do not yet have a market. The earliest versions of the personal computer, television, and automobile would have had difficulty receiving venture capital. Venture capitalists prefer products that are evolutionary or innovative, products that improve upon the design or function of a current model. The notebook computer, disposable camera, and color television were improvements over their predecessors. Venture capitalists also finance companies that produce substitutes, products that solve the same problem by offering better or cheaper alternatives.

Today, venture capitalists place the majority of their investment dollars in high-technology companies, particularly those involved in the World Wide Web, software, computer components, and biotechnology. According to *Business Week*, in 1997, 66 percent of venture capital went to technology companies, up from 60 percent just two years earlier ("Something Ventured," 1998, p. 6). While this shouldn't discourage you from seeking venture capital if you don't have a high-tech company, if you happen to be running a business involved in a high-tech market, obtaining venture capital has never been easier. Moreover, reiterating the introduction, many VCs are beginning to specialize in niche markets and industries not normally financed by venture capitalists. The flood of venture capital has increased the absolute availability of venture capital, even if the relative availability has shifted further toward high-tech companies.

Growth Opportunity: As we've already discussed at some length, you must be able to prove that your company is capable of generating significant levels of growth over the life of the venture capitalist's investment. Not only must you demonstrate this in theory, but you must also produce solid financial projections that display exactly how rapidly your company will grow and the cash flow and profit that will result. While you, the entrepreneur, bear the responsibility of projecting growth, you must ensure that your predictions are realistic and in line with forecasts from similar companies. Remember that the venture capitalist will probably have a lot of experience in your industry and will recognize realistic versus inflated financial projections. Moreover, in meetings with the venture capitalist, you will have to defend your numbers and explain your assumptions. Understanding how to create an accurate financial model will be important.

Exit Strategy: The final important point to emphasize in the proposal and discussions with the venture capitalist is the manner in which you expect the VC to exit the investment. You should not just consider exit strategies as possibilities, but explicitly plan to take the necessary steps to end the venture capitalist's involvement with your company. The VC has no interest in maintaining a long-term relationship, even in the best-performing businesses. Within three to seven years, venture capitalists expect to cash out of their investment, liquidating their equity and recognizing the gains.

Before they will invest in your business, you must convince venture capitalists that your company will be capable of going public or buying back their shares and that you are committed to this strategy.

Your Objectives

If you've decided to raise venture capital to fund your business, you should determine your objectives for acquiring this type of capital. Why do you need venture capital? Exactly how do you intend to spend the money? Are you willing to give up equity in your company to achieve your goals? Venture capitalists quickly point out that entrepreneurs should divest the notion of retaining a majority ownership stake in their company. While the entrepreneur attempts to raise as much capital as possible at the lowest possible price (i.e., giving up as little equity as possible), he or she should not expect to hold greater than 51 percent of the company after the first round of financing. Frequently, early-stage financing requires entrepreneurs to divest between 40 and 60 percent of their ownership. Second-round funding usually takes another 20 to 30 percent. After three or four rounds of financing, the founding group typically holds less than 20 percent of the company, with the CEO-founder owning around 5 to 10 percent. If you currently own 100 percent of your company, the thought of losing 95 percent of your equity may shock you. Get over it or don't bother raising venture capital. An entrepreneur once said, "One hundred percent of nothing is still nothing." Though less than eloquent, the statement proves the point. If you intend to raise venture capital, your objective should be to rapidly build a successful business in a manner that will generate substantial wealth for you and your investors. You may have become an entrepreneur for the lifestyle and other personal reasons; however, venture capitalists are not interested in that. They are investors trying to maximize their ROI by investing in high-risk businesses. You must demonstrate that you possess the same objectives and that you are willing to make the sacrifices necessary to achieve your goals.

Many venture capitalists will refuse to invest in a company in which the entrepreneur is not willing to relinquish majority ownership because it places too much power in the hands of the entrepreneur. If the company gets into trouble, the venture capitalist wants enough recourse to step in and help turn the company around, an action that often requires that the VC replace the entrepreneur and/or the management team. This is the option of last resort, however. Most venture capitalists do not wish to control, much less manage, your business, and they own greater than 50 percent only when they must do so in order to justify the amount of money they are investing. If you are unwilling to relinquish some of your equity, the venture capitalist will not believe that you are serious about aggressively growing the business. Building a successful, high-growth company requires that the entrepreneur share control, delegate management and decision-making responsibilities, and seek assistance from outside investors.

Like the venture capitalist, you may also want to avoid allowing any one investor to own a controlling stake in the company. You can prevent this situation by involving multiple investors through a syndication, an arrangement in which a leading investor (usually the initial venture capitalist) or investment bank convinces other venture capitalists to invest in your company. This relationship serves the dual purpose of raising additional capital and spreading equity over multiple parties. However, syndications can be complex to organize and can cost up to 5 to 10 percent of the capital raised.

Professional Advice

With an abundance of investment capital in today's markets, entrepreneurs increasingly expect venture capitalists to provide professional experience, advice, and management assistance, in addition to their money. This should be an important objective of any entrepreneur. You should begin the search for a venture capitalist by identifying firms that specialize in your industry. Not only will VCs have experience investing in companies like yours, but they frequently have management backgrounds running businesses that serve similar markets with comparable products to yours. It should be your objective to leverage this knowledge in order to give your company a competitive advantage and maximize the value of your capital.

VCs will also have many useful contacts within your industry. From suppliers to customers, from marketers to lawyers, venture capitalists will eagerly call upon business associates to lend their expertise. The venture capitalist may also supply part of your management team, providing people with finance or production knowledge. VC firms frequently hire consultants who can help you compose a marketing plan or perform an industry survey. If your company's situation proves particularly complex, the venture capitalist may play an active management role, spending one or two days a week helping you manage the business.

In preliminary discussions with a venture capitalist, you should quickly gain an understanding of how the VC intends to assist your company beyond providing investment capital. Be sure to choose a venture capitalist who will contribute the appropriate mix of management advice and direct involvement given your company's needs. In the commitment letter and legal documents, you will want to spell out the nature of the relationship between the venture capitalist and your business, outlining the specific services the VC will provide. Never assume that it's mutually understood or that a verbal agreement will suffice.

The Process

Obtaining venture capital financing generally follows a normal process that takes anywhere from three weeks to six months, but normally requires six to eight weeks from start to finish. First, locate one or several venture capitalists to contact. Then, submit a letter with a summary presentation and a formal proposal. If the venture capitalist likes your summary and business proposal, he or she will contact you, ask some questions, and then arrange a face-to-face meeting at his or her office to discuss your business. If the investment looks promising, the venture capitalist will begin a process of due diligence, investigating your company and the industry in much more depth. At this point in time, the VC may issue a commitment letter, making an initial promise to fund your company. Once the venture capitalist completes the due diligence process, the lawyers become involved and begin drawing up the legal papers that close the deal. Let's discuss each of these steps in more detail.

Finding Venture Capitalists: Locating venture capitalists to contact is surprisingly easy. Though most companies are private partnerships, the venture capital community is very well organized. The most frequently cited source for locating venture capital is *Pratt's Guide to Venture Capital Sources,* from Venture Economics, a division of Securities Data Publishers. *Pratt's Guide* contains an introduction discussing the venture capital industry and a list of just about every venture capital fund in the United States and Canada, including their area of specialization. Another source of information is *Galante's Complete Venture Capital and Private Equity Directory.* Similar to *Pratt's, Galante's* also databases most venture funds and their areas of expertise. A directory titled *Small Business Investment Companies* (SBICs) can be obtained from the Associate Administrator for Investment at the U.S. Small Business Administration. The National Association of Small Business Investment Companies (NASBIC) and the National Venture Capital Association (NVCA) will also provide lists of their members.

From these directories, select several venture capitalists who specialize in your industry and are located near your place of business. Venture capitalists prefer to invest in companies located nearby so that they can minimize their travelling time and maximize their contact with the companies in which they invest. Working with a venture capitalist from your city or state will also save you a great deal of money that would otherwise be wasted making trips to the VC's office. As a rule, you should only broaden your search if none of the venture capitalists in your area specialize in funding businesses in your industry. Once you have identified several venture capital firms as potential investors, you may want to carry out a little due diligence of your own to ensure that they are reputable companies. Contact other entrepreneurs who have done business with the VCs to gain a sense of their business ethics. Do a credit check and contact the venture capitalist's bank to ensure that the VC has a solid financial history and plenty of money to invest. Beyond finding capital, you are selecting a business partner. It will be vitally important to choose a firm that shares your goals and with which you can develop a strong professional relationship.

Initial Contact: Your first contact with the venture capitalist usually comes in the form of a cover letter and summary presentation attached to a proposal. VCs may receive a 100 proposals a week, of which 10 or less will actually be read. This fact alone places tremendous pressure on the entrepreneur to produce a first-rate summary presentation that will entice the venture capitalist to read and study the proposal. The summary presentation should be a three-to-five page overview written with brilliance and clarity that articulates the most important points of your business and seduces the venture capitalist into exploring a tremendous investment opportunity. An effective summary will include (1) a description of your business and its product; (2) an introduction to the management team, emphasizing the experience of its members; (3) an explanation of the amount of funding you are requesting; (4) an explanation of how the capital will be invested; (5) financial projections for the next five years; and (6) an explanation of how the venture capitalist will exit the investment. You should treat the summary presentation as a selling document that excites the venture capitalist and moves him or her to invest in your company. It should be professionally finished and cosmetically refined because it may be the most important document you compose.

Proposal: This is where the rubber meets the road. If your summary convinced the venture capitalist to read your proposal, then you have a legitimate opportunity to obtain venture capital based on the merits of your business and the potential of the investment. If you present a solid, well-written proposal, then the venture capitalist will be able to read the document and make an informed investment decision before even meeting you. It will shorten the process by reducing the amount of due diligence he or she must perform and limiting the number of meetings required to close the deal. As the name "proposal" suggests, this document should convince the venture capitalist that your company is an attractive investment opportunity. It should be succinct and to the point, only discussing topics pertinent to the venture capitalist. Unlike a business plan, which may run to 100 pages or more, the proposal should only be 20 to 30 pages in length. It should discuss how the business will succeed, omitting details that are less relevant to the performance of the company. Your objective should be to convince the venture capitalist that your company possesses a unique product and has a competent and experienced management team. It should also prove that your company will grow substantially over the next five to seven years and will give the venture capitalist an opportunity to exit the investment and recognize significant capital gains. In his *Venture Capital Handbook*, David Gladstone (1988) discusses the summary presentation and proposal at length, providing an effective format for composing these important documents.

Meetings: If the proposal impressed the venture capitalist, he or she will call you to arrange a meeting to discuss your business and a potential investment. The first meeting will most likely take place at the VC's office. The venture capitalist will want to learn more about the business, evaluate you in person, and "cut a deal" if all goes well. The VC will question you at length about your assumptions and projections, and may even inquire about your personal life. The venture capitalist wants to understand everything relevant to making the investment that could be discerned from the proposal. The first meeting will probably last several hours and may be followed up with other preliminary meetings. At some point in time the venture capitalist will want to visit your business and tour the facilities, and meet your management team and key personnel. If all goes well, the venture capitalist may then issue a commitment letter, a non–legally binding initial agreement to invest in your company. It will outline the terms of the investment and pave the way toward a formal, legal agreement.

Due Diligence: *Due diligence* is just a fancy term for the venture capitalist's investigation of your company, the industry, and the market in which he or she is investing. The due diligence process actually began when the VC read the proposal and asked the first question. The venture capitalist continues the investigation by asking even more questions, doing background checks on you and your management team, talking to customers and suppliers, analysts and competitors. The VC may even hire a consulting firm to do an intensive study of the industry and evaluate your company's growth potential.

The Closing: If you've made it this far you're nearly home. However, you should take several precautions to ensure that your interests are served and that the deal is executed according to the conditions you've agreed to. Though the venture capitalist will have a lawyer who draws up the legal documents, you should have your own attorney review them to ensure that they are both legally sound and in line with your understanding of the agreement. Then, be sure to carefully read through the documents yourself, to ensure that they coincide with the commitment letter and any other verbal transactions that took place since you began discussions. Remember that the lawyers are *not* business executives, so you shouldn't expect them to look out for your business interests. You must personally review all documents to verify that they meet your expectations.

The Exit

As we've mentioned several times already, how the venture capitalist exits the investment in your company and cashes out of the deal will be very important. Venture capitalists only invest in companies that will allow them to liquidate their investment at some point three to seven years from their initial infusion of cash. Even the fastest-growing companies represent poor investments if the VC does not have a way to recognize capital gains. Moreover, by this time the entrepreneur will probably want to break ties with the venture capitalist, and redistribute the authority that comes with such a large ownership stake in the company. This section describes some of the most common ways entrepreneurs can meet these objectives.

Going Public: An initial public offering (IPO) involves selling shares of your company in the public market, usually through a stock market like the New York Stock Exchange or the NASDAQ. Venture capitalists generally view the IPO as the most favorable way to cash out of a deal because it gives them instant liquidity. From the standpoint of the entrepreneur, an IPO also represents an attractive opportunity because it provides an opportunity to trade in equity for cash and recognize the material rewards of being an entrepreneur. Becoming a publicly traded company also generates many advantages for the business. Public companies find it much easier to raise more money by issuing bonds, offering more stock, or applying for loans. They also tend to have more credibility with customers, suppliers, financial institutions, and investors. The downside of being a public company includes having to comply with requirements established by the Securities and Exchange Commission (SEC). The operation of your company also becomes much more transparent to the public, and shareholders will pick up where the venture capitalist left off, scrutinizing your business activities and expecting substantial financial returns.

Purchase of the Venture Capitalist's Stock by the Company or Entrepreneur: You and the venture capitalist can also agree to a price at which you or the company purchases back the venture capitalist's share of the company. This returns 100 percent ownership of the company to you and other principal shareholders. Frequently, this transaction involves obtaining a loan from a bank in order to raise the cash to pay out the venture capitalist. The increased liability may become a burden on you or the company, potentially inhibiting future growth, so be sure that the business can support additional debt. Another option is to establish an employee stock ownership trust (ESOT), which is like a pension or profit-sharing plan that purchases stock in your company instead of other publicly traded corporations. It effectively buys the venture capitalist's stock, and deposits it into the trust on behalf of the employees. Be aware that ESOTs involve complex tax issues and will require the assistance of an expert with experience in employee stock ownership trusts.

Selling the Company to Another Company: You may also choose to sell your business to another company in return for cash, stock, or a note. While this gives the venture capitalist the opportunity to cash out of the investment, it typically also relieves the entrepreneur of his/her personal ownership stake, an outcome that may or may not be favorable, depending upon the entrepreneur's objectives. Frequently, entrepreneurs also exits their management role in the company, relinquishing their duties to professional managers selected by the parent company. If selling the company altogether is acceptable to you, then this option represents a viable, and sometimes more attractive, alternative to an IPO. However, if selling your business and parting ways does not sound like a favorable exit strategy, you should make this clear before involving the venture capitalist.

Raising venture capital to grow your company presents many important issues that you should carefully consider before approaching the VC community. While giving your company the cash to grow and develop, you must involve an outside investor who may or may not have interests equivalent to your own. You will have to relinquish a great deal of ownership and control of your business, and partner with an individual who has a primarily financial interest in your company. You will be expected to rapidly grow your business and take actions that allow the venture capitalist to reap large capital gains from his or her involvement. Many entrepreneurs decide that seeking venture capital does not present an attractive opportunity given their personal goals and the objectives of their companies. However, whether or not you decide to pursue venture capital financing, the education and skills you will learn from going through the process and thinking like a venture capitalist will be extremely valuable.

Angel Investors

An *angel investor* is an individual or a family that has a high net worth and invests capital in an early-stage company in exchange for equity ownership in the business. Angels sometimes accept other forms of payment (e.g., convertible debentures or loans); however, experts usually compare the investment activity of angels to that of private venture capital companies.

Estimates vary regarding the size of the angel market. *Inc.* magazine esti-mates that over 250,000 angels invested upward of $20 billion in 1996 (Gruner, 1998, p. 48). A study by Dr. Robert J. Gaston of the Small Business Administration places the number at $55 to $65 billion a year in as many as 720,000 companies (Gaston, 1996). Dr. William Wetzel Jr. at the University of New Hampshire's Whittemore School of Business suggests that approxi-mately $15 billion of the $55 to $65 billion is being invested in approxi-mately 60,000 high-risk, early-stage companies (Wetzel, 1997). The Small Business Development Center at the University of California–Irvine, be-lieves that in California alone, angels have invested $30 billion in 240,000 transactions (SBDC, *Finding Your Wings*, 1996). Though the numbers vary, they all testify to an extremely large market, two to five times the size of the venture capital industry. In *Finding Your Wings*, Gerald Benjamin and Joel Margulis (1996) state: "Simply put, private investors, or angel investors, are a primary, if not *the* primary, source of capital for early-stage and growing companies" (p. 10).

If angels represent such an important source of capital for start-ups and small businesses, one wonders why more has not been written on the topic of acquiring angel capital. Most books on small business financing speak extensively to venture capital and debt financing, barely addressing the topic of private investors. The answer to this quandary lies in the elu-sive and disorganized nature of angel investing. Unlike venture capitalists and banks, angels generally do not belong to associations or trade groups. Few newsletters or industry journals address the angel market and the en-trepreneurs seeking angel capital. To be accurate, however, modern-day angels have become much more savvy and organized in their approach to investing. Several groups have sprung up like the Band of Angels and Berkus Technology Ventures, California-based organizations that attempt to bring order and efficiency to the angel market. However, the vast major-ity of private investors remain true to their name—private.

Though angel investors value their privacy, they are not impossible to locate, contact, and approach for start-up financing. Unfortunately, books offer little assistance in this process. Acquiring angel capital usually oc-curs through informal relationships with wealthy individuals. You may be sighing with resignation, fretting because you have few wealthy friends and acquaintances with the amount of disposable capital that could help your business. However, chances are you know more people with invest-ment capital than you realize. Moreover, the scarcity of high-quality deals in today's markets has made angel investors more approachable than ever as they seek out entrepreneurs and start-ups in which to invest. After all, if we accept *Inc.*'s estimation that 250,000 investors contributed $20 billion in early-stage financing, angels represent less than 0.1 percent of the pop-ulation. Chances are slim that you know many of these individuals per-sonally. However, the process of raising capital from angel investors is not just about mining current relationships; it entails a more proactive approach of seeking out and developing new relationships, selling your idea and the business to potential partners.

A Comparison between Angel Investors and Venture Capitalists

Because experts frequently compare the two, we can understand angel investors by comparing them with venture capitalists, about which much more is known. The most significant difference between angel investors and venture capitalists is that angels are *private, and invest with their own money, using their own intuition*. They do not consider themselves in the business of investing, but engage themselves in start-up financing to generate additional wealth from capital accumulated from a previous vocation. They invest for the fun of being involved in a small enterprise and frequently mix personal goals with financial interests. Because angels value their privacy, entrepreneurs find them much more difficult to locate. No one publishes a *Directory of Angel Investors*. Locating angels requires much more legwork and creativity on the part of the entrepreneur.

Despite angels' elusiveness, several studies have been carried out in an attempt to profile the sociodemographic characteristics of the typical angel investor. International Capital Resources (ICR) specializes in linking private investors with entrepreneurs and has generated a significant amount of data on angel investors. The first, and probably most telling, characteristic is that the vast majority of angels are self-made millionaires, or billionaires as the case may be. According to the Forbes Four Hundred, 72 percent of America's wealthiest individuals are first-generation entrepreneurs, up from 63 percent in 1984 (Grover, p. 146). Most angel investors have accumulated their wealth through business, often by owning equity in a previous company that they probably started. This is an important point because many people associate a high net worth with a large income, when in fact most individuals with sizable salaries do not possess a great deal of so-called wealth. Int'l Corp. Resources identifies individuals with net worths between $1 million and $10 million as the principal group interested in high-risk investing (Benjamin and Margulis, p. 9). Generally, people with less than $1 million do not have enough play money to risk on start-up ventures. Though many individuals with more than $10 million invest in first-stage companies, many will not take the time to invest personally, but will employ money managers who invest their estates for them. Sometimes, members of this elite demographic group will commit a portion of their savings to venture capitalists, reducing their risk by entrusting their capital to venture professionals.

Angels tend to be male, between the ages of 48 and 59, with postgraduate degrees in technical fields and extensive management experience. Today's computerized economy is shifting this demographic by creating more opportunities for entrepreneurs to generate wealth faster and at a younger age. The *Wall Street Journal* reports that almost 30 percent of Americans who went into business for themselves this year were under the age of 30 (Kaufman, 1998). Many more women and minorities are becoming entrepreneurs, suggesting that the next wave of angels will be more representative of the general population.

The most significant differences between angel investors and venture capitalists lie in the contrast between their criteria for and processes of investing. As we pointed out earlier, private investors invest for personal reasons that often include motivations which are not financial. Unlike most venture capitalists, who answer to shareholders, invest all of their capital in high-risk ventures, and earn high returns on investment, angel investors are not bound by any of these criteria. They do not *have* to invest in start-ups, they most certainly do not invest all of their net worth in high-risk ventures, and they do not have to achieve a specific ROI. Because most angels are self-made millionaires, they frequently possess a desire to perpetuate the activities that brought about their own state of wealth. Investing in start-up companies is a way to relive their success and contribute to the achievement of another individual and his or her business. Many angels also invest out of compassion for the entrepreneur, the desire to alleviate misfortune, or the rush and sheer joy of high-risk investments. All of these reasons depart from those of the venture capitalist, who invests solely to maximize return on investment for his shareholders.

Understanding that angel investors possess motivations beyond ROI helps explain some of their differences from venture capitalists with respect to their investment criteria. Venture capitalists usually follow strict guidelines and procedures during the process of selecting companies and committing capital. They require a proposal or business plan, a lengthy due diligence, and a thorough investigation of the company and its management. A study by ICR discovered that 50 percent of angel investors are willing to invest in companies that lack a business plan (Benjamin and Margulis, p. 80). Moreover, angel investors supply a disproportionate amount of the capital that funds seed and early-stage companies, usually investing between $25,000 and $250,000 per deal. Venture capitalists, in contrast, tend to be more interested in later-stage companies and make larger investments with each transaction.

Although angel investors seem less formal in their criteria and process, do not assume that they incur greater risks than venture capitalists. Venture capitalists must spread investments across many companies in order to minimize their number of bad deals. Because angel investors do not have to invest at all, they concentrate more on finding the one or two good deals that will yield the appropriate personal benefits and a sufficient ROI. Angel investors also tend to take a much more active role in the management of their investments, frequently becoming a partner to the entrepreneur or holding a management position within the company. At the very least, angels often become close advisors to the businesses in which they invest, leveraging their extensive knowledge of industries and markets to help their companies grow. Unlike venture capitalists, which frequently have credentials relating to finance or consulting, angels typically have strong backgrounds managing their own businesses. They often possess a deeper understanding of the market and an intimate knowledge of the operational components of a business.

Though many differences exist between angel investors and venture capitalists, there are also many similarities. *Inc.* magazine points out that "There really isn't much difference" between many angels and their venture capital counterparts (Gruner, 1998, p. 47). Many angel investors require a well-written proposal or business plan before they'll even consider investing in your company. Angels look for companies that will generate an ROI 5 to 10 times their original investment. Most will carry out their own due diligence process before committing capital. Angels often require the entrepreneur to submit quarterly financial reports and frequent updates, involving them in the management of the company to a greater degree than most venture capitalists. Finally, most angel investors will expect to exercise an exit strategy five to seven years down the road, cashing out on their investment and ending their involvement with the company.

Acquiring Angel Capital

Because angel investors and venture capitalists exhibit so many similarities, the entrepreneur should approach angels much the same way they would approach venture capitalists. You should submit a well-written proposal, investigate the backgrounds of potential investors, locate someone with expertise in your field, and compose a deal that meets the needs of your company. The primary difference in the process, however, will be the way you locate and contact prospective investors. As we've already mentioned, most of the angel community safeguards its privacy and resists formal organization. Therefore, you will need to exercise more creativity in order to locate and develop relationships with this special class of investors.

First, you should begin your search by attending investment forums, meetings, and networks. In *Finding Your Wings*, Benjamin and Margulis (1996) provide a short list of some of the nation's larger forums and conferences. Begin by attending events near your place of business—most angel investors prefer to invest in projects close to home. Search local newspapers and investment newsletters, and talk to people involved in the investment community (e.g., investment and commercial bankers and fund managers) to learn about local forums, fairs, and seminars. The second thing you should do is build a database of potential investors, cataloging pertinent information and qualifying and ranking individuals according to their ability to meet your investment needs. Finally, you should focus a great deal of time and energy on developing relationships with angel investors. Unlike venture capitalists, angels do not have to invest their capital, and they will do so only when an entrepreneur presents an exciting opportunity that offers tremendous financial returns. A venture capitalist must invest in start-up companies, trying to optimize the mix of deals that will yield the highest financial return. An angel chooses between many more options, including other forms of investment and not investing at all. You must convince your angels that taking a great deal of risk and becoming involved with your company presents a more compelling opportunity than any other use of their money.

Alternative Financing

In your quest for financing, it is useful to consider some non-traditional forms of financing. Here are some ideas.

"Beg, Borrow, or Steal"

Actually, when you're in business, it's no longer referred to as stealing. Businesspeople use much more professional terminology like "money laundering" or "fraud," neither of which we endorse, of course. However, when you're launching a new company, you will probably become very creative in your quest for start-up capital and it will seem like you're begging for every last dollar. Don't worry, you're not alone. Nearly every business begins its life supported by bootstrap financing, acquiring funds from sources other than banks, venture capitalists, and other customary sources of capital. Interviews with the founders of companies in the Inc. 500 list of the fastest-growing private companies revealed that more than 80 percent were financed solely by founders' personal savings, credit cards, second mortgages, and multiple other forms of alternative financing. The median amount of start-up capital was about $10,000, and less than one-fifth raised outside equity capital during the five or more years they had been in business (Wetzel, 1997, p. 189). These numbers shouldn't be too surprising considering that venture capitalists only supported approximately 2,000 deals in 1997. What's significant is that the vast majority of businesses begin on a shoestring, with very little money and no formal financing.

Where, then, do entrepreneurs find the seed capital to launch a business? Well, first they dig deep into their back pockets, committing most, if not all, of their personal savings to the company. The amount of money you provide will depend a great deal upon your personal level of wealth and the amount you are willing to risk. Entrepreneurs, by their nature, tend to be young, risk-seeking individuals with few responsibilities. Having little to lose makes it much easier to sacrifice personal savings In order to start a company. Before they invest in your business, most venture capitalists and angels will expect that you've already tapped out personal resources and even stretched yourself beyond reasonable limits of debt in order to get the company off the ground. They want to see that you have personal confidence in the business and enough at stake to ensure that you're committed to the success of the company. In essence, devoting your personal resources initially will be critical to obtaining capital in the future, when the business will likely require much more money.

After entrepreneurs tap out their own cash reserves, they usually turn to friends, family, and business associates for additional start-up capital. Some entrepreneurs express a reluctance to ask relatives and colleagues for money, stating that it would be the last place they would go for funding. However, experts in small business financing point out that friends and family should be the first place entrepreneurs go to find money to launch their business. Practically speaking, relatives and acquaintances are usually much more receptive to the entrepreneur's ideas than private equity or lending institutions. They have a much better sense of your competence, commitment, and integrity. Their personal affinity for you probably gives them a heightened interest in your success and that of your business. These qualities will mean that you can raise money cheaper by paying less interest or offering less equity than a bank or venture capitalist would require. Moreover, traditional funding at the seed and start-up phases of your company's development may simply be unavailable, making friends and family the most accessible source of capital.

Unfortunately, acquiring capital from friends, family, and business associates poses the largest personal risk to the entrepreneur. Investing in a start-up company still presents a high probability that the relative or acquaintance will lose capital because you default on the loan or that equity will become worthless if the business fails. Under these circumstances, the entrepreneur merely parts ways with the venture capitalist and the company declares bankruptcy. However, neither of these options presents an acceptable resolution when the lender is a family member or friend.

Many friendships have been broken and family relations strained when an entrepreneur's business fails. Though some tension will inevitably ensue, several measures can be taken to minimize the stress and disappointment created when a company goes out of business. First, you should explain the full extent of the risk that relatives or friends accept when they invest in your company. Educate them about the high failure rate of start-ups and the consequences of bankruptcy. Treat acquaintances like institutional investors, providing a business plan or proposal if one exists. You should convince them that your company represents an attractive investment, independent of their personal relationship with you.

You may also want to put the agreement in writing, formalizing the terms and conditions of the investment. Though full-fledged legal documents are probably unnecessary, a one-page summary of the transaction should clarify the provisions for repayment and the consequences of failure. Formalizing your company's existence, through incorporation or creating a limited liability partnership, before acquiring financing will also go a long way toward depersonalizing the investment relationship (see Chapter 6). Investors understand that they are investing in a business, not just a friend. Finally, you should understand the laws regulating the transfer of capital between individuals and between an investor and a company. If you're unfamiliar with them, have a lawyer educated in small business and tax law review any documents and explain the relevant regulations governing the transaction.

Credit Cards

Once entrepreneurs have exhausted their savings and approached family members and friends, they will often leverage their personal assets to increase the amount of capital available to the business. For example, they may take out a second mortgage on their home or acquire a home improvement loan, leveraging the equity in their house to obtain more money. Another form of leveraging involves the use of credit cards. According to *Inc.*, 34 percent of small businesses used credit cards to finance expenses in 1997, 25 percent of which used credit cards "often or routinely" for both personal and business purchases (Hise, 1998, p. 50). As the credit card business becomes increasingly competitive, entrepreneurs are finding consumer credit a convenient and highly accessible form of financing. To illustrate the abundance of credit cards, *Inc.* notes that consumer credit card issuers sent out 2.5 billion applications in 1997 and over 450 million cards have been issued, nearly two for every man, woman, and child in the United States. Moreover, consumer credit limits increased by about 25 percent over 1996 levels, expanding the amount of money available through each account (p. 52).

Despite their abundance, credit cards remain an expensive form of financing. Interest rates can reach 21 percent or higher and many banks charge fees if you miss a payment or transfer balances. Entrepreneurial circles are full of horror stories of companies drowning in a sea of credit card debt. However, if managed appropriately, credit cards can provide a very effective and substantial source of capital. With a clean credit history and a solid source of income, it wouldn't be outrageous to acquire 20 credit cards worth $100,000 or more. The challenge is not acquiring credit cards, however, but managing the debt once you've begun charging against them.

Your first goal should be to pay off the balance of the cards monthly, avoiding any finance and interest charges altogether. According to *Inc.*, 60 percent of small businesses surveyed reported being able to pay off their cards on a monthly basis (p. 53). If you can't pay them off monthly, your backup plan should be to manage the credit card debt as if it's an approved loan from a bank. After all, credit cards are essentially personal loans. You should build the credit card debt into the business plan, outlining a repayment schedule and tracking the interest rates of the various cards. Once the introductory rate expires, call the credit card company and ask them to reduce the interest rate. Eager to retain your business, they will frequently reduce your interest rate from 18 or 20 percent to a more acceptable 12 or 13 percent. Credit card companies will also fight for your business by offering special balance transfer rates, often in the 4.9 to 6.9 percent range. Take advantage of these opportunities, transferring balances between companies until you've paid off the entire balance. If you transfer balances by using a check from another credit card company, the bank with the higher interest rate will sometimes recognize the competitor's check and call you to offer an equivalent rate. Another trick involves timing the closing dates of your credit card and having the account charged for expenses on the first day of each billing cycle. Sometimes you can defer the time of payment up to 90 days from the time you initially ordered a product. Finally, use the credit cards to build a solid record of repayment. Then use that history to obtain a commercial bank loan, impressing the lender with your ability to effectively manage debt. Creative strategies abound for entrepreneurs willing to stretch their credit and their mind in order to finance a new business. Just maintain a solid credit record and keep an eye open for opportunities to save money.

More Sources of Capital

The sources of capital available to young companies seem almost as varied as the businesses themselves. Entrepreneurs continue to innovate in their never-ending pursuit of investment funding and they've turned up some creative methods for obtaining the next infusion of cash. The following are a few more nontraditional sources. We encourage you to research sources that seem applicable to your company's situation and capital needs.

Joint Ventures and Strategic Alliances: By joining forces with a more developed company, your business can tap into the financial resources and capabilities of a larger firm. Of course, you must have something to contribute to the relationship as well, for example, technology, expertise, or a product that the partner can use. With a partnership, two companies have a mutual interest in each other's success and they pursue markets with a combined strength that is greater than their individual capabilities.

Lease Financing: Banks issue loans to individuals when they have collateral to put up as a guarantee of payment. Companies can also leverage their assets to raise additional capital by using the equipment they lease as collateral. Through lease financing, you can avoid a down payment and obtain a loan that might otherwise be inaccessible.

Licensing: High-tech companies frequently license their technology to other companies that then turn around and apply the technology to their own products. In return, the licensee pays a royalty or fee to the licensing company. Businesses can also license brands, production methods, or anything else another company can use.

Franchising: Companies can also franchise their business, selling the right to use their name, apply their production process, and sell their product. Restaurants frequently franchise their businesses in order to raise more money and expand the number of company stores. Jamba Juice franchised 12 stores that raised $75,000 and 4 percent of sales per year. With the capital, Kirk Perron, Jamba Juice's founder, was able to open enough stores to attract the attention of venture capitalists who helped him grow the chain to 90 stores (Grover, 1998).

R&D Arrangements: R&D limited partnerships occur when a larger company gives a small business a contract to research a technology that can benefit the larger partner. Depending on the agreement, once the technology has been developed, the partners can form a new company, one company can purchase the technology and bring it to market, or the two can form a financial agreement and part ways. R&D arrangements offer an excellent opportunity to raise seed funding for a young company with a proprietary technology.

Incubators: A number of corporate and university incubators provide some combination of capital, physical space, and technical assistance to seed and start-up companies to develop products and launch new businesses. If it's a corporate-sponsored incubator, the corporation providing the capital may form a licensing agreement with the start-up, purchase a share of the new company, or fold it back into the corporation, depending on the terms of the incubation agreement.

ESOPs and Management Buyouts: In an employee stock ownership plan (ESOP) or management buyout, the employees of the venture buy ownership in the company through the purchase of stock or options. In order to purchase shares, employees will frequently forgo some of their salary, reducing the company's cost of labor and conserving cash. Management may also purchase the company with cash, providing a direct infusion of capital and keeping the ownership of the business in the hands of some of its closest constituents.

Loans

Thirty-eight percent of small companies used bank loans to finance their businesses in 1997 (Hise, p. 50). However, up to this point, we've barely mentioned commercial banks as an important source of capital, choosing instead to highlight venture capital, angels, and alternative sources of funding. We have de-emphasized the potential of debt because many seed and start up companies simply cannot qualify for loans from banks. Unlike angel investors and venture capitalists, traditional banks are creditors, not investors. Specifically, most banks are short-term lenders, granting 30-to-90-day loans and charging interest on the debt. Unlike investors, which experience the upside potential and downside risks of an investment, lending institutions only expose themselves to the downside risk of financing a small business. They do not claim a share of the company's profit or realize capital gains from the appreciation of the company's value. If the company succeeds they simply receive consistent payments against the loan amount. If the business fails, the entrepreneur will most likely declare bankruptcy and default on the loan, forcing the bank to possess its assets or sue the owners.

Although lending money is the business of banks, accepting a great deal of risk is not. Unlike venture capitalists, the potential reward of lending to a start up does not increase with the potential risk associated with the loan. Therefore, the objective of a commercial bank is to make loans to companies and individuals that carry little risk of defaulting. To hedge against that risk, banks frequently require companies to provide collateral equivalent to the value of the loan. Moreover, before it issues debt in the first place, a bank carries out its own version of the due diligence process, ensuring that the company will be able to make consistent payments against its debt. This means that your company must at least generate revenue, and most likely a profit, before a commercial bank will even consider your loan application. Considering that many high-growth start-ups fail to produce either revenues or positive net incomes in their first several years of operation (particularly high-tech, Internet, and biotech companies), bank loans simply cease to be a viable financing option for many businesses. However, if you think that your company may be a candidate for a bank loan, then the best advice we can give is to purchase several books specifically addressing debt financing and the process of obtaining a loan. We give several recommendations in the "Sources of Information" section at the end of this chapter. Acquiring and managing debt can be a complex and difficult process, often proving to be more complicated than approaching venture capitalists. It is important that you have a strong grasp of your company's financial status and a solid understanding of the procedures for obtaining a loan.

The Basics

The most common form of bank loan is a 90-day short-term *unsecured loan*. Standard variations include loans made for periods shorter than 90 days (i.e., 30 or 60 days) and loans extended for up to a year and backed by collateral. These are known as *secured loans*. If you're familiar with accounting, you've probably already figured out that a short-term loan represents a current liability on your company's balance sheet, indicating that debt must be repaid within a year. Bank loans typically have an annual interest rate several points above the prime rate, much like consumer credit cards. In the past, the most common approach was to apply a simple interest rate to the loan, requiring that the debtor pay fixed payments over the life of the loan. More recently, banks have been charging a floating or variable interest rate, allowing the interest charges to vary according to fluctuations in the prime rate. Another trend has been to price the loan at a rate above the marginal cost of funds, which is typically reflected by the interest rates on certificates of deposit (CDs). This rate fluctuates daily according to changes in money market rates. In general, the amount of interest paid on a loan will depend on (1) the dollar amount of the loan, (2) the period of the loan, (3) the nominal annual rate of interest, (4) the repayment schedule, and (5) the method used to calculate the interest.

Often entrepreneurs can forecast the cash flow of their company and anticipate future periods when they will require money to pay for supplies or build up inventory. Instead of borrowing the cash now and paying unnecessary interest, they can apply to a bank for a line of credit—an assurance by the bank that, as long as the company remains financially healthy, the bank will lend the company a specific amount of capital. This does not guarantee that the bank will lend the money, rather it ensures that when the business wants to draw against its line of credit, the bank will review the company's current financial statements to verify that it still qualifies for the loan. Under certain circumstances, a business can obtain a guaranteed line of credit that promises the company that the bank will lend it money regardless of its current financial position. As you can well imagine, banks charge extra for the guarantee, typically 1 percent a year on the unused portion of the line of credit. Moreover, a bank will frequently require that entrepreneurs maintain a compensating balance, holding a specific amount of money in their checking account without interest.

As we mentioned earlier, banks will frequently require collateral from the entrepreneur in order to reduce the risk of making a loan. Collateral may be in the form of any asset that has measurable value, including equipment, property, or inventory. If the entrepreneur defaults on the re-payment of the loan, the collateral becomes the possession of the bank, which may sell the assets in order to recoup its losses from the loan. With a small business, banks often require that the entrepreneur and his or her key managers personally sign for the loan, offering their personal posses-sions as collateral. Obviously, this puts the entrepreneur at great risk. However, the rationale of the banker dictates that if you're not willing to put up personal collateral for the loan, then the deal is too risky for the bank, and the bank will deny the credit altogether.

Though commercial banks and venture capitalists differ along almost every dimension, the one thing that's important to both is your business plan. Having a well-articulated, accurate business plan with solid num-bers that predict positive financial performance will be important to ob-taining a line of credit from a bank. However, unlike the venture capitalist, the banker does not search for outrageous growth rates and a high poten-tial return on investment. In fact, the banker could probably care less how rapidly your company grows. He's interested in ensuring that your com-pany will continue to remain healthy, producing financial results that will allow you to repay the loan according to the terms of the agreement. You must be able to validate your financial projections and explain your as-sumptions in a manner that convinces the banker that you run a sound business.

The Small Business Association

In 1953, Congress formed the Small Business Administration (SBA) to pro-vide financial assistance, advice, and counseling to small businesses. In 1996, the agency had over 100 offices and guaranteed authorization of over $10 billion worth of loans. Today, the SBA continues to be a valuable re-source for small businesses as the largest source of long-term financing in the country. Through 7(a), the SBA's General Loan Program, private lenders grant loans to small businesses and the SBA guarantees 70 percent to 90 percent of the loan amount up to $750,000. These guarantees reduce the risk to banks and increase the amount of funding available to small busi-nesses. A small business accesses SBA funding through its local bank, ap-plying for an SBA-guaranteed loan after it's been denied a commercial loan. The SBA also supports business development efforts through its re-source partners: Small Business Development Centers (SBDCs) and the Service Corps of Retired Executives (SCORE). SBDCs provide management assistance and counseling, seminars, and workshops to small businesses. The SCORE program consists of more than 12,000 retired and active execu-tives and small business owners who volunteer their professional manage-ment expertise to help young companies. The SBA also licenses Small

Business Investment Companies (SBICs), the only type of investment firms that can legally issue loans and own equity in start-up companies. They operate much like venture capital firms and were discussed earlier in the section on venture capital. You can contact the SBA to learn more about its programs by visiting its web site, www.sba.gov, or calling its toll-free number, 1-800-859-INFO or 1-800-697-INFO.

Commercial loans continue to be a popular source of small business financing. However, obtaining credit can be a challenge for a new company with little cash flow. Even if your company can't qualify for a loan today, begin researching the loan application process and contacting bankers. When your business becomes financially stable, a credit line will likely become a valuable resource for cash.

Conclusion

The U.S. economy is an extremely favorable environment for launching a new business and raising the capital to make it succeed. Entrepreneurs financing start-ups face a myriad of choices, many of which were not available a few years ago. However, the competition for capital remains fierce and the process continues to be complex and arduous. Before you raise money, you should carefully examine your company's needs, projecting how you will use the capital to help the business grow.

Then you should survey the financing opportunities available to you, eliminating options that are inaccessible or too expensive. Remember that raising money always comes at a price and your objective should be to raise only the amount you need at the cheapest price possible. Ideally, you should be able to prove that utilizing the capital to fund your start-up will yield a greater return to the company's shareholders than the cost incurred for acquiring and using the money. Once you've identified the most relevant sources of capital, you should gain a detailed understanding of the process for obtaining the money. Plan and budget for both the time and expense of raising the capital, understanding that acquiring the cash could take several weeks or many months.

Carefully construct the necessary documents, recognizing that you are selling the company to outsiders, asking them to trust and believe in your ability to manage a stable and growing business. Finally, you should understand the personal side of raising money. Whether you're approaching family members, venture capitalists, angel investors, or bankers, you will have to develop partnerships based on strong business and personal relationships. Good luck and happy hunting.

Chapter 4

꒜꒐ꕥ ꒜꒐ꕥ ꒜꒐ꕥ ꒜꒐ꕥ

The Business Plan

E very traveler standing nervously at the edge of foreign territory clutches a single, irreplaceable item: the map.

Your business plan is your map through the jungle of today's business world. It will guide you step-by-step through every aspect of the start-up process. By meticulously detailing a proposed company's market competition, strategies for implementation, and financial projections, the business plan reveals to the entrepreneur the golden path to vast fortunes or, as the case may be, potential pitfalls or barriers to entry.

A good map provides a clear, succinct route to follow. The business plan is very important in convincing potential investors to part with their hard-earned cash. Within the pages of your business plan, a prospective investor must clearly see the company's purpose, philosophy, plan of action, expected challenges, and path for future success.

This chapter will provide you with an analysis of each major section of the business plan, hints on writing and researching the various sections, and the critical questions and concerns that each section should address. Highlighting this information are samples of hypothetical business plans. Consider the material carefully. Do the research. Put in the time. This early preparation will reward you with a business plan better able to get funding and prove you are prepared for the difficult journey ahead.

Why a Business Plan Is Necessary

With all due respect to the romantics among us, money makes the business world go around. Blood, sweat, tears, determination, heart, and the infinite list of other business catchwords are all important to a start-up, but money is its lifeblood. Money gives entrepreneurs a chance to test

---

As this is a basic framework of The Business Plan, the specific plan for your business might look very different and should be formulated with the help of professional advisors.

their business savvy; a lack of money forces them to wonder what might have been.

Let's begin this chapter with a sobering thought: In order for a business idea to be able to leave the drawing room and stand on its own two feet, the financial capabilities necessary to see the idea through to completion must be obtained. This fact of business creates an apparent paradox for the new entrepreneur. You are starting a business with the intention of making money—but it usually takes a substantial amount of money simply to get the ball rolling.

Lest the hopes and dreams of the less affluent entrepreneurs be immediately crushed, remember that a lack of personal wealth is not a death knell for a young business. During our college years, most of us discovered the concept of extended credit. Simply stated, a vast majority of start-ups must initially borrow money, with the agreement to pay it back at a later date.

For those whose memory of economics has faded, we have outlined the basic process by which you can obtain credit. Here is our eight-step crash course:

1. Determine how much money is needed to start your company.
2. Convince an investor that your company will be profitable.
3. Prove to the investor that your company requires the predetermined amount of money.
4. Ask the investor for support in funding the company.
5. Offer either incentives, interest, or collateral for the investor's contribution to your company.
6. Make arrangements to pay back the borrowed money.
7. Begin your company and collect revenues from your service or product.
8. Pay back your investor under the stated terms.

From the time of Julius Caesar to that of Bill Gates, this basic process of raising money has remained essentially the same. What has changed, however, is the manner in which the process is organized and conducted. Most notably, the presentation of a formal business plan has become standard procedure in seeking financial backing from all major sources of start-up funding.

Banks, venture capitalists, and private investors want to see your company on paper. They want a clear picture of what your company is trying to accomplish, why it will be successful, who will be your competitors, how you intend to market your product or service, and who will manage the company.

Of course, every business plan will vary with respect to its proposed product or service. Nonetheless, certain guidelines or general rules are expected to be followed in the business plan's preparation. In this chapter we will provide a greater understanding of these general rules in nontechnical language that can be understood by readers who lack extensive business backgrounds.

The Goals of a Business Plan

Before we describe the components, we will explain the goals of the business plan. Properly constructed, a business plan will provide you with a road map and a chance at obtaining the funding you need.

Financial Funding

Your business plan provides an outline of your company's goals, procedures, competition, and projections for (usually) the first five years of operation. If the prospective investor believes that your written proposal falls short in addressing any of these concerns, he or she simply will not support your project. Thus, before any other claims about the greater purpose of a business plan can be discussed, the first goal must be made very clear: A business plan's first objective is to acquire funding for a start-up company.

A mistake common to many new entrepreneurs is the assumption that the ideas presented in a business plan alone are enough to convince a prospective investor of a company's worth. Acting on this assumption, the new entrepreneur spends less time putting together a sharp-looking business plan and more time getting a head start in business operations. Beware. A sloppy, poorly drawn map is likely to result in lost investors—and an early death for your business dreams.

Before falling victim to this common mistake, consider for a moment what a business plan reveals to a prospective investor beyond the who, what, where, and how of your company.

■ *A well-written business plan reveals that you are a capable individual with more than just the aspirations for success.* It is your primary—and in many cases your only—means of convincing investors that you also have the tools to make your dream a reality.

■ *A business plan reveals that you are a professional.* In lieu of any personal relationship with a prospective investor, the business plan is a representative sample of your work and therefore an indicator of your abilities. It's only natural for an investor to assume that a hastily prepared business plan indicates inattention to detail. Likewise, a well-written yet incomplete business plan indicates a lack of ability to follow through.

■ A *business plan reveals that you are prepared.* It displays a level of expertise in the field you are choosing to enter and a solid knowledge of the current market environment. A comprehensive, well-prepared business plan provides you with credibility in the eyes of prospective investors and gives added assurance that their investment is well worth the risks.

■ A *business plan reveals vision.* Your business plan shows that you have considered future concerns and have planned to meet their challenges. Additionally, it makes known the greater opportunities that lie ahead for your company. A winning business plan states not only the immediate need for your product or service but also the greater potential of your company to meet the needs of the future marketplace.

As each of these statements suggests, a business plan creates an impression beyond the immediate viability of the idea itself. It helps the prospective investor to recognize your qualities as an individual and serves as a sample of how you will operate your business. As both a plan of action and a testament to your abilities, a well-written, carefully researched proposal will help you find the funding to begin business operations.

A Map for the Early Years

A financial commitment to your product or service signals only the beginning of your journey. Your business plan also proves critical once funding has been secured. The first few years are the most critical for a start-up company, and you will need your carefully prepared and detailed map to help you navigate through the hazards and potential pitfalls of today's business environment.

The preparation of a business plan forces you to ask difficult questions concerning issues such as sales strategy, customer support, and product pricing. As you begin business operations, a carefully prepared business plan will provide you with implementation strategies: It will tell you where, how, and who to advertise your product to; it will establish how the company will service the concerns of customers; and it will suggest a competitive pricing strategy for your product or service.

A business plan also provides a perfect way to communicate your vision to your new company's personnel. Within a neatly packaged document, newly hired employees will be able to understand the purpose of the company, the strategies for achieving its goals, and their role within the larger context of the business. It also serves as a useful tool for critical self-evaluation along the way. At various stages of the start-up process, the questions "Are we on plan? If not, why?" must be asked and answered.

A Word of Caution

One entrepreneur dreams of conquering the microprocessor empire by the age of 21. Another envisions running a local fish bait shop. Regardless of their size, all business dreams are similar in requiring careful planning to become successful.

In its simplest form, a business plan represents an entrepreneur's attempt to put his or her dream onto paper. Taking a long, hard look at your dreams can be an emotional roller coaster. Before completing your business plan, you will be convinced that your ideas are doomed to failure. An hour later, you will be assuring yourself of seven-figure profits in the first month of operation. Considering the intense investment of time and effort required to prepare a business plan, the highs and lows encountered along the way are only natural. Nonetheless, you must be aware of the distinction between momentary panic attacks and an idea that simply isn't viable.

A sobering fact of business is that 80 percent of all start-ups don't even make it into their fifth year of operation. For many of these failed companies, their business plans replaced an honest assessment of the market's potential with written refusals to abandon hours upon hours of hard work. From the very first sentence of your business plan to the concluding paragraph, you must avoid the temptation of falling in love with the dream—and becoming blinded to reality. Instead, let the dream's potential serve as the foundation of your commitment. The following warning addresses a common, yet understandable, error made by new entrepreneurs: Don't become attached to a business idea—become attached to a business idea's potential.

The experts do not lie when they say the obstacles to success are many. Don't start your journey with a map drawn using rose-colored glasses and scattered with idealistic assumptions.

Research and analysis are the final authorities in assuring you that a business dream has potential. Many times these cold-hearted authorities will force you to ditch your ideas and start fresh. To be sure, a lot of hard work will have gone to waste for very little result—but it's nothing compared to the many hardships, financial and otherwise, that you could have suffered by committing yourself to an impotent, unrealistic idea.

Start with a business plan based on sound research and assumptions. Doing so will give your company every advantage in the race to survive, and it will give you the necessary confidence to put your idea into action.

General Tips on Writing a Successful Business Plan

All communities develop their own language, and the business community is no exception. An otherwise well-written business plan that does not use the language of business is likely to be viewed either skeptically or less seriously by prospective investors. Whether your subject is market competition or company management, make every effort to follow these simple guidelines to the practical and stylistic elements of business writing.

Write Professionally, Not Academically

First and foremost, the business plan provides analytical evidence of your company's potential for success. Present this evidence through concise, purposefully written sentences that directly address the concerns unique to each section of the business plan. In contrast to a college essay or paper, a business plan should do the following:

■ Keep paragraphs short and blocked.

■ Reserve quotations and anecdotes for those cases where the information confirms claims in market research or is necessary to fully answer the concerns of the investor.

■ Be sparing with essay-writing words and phrases such as *therefore, to be sure, however, consequently, hence,* and *thus.*

■ Minimize use of colloquial phrases.

■ Utilize phrases such as "the Company strongly believes . . ." and "the Company feels confident that . . ." as opposed to "it would seem . . . ," "we hope . . . ," and "this might suggest . . ."

This does not imply that business writing should be dull or bland. A well-written business plan can follow these guidelines and still prove engaging and unique. However, a business plan that reads too much like a college essay risks being interpreted as a sign of business inexperience.

Base Predictions on Statistical Evidence

One of the most challenging aspects of writing a business plan involves predicting the potential market for your product or service. Since the details of your company's early years are speculative, this material comes under the most intense scrutiny from prospective investors. To make your predictions more accurate and convincing, be sure to include actual statistics in formulating each step of your analysis. Make sure that all assumptions have a numerical foundation. For example, do not simply state: "The rapid growth of the Internet fuels speculation that a virtual office business would prove profitable." Instead note: "*Computer* magazine lists the market of Internet servers as increasing by 80 percent in the past three years. This trend provides strong indication that a virtual office business would prove profitable." By providing actual numbers for the prospective investor to analyze, your business plan uses market history, not wishful thinking, to create an accurate picture of future possibilities.

Use Bullets

Don't force your prospective investor to search through paragraphs of information to find your business plan's key points. Bullets (•), spacing, character size, and character quality (such as **bold,** *italics*, and <u>underline</u>) draw immediate attention to evidence suggesting a market's viability, your product's advantage over competitors, effective sales strategies, and so forth. Make your business plan reader-friendly—and ensure that important considerations are not overlooked by casual readers.

Consider Technology

In today's world, technology is key to the efficient, smooth operation of all aspects of business. As you prepare your business plan, consider the technology available to assist in the production, marketing, or sales of your product or service.

Invest in Business Software

The purchase of a good word-processing and spreadsheet package will prove to be a worthwhile investment. Most word-processing programs today deliver a professional-quality format and come packaged with chart-ready capabilities. A good spreadsheet program gives you the capability to adjust strategic variables such as service pricing and personnel wages, providing information on future revenues with only a few keystrokes. Most spreadsheets today can also produce tables from these supplied variables. Presenting information graphically makes your research more accessible and lends a professional appearance to your business plan. Business plan writing software is also available, and is useful for guidance purposes.

Look at Other Business Plans

Looking over the different formats, writing styles, presentation of information, and general structures of various finished business plans can provide great insight into strengths to be emulated and weaknesses to be avoided. In addition to providing business plan samples in this chapter, we have listed in the Appendix several books that provide quality examples. Also, an Internet search using the search term "business plans" should produce an appreciable amount of possible models. A standard warning with using the Internet though: Many of the samples lack the professional qualities of clarity, format, and research that highlight a successful business plan.

Don't Sell the Farm

The best business plan cannot be copied. Even if the product of your hard labor were to fall into enemy hands, only you should be able to reproduce the company outlined on paper. Here are a few ways to protect an idea.

- *Do not specify the exact methodologies of your service.* It is sufficient to write "the Company plans to accomplish [goal of service] through [service A, service B, and service C]" without providing the intimate details of services A, B, and C.

- *Do not reveal the operation of exclusive technology.* Use phrases such as "proprietary technology developed by the Company allows the product to . . ." instead.

- *Assemble an irreproducible management team.* Human capital simply cannot be copied.

- *Do not reveal the dynamics of your service strategy.* A good business plan can provide in-depth detail about a proposed service and the means by which it will market the service without revealing how these elements work together.

A fine line exists between too little information and too much. Yet in order to ensure protection from the harsh realities of the business world, your business plan must be able to convince the prospective investor that you can offer a unique benefit or advantage over competitors without giving away the exact specifics of how you plan to accomplish this task.

Proofread, Proofread, Proofread

A successful business plan must be error-free and grammatically correct. While word-processing programs do an acceptable job of correcting common mistakes, they will not tell you how smoothly sentences flow or how clearly ideas are being expressed. Before presenting your business plan to a prospective investor, ask people you trust to read over the document and provide feedback as to which sections need revising, which sections lack information, and which sections seem overly repetitive. Demand absolute honesty from your readers, and be sure to ask them to express any concerns that the business plan doesn't completely address. After all, if your personal friends aren't convinced by your proposal, prospective investors will be highly unlikely to risk their money.

Make a Good First Impression

Since you have already spent hours researching and writing your business plan, it only makes sense to give it the highest quality presentation. As mentioned previously, the format of your proposal should be neat, professional, and easily accessible. In addition, be sure to print your business plan in a conservative, well-recognized font. Times New Roman is generally accepted as the standard font for most publications. The business plan should be printed on heavyweight cotton fiber paper and presented in a spiral-bound, clear plastic binder. If possible, you should consider getting professional help in making your proposal as attractive as possible. A few extra dollars spent on these considerations will help you create the best possible first impression in the eyes of a prospective investor. Do not go overboard in this area, though, as the potential investor may get the idea that you are a poor money manager.

Consider Outside Help

Especially for new entrepreneurs, assembling an experienced management team often proves to be a difficult task. As a general rule, your management team must possess (or develop) skill in business finance, marketing, operations, and management. If your company appears weak in any of these areas, consider adding qualified consultants to your business plan. Not only can they strengthen your company's position for funding, but they can also provide needed assistance during the critical first months.

Use the Internet

The impact of the Internet on the business world demands special attention. Today, virtually all companies maintain a web site and/or utilize computer media in some aspect of their business. As more and more households become connected, these web sites provide ready advertisement and instant information on the product or service being offered. While the use of the Internet is obviously not a requisite for doing business in the 1990s, utilizing this technology in the marketing, sales, or service of your product could prove to be quite rewarding. As you prepare your business plan, consider how this powerful tool can be used in reaching or maintaining relations with your target population.

It is easy to fall back into old habits. Check periodically to make sure that your business plan keeps the foregoing tips in mind. Frequent and early reminders about form and style will make revision much more bearable as you progress toward a finished product.

The Business Plan

Although business plans differ with respect to style or format, prospective investors consider the following elements to be essential components of a business plan:

- Cover letter
- Title page
- Table of contents
- Executive summary
- Business identification statement
- Management and personnel list
- Market research
- Services description
- Marketing strategy
- Competition overview
- Financial projections
- Appendix, including resumes and/or glossary.

The following is a breakdown of the information needed in each section of the business plan and the questions that each section must answer. (All companies, individuals, and information provided in the business plan samples are fictitious. Resemblance to any actual company's business plan or name is purely coincidental and is not intended to provide proprietary information about any particular industry or company.) Prior to presenting the plan to a prospective lender or investor, you should obtain a signed nondisclosure agreement from him or her.

Cover Letter

A cover letter gives you the opportunity to clearly identify yourself, your business, and the amount you are requesting for funding. It should be approximately a page in length, written on company stationery, and provide the following information:

- Business information (name, address, URL listing, telephone, fax, contacts)
- Brief company description
- Financial requirements

The sample cover letter provides a model for presenting this information to a prospective investor.

———————————— ✢ ✢ **SAMPLE** ✢ ✢ ————————————

[Company Logo]
[Company Address]

[Date]

[Investor]
[Investor's Address]

Dear _____ :

[Company] is a _____ business specializing in _____ . [Company] is requesting a loan of $ _____ for the successful implementation of the enclosed business plan. Repayment is anticipated over a period of _____ . As collateral for a financial commitment, [Company] is offering [incentives].

[Company] will greatly appreciate your serious consideration of this loan request. Should further information be required, please contact [Company] at [phone number].

Sincerely,

[Signature]

[Printed Name]

[Title]

Enc.: Business Plan for [Company]

———————————————————— ✢ ✢ ✢ ✢ ————————————

A statement of confidentiality should be attached to your cover letter. This paragraph informs the prospective investor that information in your business plan is strictly confidential and may not be released without your written authorization. A business plan number should also be included on this page for your own reference. A standard statement of confidentiality is given in the sample.

SAMPLE

[Company Logo]
[Company Address]

This memorandum does not constitute an offer to sell or a solicitation of an offer to purchase securities. This business plan has been submitted on a confidential basis solely for the benefit of selected investors and is not for use by any other persons. Neither may it be reproduced, stored, or copied in any form. By accepting delivery of this plan, the recipient acknowledges and agrees that (1) in the event the recipient does not wish to pursue this matter, the recipient will return this copy to [Company] at the address listed above as soon as practical; (2) the recipient will not copy, fax, reproduce, or distribute this Confidential Business Plan, in whole or in part, without permission; (3) all of the information contained herein will be treated as confidential material. Agreement executed by the recipient prior to, or contemporaneously with, the receipt of this confidential business plan.

Business Plan No. _____   Provided to _____

Company _____

Date _____

Title Page

The title page signals the beginning of your business plan. A large, color company logo should appear on the top half of the page. See the sample title page.

SAMPLE

[Company Logo]
[Company Name]

REQUEST FOR FINANCING

CONFIDENTIAL

Table of Contents

The table of contents provides a ready reference for the prospective investor. Since page numbers can be added only upon completion of the document, the table of contents should be prepared last. See the sample table of contents.

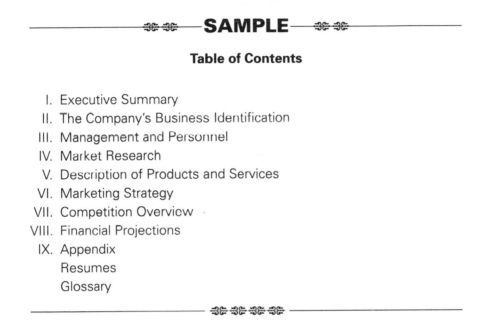

──────────── ❧❧ ──**SAMPLE**──❧❧ ────────────

Table of Contents

I. Executive Summary
II. The Company's Business Identification
III. Management and Personnel
IV. Market Research
V. Description of Products and Services
VI. Marketing Strategy
VII. Competition Overview
VIII. Financial Projections
IX. Appendix
    Resumes
    Glossary

──────────── ❧❧❧❧ ────────────

Executive Summary

The executive summary summarizes the main points of your business plan in two to three pages. This section of the business plan proves especially important in selling your idea to the prospective investor. In only a few paragraphs, you must convince the reader that (1) a significant business opportunity exists in the market and (2) your company's product or service will effectively exploit this business opportunity. An executive summary should provide the following information:

- Brief background of market
- The business opportunity
- Your company's strategy to exploit this opportunity
- Your company's request for funding

The executive summary should be your business plan condensed to its finest elements. For this reason, most entrepreneurs reserve writing this section for the very end. The sample shows an executive summary for a hypothetical consulting firm.

SAMPLE

I. Executive Summary

Last year, 25,000 aspiring chefs applied to the Ray's Culinary School. This number represents more than a 10 percent increase of the previous applicant pool, and a 17 percent growth from 1987. While the number of applicants has increased dramatically, the number of students accepted has reached a plateau of 1,500.

These alarming statistics reveal an increasingly larger pool of prospective chefs vying for limited openings at culinary schools across the country. The question remains, however, exactly how a prospective applicant can rise above the competition and gain acceptance to these institutions. While common knowledge dictates requisites of stellar recommendations, varied restaurant experience, and multiple culinary awards, this checklist proves insufficient in addressing the means by which these goals can be attained. M&R Food Consultants (M&R) has identified this significant market opportunity and has developed a service program ideally suited for structuring and planning a career in the culinary arts.

M&R believes that the ability to gain acceptance into culinary institutions requires commitment and understanding beyond that offered by current guidebooks or references. A career in food preparation demands the preparation of an individual during formative secondary-schooling years and beyond in order to ensure the greatest possibility of acceptance. The M&R program addresses these concerns of prospective applicants. Based on multiple interviews with top chefs, extensive background research, and personal experience within elite restaurants, the M&R program provides information and strategies that might otherwise be overlooked by individuals lacking extreme familiarity with the admissions process.

To satisfy the various needs of prospective culinary school applicants, M&R plans to offer the following services:

- Cuisine presentation
- Culinary school test preparation
- International food preparation
- Spices/condiments
- Elite culinary school reports

■ Chef profiles
■ Admissions guidelines
■ Alumni contact lists
■ Special foods preparation

The application process distinct to culinary institutions has been severely underserved. M&R Food Consultants recognizes this market potential and has developed a program that aims at maximizing an individual's appeal to these schools. Beyond detailing the importance of various criteria in the application process, the M&R program provides individualized attention to the applicant's strengths and weaknesses and, more importantly, prepares both long-term and short-term strategies with these considerations in mind.

M&R aims initially to establish an office in Vancouver, B.C. (Canada), and eventually to expand in response to market considerations. As the home of the renowned Che' Quakee and YukJan restaurants, Vancouver provides an attractive environment from which to base a consulting firm of this nature. Assuming a funding commitment for spring 1988, M&R expects to procure a clientele and begin providing services for the summer 1988 application season.

The influx of applicants to culinary institutions has created an attractive investment opportunity with high return. The M&R market entry plan targets those members of the professional community driven to provide themselves with every advantage in gaining acceptance to these institutions. Consulting services, accordingly, will be aggressively priced and distributed through a combination of direct and indirect sales channels. M&R estimates potential market revenue of $7.9 million in five years.

M&R Food Consultants is seeking a commitment of $354,200 for market entry and an additional $20,000 to fund continued implementation of the business plan. This commitment will enable M&R to be first to market and, furthermore, to gain and maintain the position of market leader in culinary consulting.

Business Identification Statement

The business identification statement provides a detailed account of your business's specifications, history (if any), purpose, and organization. This portion of the business plan should include the following:

■ Precise legal description of the proposed business
■ Outline of the business's history
■ Business location

- Projected operating schedule
- Projected list of operational requirements
  Office space requirements
  Office machinery and equipment
  Outside services
  Production materials
  Technical assistance
- List of outside contractors
- Goals of the proposed business

Many business plans integrate the management and personnel list or the services description, or both into the business identification statement. If you choose to include either of these categories, be sure to clearly identify each with prominent subheadings. For purposes of explanation, this chapter shows the *management* and *services* sections as separate parts of the business plan.

The sample is a business identification statement for a hypothetical security alarm company.

──────────── ❀ ❀ **SAMPLE** ❀ ❀ ────────────

II. The Company's Business Identification

In 1982, Dr. Richard Gould began development of a prototype for the IS-Block security system in his office at Smith and Holmes. He resigned from his position as Director of Engineering a year later in order to devote all of his time and resources to the further development of the system, market research, and continued work toward the first release.

Fox Security Systems will be the name given the distributing company of the IS-Block security system. Fox Security Systems will be established as a "B" Corporation (Delaware) and will be located in the Greater Milwaukee area. The Company believes recently graduated electro-mechanical engineers from a number of excellent engineering programs in the Milwaukee area will be the source of the creative talent required to make the Company successful. The Company also believes that a significant number of electronic boutiques in the Milwaukee area will provide a source of competent sales and support skills.

Fox Security Systems aims to begin production of the IS-Block in mid-January 1986 and begin distribution and sales in early June. These release dates will allow Fox Security Systems to be the first to market with thermo-sensory trace mechanisms for the detection of intruders into secured buildings and offices. Continuing from its entry IS-Block system, Fox Security Systems will be positioned as the preeminent supplier of professional security monitoring devices, with a product family that addresses the safety lifecycle from prevention, through detection, to notification of proper authorities. Fox Security Systems has developed proprietary thermo-sensory technology that allows many possible intruders to be tracked from their point of entry to their exit from the establishment. The IS-Block is the first such security alarm that both utilizes this technology and can be implemented in all building frames.

Fox Security Systems has determined that funding will be required in four major areas: (1) electronic components, (2) research and development, (3) sales and marketing, and (4) office expenses and equipment. The table outlines the projected percentage cost of total revenues for each major cost driver from 1986 to 1990.

Percentage Breakdown of Projected Expenses for Fox Security Systems, by Year

Expense	1986	1987	1988	1989	1990
Electronic components	16%	11%	11%	11%	11%
R&D	12%	5%	6%	6%	7%
Sales and marketing	28%	20%	20%	19%	20%
Office expenses and equipment	20%	9%	8%	7%	6%

Initial production of the IS-Block will be contracted to Values Engineering, a local university–based electromechanical production plant. By 1987, Fox Security Systems will have developed the capabilities and purchased the machinery necessary to take over this aspect of business. (Please refer to the attached financial projections for the specifics of each major cost driver and a breakdown of expenses.)

The trend toward specialization today as well as the customer's desire to purchase complete systems is driving the need for partnerships. Bundling its products with competitive physical-entry barriers will allow Fox Security Systems to penetrate accounts at a higher rate. By balancing technological advances with proven physical-entry barriers, the Company strongly believes that it will be able to extend its offerings to a broader customer base. Accordingly, Fox Security Systems sees these companies as important opportunities for product integration.

————————————— ❧ ❧ ❧ ❧ —————————————

Management and Personnel List

Most prospective investors consider your management team to be either the greatest weakness or the greatest strength of your proposed business. These individuals must possess a blend of business experience, pragmatism, and vision to both direct day-to-day operations of the company and make long-term policy decisions. In preparing the management and personnel list, be sure to do the following:

- Present key management (business experience, strengths, leadership qualities).
- Detail individual titles and responsibilities (management, finance, marketing, operations).
- List key outside support personnel.
- List required staff and responsibilities.
- If applicable, list the board of directors and their stock allocations.
- Attach resumes of key management in the business plan's appendix.

As indicated in the general tips section of this chapter, many new entrepreneurs have difficulty assembling an experienced management team. Accordingly, individuals in key positions will come under increased scrutiny from prospective investors. If any individuals in your company have been slated to perform tasks above their present abilities, strongly consider adding qualified consultants as temporary members of your staff. In addition to strengthening the business plan in general, experienced business consultants can help direct company operations until your management team is ready to take control.

The sample management and personnel list describes the management team of a hypothetical land management company.

SAMPLE

III. Management and Personnel

The management and personnel of a company form what is called it's "Human Capital." Some would say this human capital is the backbone of the company. It is very important to make the expertise and qualifications of your team clear.

Biographies

Wood Bryk Land Management, Inc. was founded and is managed by the following land management professionals:

Name	Position
Jamison Chustz	Founder, Chairman of the Board, President
Hilary Imes-Hunter	Founder, Director of Operations

Name	Position
Ellen Bellizzi	Executive Vice President, Marketing
Mark S. Constanzo	Vice President, Finance
Andres Krim	Controller

Jamison Chustz Chairman, President

Mr. Chustz has over 15 years of senior-level land management experience. Prior to cofounding Wood Bryk, Mr. Chustz spent five years as Chief Executive Officer of Cambridge Realty Consultants, a leading land purchasing company in Boston. Previously, Mr. Chustz has organized land management programs in Mississippi, Illinois, and Wisconsin, where he oversaw $100 million in purchases and a budget exceeding $20 million. Mr. Chustz has served as director on numerous boards, both locally and nationally, including publicly traded land management companies such as Siesta Beach Partners and American Trust Land Corporation.

Hilary Imes-Hunter Founder, Director of Operations

Ms. Imes-Hunter has over 20 years of senior-level land management experience. Before cofounding Wood Bryk, Ms. Imes-Hunter served as Chief Operating Officer for Lowell & Holworthy, Inc., a leading land acquisition firm with over 5,000 employees at 23 sites in 10 states. Lowell & Holworthy operates the largest network of comprehensive surveying and land evaluation facilities in the United States. Prior to joining Lowell & Holworthy, Ms. Imes-Hunter worked as an administrator in the Federal Land Development Department.

Ellen Bellizzi Executive Vice President, Marketing

Ms. Bellizzi has spent a majority of her career as an advertising and marketing consultant for private companies. Prior to joining Wood Bryk, Ms. Bellizzi was employed by Palm Gardens Resorts, a resort company with over $300 million in revenues. While at Palm Gardens, Ms. Bellizzi was instrumental in increasing resort attendance by 245 percent over five years. Previously, Ms. Bellizzi had been employed by Lowell & Holworthy, Inc.

Mark S. Constanzo Vice President, Finance

Mr. Constanzo has over 10 years of land management experience. Prior to assuming financial duties for Wood Bryk, Mr. Constanzo served as Chief Financial Officer of Superior Land Management. In that role, Mr. Constanzo was responsible for all financial activities of the $400 million publicly traded company, including a leveraged buyout, numerous acquisitions, an initial public offering, and subsequent merger with Lowell & Holworthy, Inc.

Andres Krim Controller

Mr. Krim has eight years of experience in land management. Prior to joining Wood Bryk, Mr. Krim served as the Corporate Controller of Palm Gardens Resorts, where he was responsible for the assimilation and integration of all acquisitions, the accuracy of that company's books, Securities and Exchange Commission reporting requirements, and the administration of the company's pension plan. Previously, Mr. Krim worked for Harbach Partners.

Recruitment of Additional Key Management

Wood Bryk Land Management, Inc. recognizes the need for a high-level individual with prior surveying experience to assume the role of Managing Director. The Company has retained the services of a recruiting firm to identify candidates. Wood Bryk expects to have the individual in place no later than January 1, 2000.

Land Advisory Board

Wood Bryk has established a Land Advisory Board to be comprised of some of the leading surveyors and land developers throughout the United States. Chaired by Mr. Chustz, the Land Advisory Board will advise the Company on demographics, geographical considerations, and new procedures. Wood Bryk has identified and is in discussions with several potential candidates for the Land Advisory Board.

------------------------------ ❦ ❦ ❦ ❦ ------------------------------

Market Research

Before lending money to your company, prospective investors must be convinced that the current market conditions both demand and can successfully sustain your product or service. The market research section of a business plan serves this purpose by outlining the potential market for your product or service. As noted earlier in "A Word of Caution," take the time to do a complete, in-depth, and honest evaluation. Beyond lending credibility to your business plan, a well-written market research section can often provide insight in designing your marketing strategy, reveal the weaknesses of your competitors, highlight underdeveloped niches, or warn of potential barriers to entry. For these reasons, most experienced entrepreneurs choose to write the market research section first.

A good market research section should contain the following information:

■ General description of the market (e.g., auto industry)
■ Specific description of market (e.g., car horn manufacturers)
■ Recent market trends

- Analysis of market niche (i.e., characteristics, market penetration, potential share, stability, growth, sales volume, limitations)
- Sources of market strength and weakness (i.e., location, customer service, quality of product, marketing strategy)
- Concise statement of the business opportunity and your ability to take advantage of that opportunity

Use statistical evidence whenever possible to illustrate trends or back up claims. In addition, the research section of your business plan should cite all supporting documentation in footnotes or endnotes, whether from industry experts, trade reports, government studies, surveys, periodicals, or academic journals.

The sample shows a market research section for a hypothetical legal partnering firm.

❄❄ SAMPLE ❄❄

IV. Market Research

Legal Representation Industry

There are a number of powerful fundamental trends reshaping the legal representation community. A reduction in per case reimbursement across virtually all classes has dramatically changed the business environment for lawyers. Paperwork has mushroomed, attorneys are working harder, and more risks are being assumed. Despite these added hassles, *Big Money Magazine* reports that attorneys are taking home 9 percent less salary than five years ago.

Touhls Brothers believes that most independent attorneys, including divorce attorneys, are inadequately prepared to respond to these challenges. Divorce attorneys are highly fragmented, practicing individually or in small groups of two to three. Accordingly, they are unable to expand quickly enough to spread increasing overhead costs over a larger client base and, more importantly, frequently lack sufficient capital to cover the soaring costs of liability insurance.

There are many law firms in the Midwest with reputations for providing quality divorce services. The Company has gathered and analyzed extensive demographic and firm information for each state. The respective number of firms providing divorce services with at least three certified divorce attorneys is as follows: Michigan—44, Illinois—51, Indiana—21, and Ohio—66. Of these 182 law firms, however, only 16 have utilized partnering opportunities such as the one proposed by Touhls Brothers.

In December 1983, an *Arkansas State Legal Journal Dailey* survey noted a growing percentage of firms expressing "high" to "very high" interest in pursuing partnering agreements. The survey noted several key motivating factors of this trend: "While traditionally attorneys have been independent in nature, changing administrative challenges have forced many private practices to consider networking with nearby firms. Most independent attorneys say the time demands of running a law practice today coupled with an uncertainty factor of future demands simply make the choice of joining an attorney network a necessity."

The increased desire of independent firms to partner with larger legal organizations has created enormous market opportunity for Touhls Brothers and other legal administrative companies (LACs). LACs provide expert management, sophisticated information systems, access to low-cost capital, economies of scale, contracting leverage, and financial stability for attorneys.

At the present time, none of the over 15 LACs focuses exclusively on divorce representation. These publicly traded and privately held LACs command substantially less than 5 percent of a market that exceeds $150 billion per year.

Market Analysis of Divorce Representation

The market prospectus for divorce services partnering appears very promising. Many of the current and forecast pricing pressures on attorneys, particularly specialists, are driven by supply and demand. On this basis, the *New York Lawyers Journal* listed divorce law as being one of the single most productive specialties, particularly relative to the specialties pursued by several public and privately held LACs. According to a 1983 study by the Janis Group, the need for specialists is expected to decline by 8 percent from current levels over the next several years. In contrast, the same study forecasts a need for a 14 percent increase in the number of practicing divorce lawyers.

1. *Divorce rates.* Divorce attorneys account for approximately 75 percent of legal visits for individuals between the ages of 23 and 55. The *National Legal Newsletter Daily* indicates this figure will most likely increase to 80 percent of all legal cases by the turn of the century.

2. *Demographics.* The size of the current married population, general marrying-age population (18–35), and projections for the future are favorable for divorce services attorneys. Married couples currently represent 42 percent of the population over 18, and 74 percent of the population over the age of 32.

3. *Market dominance.* A key element of LAC strategy is to dominate markets the corporations enter. "Domination" is defined as the ability to provide at least 25 percent of divorce services. In

contrast to civil or tax attorneys, fewer divorce attorneys are needed in order to achieve local market dominance. For example, to adequately serve a population of 100,000, approximately 5 divorce service attorneys are required. In contrast, the same population demands 20 tax attorneys. LAC's improved networking capabilities allow market dominance to be established more quickly and, in turn, allow its attorneys to benefit from this marketing position.

4. *Attractive option for divorcing couples.* Surveys by the Government Council of Family Research and Statistics indicate that a network of legal services specializing in divorce proceedings prove to be highly accommodating to divorcing couples. The services offered were seen to be of higher quality, more convenient, and more cost-effective than general practices in the surrounding areas.

The Opportunity

The changes in the legal representation industry, combined with the aforementioned characteristics of the divorce representation market, have created an opportunity in divorce services management. Currently, over 10 LACs are traded on the public market, falling into two categories: multiple specialty and single specialty. Acquiring the services of a LAC has proven to be a rewarding decision for attorneys, providing them with financial security and ease of contract and client management. There are numerous single-specialty LACs focusing on areas such as tax, civil, and corporate law. However, there are no LACs for divorce practices in the Company's target market. Touhls Brothers has initially targeted in excess of 500 private practice divorce services across the Midwest. Further, the Company's market research indicates that very few divorce services in the target markets have been approached by other LACs. At the same time, surveys by *The Midwestern Law Quarterly* indicate that divorce attorneys have begun to see the positive impact LACs have had on other specialists and have become amenable to affiliating with a LAC. This evolution in the marketplace will help Touhls Brothers meet early acquisition requirements. Accordingly, the Company's market timing is most opportune.

––––––––––––––––––––– ❧❧❧❧ –––––––––––––––––––––

Description of Products and Services

The product or service that you intend to offer lies at the heart of your business plan. When viewing the services description, the prospective investor wants to know how your product or service differs from competitors', its added value to the customer, and how it will work or be used. The services description should include the following information about your product or service:

- Detailed description of your product or service
- How the product or service addresses the stated business opportunity
- How the product or service differs from competitors'
- Added value to customers of the product or service
- Sales cycle of the product or service (seasonal, product-life, prospective warranty)
- Future product or service plans
- Customer service and product support
- Trademarks, patents, copyrights, and government regulations concerning your product or service
- Risk factors unique to the production, delivery, or service of the product or service

A frequently overlooked aspect of this section is the future offerings of your company. Be sure to discuss not only why your product or service will be competitive in the present environment but also how you intend to remain competitive years down the road. In addition, subheadings such as "Risk Factors," "Future Product and Service Plans," "Customer Service and Product Support," "Features Comparison," and "Value Proposition" should be used for improved clarity and structure. The sample shows services description for a hypothetical software company.

⋙⋙ SAMPLE ⋘⋘

V. Description of Products and Services

Product Description

Pitch-Count 2000 is a powerful tool that analyzes the performance statistics of baseball pitchers and hitters. The baseball statistics software allows an individual to determine pitch frequencies, pitch specifications, hitter's tendencies, and hitter's plate coverage. Some of Pitch-Count 2000's features are

- Highly advanced graphical user interface that helps third parties easily analyze pitch velocities and placement
- Isolation screens to help pinpoint and analyze performance problems
- Windows 95, Windows 98, JavaScript, and Macintosh compatibility

- Instant data charts which can compile, sort, and view statistics using various graphical mediums
- Detailed analysis of individual pitchers' pitch location, pitch counts, pitch selection, pitch patterns, and pitch effectiveness
- Detailed analysis of individual hitters' field strengths, hitting zones, pitch preference, left vs. right analysis, and situational effectiveness
- Comparative views of individual performance in day, week, month, or year-long comparison charts
- Selection features that allow great flexibility in designating which statistics are displayed for each pitcher or batter

Pitch-Count 2000's highly advanced graphical user interface and statistical analysis have previously been unavailable to professional teams and serious baseball enthusiasts. A pitcher or hitter's performance can now be analyzed, detailed, and documented at many intricate levels. Game-time operation allows third parties to retrieve information on individual hitters or pitchers for each at-bat. Other baseball statistics programs are unparalleled in accuracy and cannot offer instantaneous access to a particular player's profile.

Kearnajay Software's plan includes the availability of the Pitch-Count 2000 to major league baseball teams by spring training of 2002, with availability to the public in the winter of 2002. A production version of the baseball statistics software has been started and is over 50 percent complete. Kearnajay Software sees no future complications and believes the product will be ready for testing on schedule. Sample screenshots of the program can be seen in the appendix.

The Company believes that the testing of the Pitch-Count 2000 by major league baseball organizations will be extremely important to the success of its products. All of Kearnajay Software's products will be of such a technical nature that user interface and extensive testing practices must be established. The Company has secured commitments for testing from its early design evaluators as well as the Pittsburgh Pirates, New York Mets, Florida Marlins, Minnesota Twins, and Chicago Cubs. The product will be released to other interested professional baseball organizations for testing as well.

Kearnajay Software has identified many opportunities for future enhancements to the base product. The following will be structured as upgrades or add-ons:

- Memory mapping of pitch trajectories
- Video playback of five previous at-bats

- ■ Pitcher-hitter matchup statistics
- ■ Infrared relay of information to remote computer

Since Kearnajay Software has programmed Pitch-Count 2000 with extensibility in mind, research and development costs for such upgrades will be significantly smaller than for the original product. The table gives an idea of the comparative features of products currently in the marketplace.

Features of Pitch-Count 2000 Compared with Those of Other Products

Features	Pitch-Count 2000	IMSA Stat-Mate	Yenseal Ball Tracker	Hardball Stat-Master
Highly advanced graphical user interface	•		•	
Comprehensive player profiles	•			
Accuracy of pitch velocity	•		•	
Pitch-count tendency evaluation	•			
Hitter's field strengths	•		•	
Day, week, month, year statistics	•		•	•
Macintosh-compatible	•			•
Video strike zone analysis	•			•

Future Product Plan

Pitch-Count 2000 addresses a present need in the marketplace and establishes a strong initial product from which to leverage future offerings. As strong interest from major league baseball organizations attests, there is already a demonstrated market for the product at the professional level. Pitch-Count 2000 is near completion and will immediately give the Company an opportunity to accomplish the following goals:

- ■ Generate significant revenues and become profitable.
- ■ Establish brand-name recognition for Kearnajay Software.
- ■ Establish a superior support infrastructure for future products.
- ■ Position Kearnajay as the leading provider of sports statistical software.

Once Pitch-Count 2000 establishes market reach, Kearnajay Software will follow up with its strategy to create football and basketball statistical software. As competition intensifies, Kearnajay Software will have established its niche validity and will be well positioned to prosper as a market leader, as well as a niche player delivering early into these market segments.

Service and Support Plans

Since Pitch-Count 2000 will be of a technical nature, quality electronic support of its products will play a key role in the Company's reputation. The Company intends to utilize technology and automated systems to lower support costs and reduce the time required to solve customer problems. Specifically, Kearnajay will establish a troubleshooting bulletin board on its Website (www.kearnajay.com), offer e-mail technical support, and provide a telephone hotline during standard office hours.

Value Proposition

Kearnajay Software's initial product is designed to deliver value to its customers in two major ways.

1. *State-of-the-art product.* Pitch-Count 2000 effectively compiles statistics aimed at revealing player performance. It is the first software available that gives baseball managers, coaches, and enthusiasts the ability to track a player's effectiveness and determine where improvement is necessary.

2. *Instantaneous information.* Pitch-Count 2000's ability to compute in real time allows for immediate and accurate statistical analysis. The varied and flexible statistical views available with Pitch Count 2000 can quickly isolate a particular game's pitching and hitting patterns for use by managers and coaches.

Copyrights

Kearnajay Software plans to protect its proprietary video recognition/isolation technology. It will rely on a copyright and contractual provisions to enforce intellectual property rights in Pitch-Count 2000 and future products. The Company does not currently hold any patents for its techniques but will most likely choose to file applications in the future.

Risks

Kearnajay Software's Pitch-Count 2000 is dependent on particular computer language features, operating systems, and processor architecture. The Company's primary systems target will be the newer versions of Windows from Microsoft such as Windows 95 and Windows 98. Their success and general acceptance, the Company strongly believes, will continue into the next decade.

The success and acceptance of these products at the professional baseball level will be vital to the success of Kearnajay Software. Recent preseason agreements with the Pittsburgh Parakeets and the New York Bluebirds indicate that the Company's target audience realizes the potential advantage Pitch-Count 2000 could bring to professional baseball teams.

Marketing Strategy

The *marketing strategy* section of your business plan details the strategy you intend to use to generate sales for your product or service. A good *marketing strategy* section will do the following:

■ Clearly state the target market.

■ Describe the distribution strategy of your product or service.

■ Describe your strategy to promote sales.

■ Describe the pricing strategy of your product or service.

■ Describe how you intend to advertise your product or service.

■ Define the benefits of your product's service strategy over the competition.

When designing a marketing strategy, keep your *market research* and *competition* overview in mind. If certain benefits of your product or service have been ignored by the competition, try to formulate your strategy to capitalize on these shortcomings. Additionally, be sure to examine your competitors' marketing strategy. Adopt their most effective features, and add to yours what their marketing strategy lacks.

The sample shows a marketing strategy section for a hypothetical microwave oven company.

SAMPLE

VI. Marketing Strategy

Overview

PIPA Industries's marketing strategy stresses the fact that our product is superior to others in the market. To prove the value of our K-Line Microwave Oven, the Company focuses on the energy efficiency and added value demonstrated by many tests. Surveys indicate that these two areas are of greatest concern to the customers who purchase our products.

Our products are seen by consumers as a time-saving tool. This unique advantage over conventional ovens can be exploited to arrive at a winning position in the consumer's mind. By equating time with money in the mind of the consumer, we reposition our product from a cost to an investment. The K-Line Microwave Oven can be portrayed as a smart investment for any family.

Target Market

Market research indicates that the vast percentage of microwave ovens purchased in the United States are purchased by women with young families. The typical customer for this product is a married woman earning between $20,000 and $35,000 per year with two to three children between the ages of 3 and 15.

The principal reason given in surveys for buying a microwave is convenience. Most women are trying to raise a family and work at the same time. The microwave oven provides an easy way to prepare a meal in a short amount of time. The Company's target market is generally familiar with microwave ovens and is readily receptive to the proposed marketing approach. It is important to point out that the K-Line Microwave Oven marketing strategy stresses energy efficiency and added value, the two top criteria given by women in selecting a model.

Advertising and Promotion

PIPA Industries recognizes that the key to success at this time is extensive promotion of the K-Line Microwave Oven. This must be done aggressively and on a wide scale. To accomplish sales goals, PIPA Industries will require an extremely capable advertising agency and public relations firm.

The Company plans to do most of its advertising on television and radio in suburban metropolitan areas. PIPA Industries has hired JVT Enterprises for the television and radio marketing strategy. This relationship has proven productive and has lasted since the inception of the company. JVT Enterprises has the buying power and the technical and marketing expertise necessary for a successful campaign. PIPA Industries is also working closely with Lascelle Media Consultants for additional mass media strategies. The Company feels that this type of advertising will establish PIPA Industries as a professional, reliable corporation and will give the Company immediate public awareness.

Additionally, PIPA Industries will select primary publications with highly specific market penetration to portray a positive corporate image, superior products, and quality service. The Company plans to work with a reputable advertising agency to maximize ad life with monthly exposure of the advertisements. To get the most out of our promotional budget, the periodical coverage will focus on three targeted audiences: (1) working mothers, (2) households concerned about home value and energy efficiency, and (3) young families.

Advertising Campaign

PIPA Industries believes that the best way to reach potential customers is through an intense advertising campaign promoting the company's basic slogan, "Your Time Is Important to Us." To maintain our image, the delivery and tone of promotional statements will stress family and suggest that time spent cooking could be spent with the children.

Distribution Strategy

PIPA Industries plans to sell the K-Line Microwave Oven through local and national distributors. It is important to select reputable distribution channels already in existence and staffed with professionals possessing appropriate backgrounds and clientele. This marketing approach is advantageous in that it utilizes professionals involved with parallel products and services. All distributors will have expertise and have been practicing in their field for a long time.

PIPA will determine which distributors to approach in accordance to testing currently in progress. These tests specifically reflect the customer profiles, geography, reputation, and market strength of distributors. At this time, suburban and metropolitan areas show the highest level of consumer interest.

The primary means of supplying distributors will be through Company sales representatives. An advantage to this approach is that it allows more flexibility and options with which to respond to special needs and circumstances of the market environment. This will reduce shipping time and increase customer satisfaction. To date, none of our competitors has been able to achieve this goal.

Competition Overview

The competition overview details the companies that will compete either directly or indirectly for the same market share that your product or service aims to capture. A good competition overview will do the following:

■ Identify all competitors' strengths and weaknesses.

■ Identify all competitors' market share and financial status.

■ Describe how competitors are marketing their products or services.

■ Detail the advantages of your product or service over the competitor's product or service.

■ Foreshadow any potential competitors in the market.

Many business plans also include an analysis of a successful noncompeting company that offers a comparable service or product in another market industry. By outlining how this company gained market share, you provide the prospective investor with a profitable model from which your business might be structured.

The sample shows a competition overview of a hypothetical gargoyle-sculpturing company.

─────────────── ❀ ❀ **SAMPLE** ❀ ❀ ───────────────

VII. Competition Overview

The ability to offer superior beauty along with full water guidance capabilities from rooftops or eaves makes Creative WaterWorks gargoyles a unique addition to any building or business. Creative WaterWorks gargoyles perform in virtually all situations where water guidance systems can be added.

Although Creative WaterWorks gargoyles are unique in today's market, there are a few direct competitors in the U.S. and Canadian business sector. North American Rooftops enjoys approximately 70 percent of the gargoyle market share, Seokim Drafting owns 25 percent of the market share, and freelance sculptors hold the remaining 5 percent. Currently, competitive threats come primarily from the first two mentioned companies.

1. *North American Rooftops.* North American Rooftops is a $23 million provider and marketer of building accessories based in Sarasota, Florida. The company is a division of Buckner Housing, a public company with $800 million sales. The division sells shingles, stucco, and roofing supplies. The recent trend for the division has been static, as the parent has not provided working capital to support new designs and roofing techniques. Although North American Rooftops remains the largest direct competitor to Creative WaterWorks, recently released budget proposals for North American Rooftops indicate a continued emphasis on maintaining a lead in the shingle and stucco market. Funding for gargoyle production remained steady in most categories and significantly dropped in research and development.

2. *Seokim Drafting.* Seokim Drafting recently entered the gargoyle sculpturing business after initially concentrating in fountain sculpturing since its formation in 1979. The company's net sales for gargoyles was estimated in 1992 at $4 million. Market research indicates that Seokim Drafting will remain a for-hire, freelance sculpturing company and will not attempt to mass-market its gargoyle products as Creative WaterWorks plans.

In all test studies, the products by Creative WaterWorks scored appreciably above the common rules of the product performance requirements as set forth by U.S. regulations. In addition, market research indicates that the performance of Creative WaterWorks gargoyles is superior to other gargoyles on the market in the great majority of testing categories and equal in the remaining. The table illustrates how Creative WaterWorks gargoyles compare with the competition in all major testing categories as scored by *Research Associates and Consumer Guidebooks.* The scoring reports indicate that the competition is faring well in the gargoyle market. However, Creative WaterWorks proves superior in both quality and price.

Performance Test Scores of Creative WaterWorks Gargoyles Compared with Major Competitors, by Category

Categories	Creative WaterWorks	North American Rooftops	Seokim Drafting
Product line	A–	A–	N/A
Quality	A	B	A
Distribution	A	A–	C
Price	A–	B	C
Installation	A–	A–	A–
Water guidance	B+	B	B+
Appearance	A	B–	A
Durability	A	C	A
Warranty	A	B+	A

In considering the potential for additional competitors in the gargoyle market, the Company believes that the time to market is of paramount importance. An early entry would prove beneficial in two critical ways: First, it would allow Creative WaterWorks to capture the immediate market share for cost-effective, quality gargoyles before North American Rooftops and Seokim Drafting could execute similar business strategies. Second, it would establish name recognition for Creative WaterWorks as the leader in gargoyle sculpturing.

The Company seeks immediate and continued financing in order to ensure the timely execution of its business plan. With this given support, Creative WaterWorks believes an effective marketing strategy can be implemented from which to maintain a lead over current and future competitors.

Financial Projections

The financial projections present your product or service to the prospective investor in monetary figures. This section should include your company's projections for the first five years and should be broken down into monthly increments. Although the financials of business plans vary, the most basic components of this section are as follows:

- *Profit and loss statement.* Net difference between the total revenues and total costs of your company's service or product
- *Balance sheet.* Profile of your company's assets, liabilities, and equity
- *Cash flow statement.* Profile of your company's actual net income

Most new entrepreneurs without accounting experience find the financial projections a very difficult section of the business plan to prepare. Since figures are viewed in meticulous detail by prospective investors for accuracy and realism, do not attempt to "wing it" or assume values for unknown variables. If assistance is needed, either consult business accounting books (available at any bookstore or library) or obtain the temporary services of an accounting firm. Even with outside help, however, you should become intimately familiar with the derivation of each statistic and what it represents, especially if questions arise in presenting the business plan to investors.

The detail with which financial projections are compiled extends beyond the limitations of this chapter. For more information, be sure to check out the sources provided in the Appendix. These sources outline additional financial considerations such as depreciable assets, financial assumptions, and break-even analysis that you might choose to include.

The sample shows the three basic components of the financial projections for a hypothetical electronics merchandise shop.

───── ⋇ ⋇ **SAMPLE** ⋇ ⋇ ─────

VIII. Financial Projections

With funding by December 1996, XBH Portables believes that first-year profits can be generated because of management's ability to successfully implement the business plan on time and within budget, the low cost of reaching the initial target market, and the year-long sales cycle. We have provided the Company's starting balance sheet, a profit and loss statement, and a cash flow statement (see pages 147–149). XBH Portables believes it has captured all relevant expenses associated with the revenues planned over the five-year period.

───────────── ⋇ ⋇ ⋇ ⋇ ─────────────

Conclusion

Despite any claims to the contrary, no book can make writing a business plan a painless experience. Long hours, intense research, and endless revision are very much a part of the process. Considering the time and effort necessary for beginning a company, though, it is only fitting that this first step be a precursor to what lies ahead.

Take the time and effort to prepare a respectable business plan from the very beginning. Convince yourself that proper planning is not just desirable, but necessary. A well-written business plan gets you to the market before the competition and also better prepares you and your company for the critical early years.

Simple luck is certainly a factor in the success of a fledgling business, but don't forget that simple luck is made infinitely more possible through good planning.

Starting Balance Sheet
Assets and Liabilities of XBH Portables
September 1, 1996

Assets

Current Assets

Investment 1	$ 1,000
Investment 2	6,000
Investment 3	55,000
Investment 4	45,000
Investment 5	20,000
Total Current Assets	$127,000

Fixed Assets

Office-Showroom	$150,000
Furniture, Equipment	15,000
Company Van	20,000
Total Fixed Assets	$185,000
TOTAL ASSETS	$312,000

Liabilities

Current Liabilities

Office-Showroom Mortgage	$ 400
Office-Showroom Tax Payment	200
Office-Showroom Maintenance Fee	90
Credit Cards	50
Total Current Liabilities	$ 740

Fixed Liabilities

Mortgage Balance	$100,000
Total Fixed Liabilities	$100,000
TOTAL LIABILITIES	$100,740

Total Net Worth

TOTAL ASSETS LESS TOTAL LIABILITIES	$211,260
TOTAL LIABILITIES & NET WORTH	$312,000

Profit and Loss Statement
Projected First Quarter 1997

	January	February	March
Net Sales	$30,000	$32,000	$38,000
Cost of Sales	18,000	19,200	22,800
Gross Profit	*$12,000*	*$12,800*	*$15,200*
1997 OPERATING EXPENSES			
1. Sales Salaries	$ 1,800	$ 1,800	$ 1,800
2. Payroll Taxes	360	360	360
3. Advertising	1,200	1,200	1,200
4. Store Supplies	500	250	250
5. Auto Expense	300	200	200
6. Travel	1,200	600	600
7. Telephone	200	150	150
8. Utilities	190	200	200
9. Miscellaneous	1,200	640	760
10. *Total Operating Expenses*	*$ 6,950*	*$ 5,400*	*$ 5,520*
1997 FIXED EXPENSES			
11. Rent	$ 2,000	$ 2,000	$2,000
12. Insurance	425	425	425
13. Taxes	180	192	228
14. *Total Fixed Expenses*	*2,605*	*2,617*	*2,653*
15. *Total Expenses*	*9,555*	*8,017*	*8,173*
16. *Net Operating Profit*	*$ 2,445*	*$ 4,783*	*$7,027*
OTHER EXPENSES			
17. Loan Payment	$ 624	$ 624	$ 624
18. Depreciation	117	117	117
19. *Total Other Expenses*	*$ 741*	*$ 741*	*$ 741*
Total Profit before Income Taxes	$ 1,704	$ 4,042	$ 6,286
Income Taxes (6.7%)	114	271	421
Net Profit after Income Taxes	*–$ 1,590*	*$ 3,771*	*$ 5,865*

Cash Flow Statement
Projected First Quarter 1997

	January	February	March
Cash on Hand	$63,575	$54,920	$ 62,119
Cash Receipts			
Cash Sales	12,000	12,800	15,200
Credit Card Collections	18,000	19,200	22,800
Loans	0	3,000	0
Total Cash Receipts	$30,000	$35,000	$ 38,000
Total Cash Available	$93,575	$89,920	$100,119
Cash Paid Out			
Merchandise	29,000	18,000	19,200
Gross Wages	1,800	1,800	1,800
Payroll Expenses	360	360	360
Outside Services	1,000	576	684
Office Supplies	500	250	250
Maintenance/Repairs	0	0	250
Advertising	500	1,600	1,200
Auto Expenses	300	200	200
Accounting	200	200	200
Rent	2,000	2,000	2,000
Telephone	200	200	150
Utilities	190	190	200
Insurance	425	425	425
Real Estate	100	180	180
Travel	1,000	900	600
Miscellaneous	1,000	920	700
Total Cash Paid Out	$38,655	$27,801	$ 28,399
Cash Position	$54,920	$62,119	$ 71,720

Chapter 5

ఇ౬ ఇ౬ ఇ౬ ఇ౬

The Importance of Industry

I t's a big sea. You're a small fish. The only way that you're ever going to survive is to know your environment and master your domain. Simply getting acquainted with your surroundings is not enough. You must understand the habits and characteristics of all the other fish in the sea, from the smallest minnows to the biggest sharks. Where do they gather? What do they feed on? When do they thrive? Meanwhile, you must also develop a comprehensive knowledge of the sea itself, knowing about its currents, temperatures, and pressures. Missing any one of these pieces of information could prove disastrous. Just imagine—it wouldn't be very pleasant to unsuspectingly enter shark-infested waters or to attempt to swim against a strong current, would it? And just think how much easier your life would be if you discovered an alternative source of nourishment, freeing you from the constant grind of competing with other fish for food.

Like the sea, each industry includes several important components. The specific industry your business falls within is composed of all the other companies providing a similar product or service to yours, as well as all other businesses involved in the production or development of the good and the suppliers and distributors of the product or service. For instance, the exercise equipment industry involves a number of integral players: the producers of the finished exercise machines and the tools used to build the machines, the suppliers of the appropriate machine parts, the independent sales representatives, and the trade and retail outlets. Lacking any single category of these contributors, the exercise equipment industry would suffer fatal damage from a discontinuation in the progression from the conception of the products to their consumption.

An entire sea includes more than just the different types of fish in it; it also encompasses the aquatic environment in which the fish swim. If a fish knows when to swim with certain currents and when to step aside for a moment, it can get to its destination quicker and more efficiently. A fish also operates most effectively in its niche, that particular place where the fish finds factors such as temperature and water pressure most suitable for its well-being.

The life of a fish certainly doesn't seem very difficult. Then again, you're not the one who has to live in constant fear of sharks and octopuses, among other ocean-dwelling predators. Starting your own business probably doesn't seem too complicated at first glance either. But considering the rapid expansion of industry sizes along with the vast wealth of resources available in this day and age, you may find it more challenging than you had ever imagined.

A Broader Perspective

It's a bigger world. You're still a small fish. Fortunately, the secret to survival is well within your grasp. As the new entrepreneur on the block, the key not only to your survival, but also to your success, lies in conducting research in your prospective industry both before and during your entrepreneurial endeavor. Even the most innovative and promising ideas will fail as a result of poor industry conditions. Eager entrepreneurs often either fail to recognize the unfavorable industry climate or lack the patience necessary to weather the conditions. Even when they do recognize turbulent periods, some entrepreneurs jump the gun and introduce their ideas at the first sign of tranquillity, unaware of the fact that they are only in the eye of the storm.

So what does all of this mean for you? You probably already know that competition would be a vital part of the entrepreneurial experience, and you probably already know that successful businesses are familiar with their respective industries. This chapter will teach you the most effective means of researching your industry and competition. With the expansion of technology (especially in the realm of computers) in recent decades, an abundance of information can become available both cheaply and easily to anyone who desires it. However, this abundance of information may overwhelm the unprepared, inexperienced businessperson.

That's where we come in. Although local libraries, government agencies, and the Internet provide plenty of available resources, this information is worthless without a means to analyze it. We aim here to provide you with the necessary tools. By the end of this chapter, you will know how to do the following:

- Effectively learn from your competition.
- Research your competitors and industry cost-effectively.
- Correctly and profitably identify current trends and conditions in your industry.

■ Recognize the hottest upcoming trends for the twenty-first century.

■ Interpret basic economic concepts and recognize common misconceptions.

■ Develop your own plan of research.

NOTE: *Research?*

The word *research* sends shivers down many of our spines, as visions of 50-page thesis papers dance in our heads. However, you must realize that knowing your industry is serious business, and dedicated research is the only way you're going to familiarize yourself with your industry. Conducting research for business is just like participating in a big scavenger hunt. The hunt itself may be tiresome, but when you discover the information you need, not only does a feeling of self-satisfaction envelop you, but profits could soon be filling your pockets as well.

But first, let's get back to business.

Put Your Business to the Test

Before even introducing your idea, you should examine your industry climate. This involves some self-evaluation of your relative position and situation within the industry. You should be able to predict the level of performance of your business under practically every possible set of circumstances. Asking yourself the following questions will give you a solid introduction to your industry.

How Will Your Individual Business Cycle Relate to the Overall Business Cycle? Like everything in life, the overall business cycle experiences ups and downs. Generally speaking, there are booms in which the majority of the people enjoy prosperity, and there are recessions in which the majority of the people don't. Unfortunately, your business is not immune to this roller-coaster ride. However, by knowing how the peaks and troughs of the country's business cycle affect your individual company's cycle, you can smooth out your own ride and mitigate any drastic climate shifts your company must endure.

For instance, the business cycles of substantial consumer goods such as housing and luxury automobiles usually run simultaneously with the overall business cycle. These products and services are thus very *cycle sensitive*. Goods not sensitive to the collective business cycle are termed *countercyclical*; whenever the nation suffers from a recession, these goods become more popular (and vice versa with economic surges). If you plan to start a business in the discount department store or used automobile industry, slower growth for the entire economy may actually increase the demand for your goods (Abrams, p. 67).

HINT: *Think about* It

If you think about it, this makes perfect sense. During times of recession, people generally search for better deals, that is, cheaper goods. Discount stores and used product distributors provide ideal sources of these goods, and thus their sales increase.

Will Seasonality Influence the Prosperity of Your Enterprise? If you've ever been to a seafood restaurant, you have probably noticed that not all of the prices are listed on the menu. Rather, the prices for dishes including lobster often are stated as "Dependent on Season." Lobsters thrive during different seasons around different parts of the country, and restaurant owners must compensate for these irregularities by altering their prices. Since they know prices will consistently change, they can save money on menu costs by printing a note for lobster dishes rather than creating many menus with different prices.

You must recognize whether the seasons influence the popularity of your good. If they do, will your business prosper in the summer or the winter? Perhaps the most recognizable industries dependent upon seasonal changes are those related to popular holidays—turkeys during Thanksgiving, flowers on Mother's Day, chocolates on Valentine's Day, and especially goods strictly related to their holidays, such as Christmas trees (Abrams, p 67).

How Will Industry Regulations Affect Your Business? When considering the effects of regulations on your industry and business, you must take into account regulations at all possible levels—from national to state to county. Some common rules involve environmental regulations, health and safety regulations for your workers, and product claims controls. Others involve the fairness of trade, deregulation factors, and licensing restrictions.

Environmental regulations will be some of the most important, as environmental concerns become increasingly prominent in our society. Just as recycling and pollution control techniques have become more prominent in the past two decades, people will increasingly demand environmental protection legislation. But as the environmental industry itself is taking off, you can actually benefit from these restrictions. The smartest businesses will discover innovative means to minimize their costs and maximize their benefits from the regulations (Abrams, p. 67).

Are There Any Other Possible Barriers to Entry? Besides industry regulations, many other factors could discourage your new business. For instance, some industries are already very mature, making it difficult for newcomers to garner much success. This issue will be discussed in detail when we explain the industry life cycle.

You also need to check if other companies have already won the rights to certain technologies that may give them a major competitive advantage. In addition, some industries are just very expensive to enter. The fixed initial startup costs of plants, equipment, and technology—along with the myriad of regulations and certifications—could be unbearable for an individual businessperson. Before entering any industry, you must carefully weigh the benefits and costs (Allen & Price, p. 149).

HINT: *Get Personal*

When comparing the ups and downs, don't forget to factor in your own personal response to fulfillment or disappointment. What does joining this particular industry actually mean to you? Is your interest in this industry strong enough to support the stress that comes with dealing with the obstacles you'll encounter?

How Will Technology Affect Both the Larger Industry and Your Specific Business? Technology has experienced rapid growth and numerous innovations in recent years and will undoubtedly affect both your industry and your company in multiple ways. The primary source of expansion stems from the vast (and exponentially growing) realm of the computer industry. Because different forms of technology are constantly undergoing improvements, it is impossible to predict the state of technology in the future. But you can estimate growth in your industry by examining the current trends in technological growth affecting your industry. Have improvements remained stagnant in recent years, or do they show signs of continued development? You can benefit immensely by entering an industry with increasingly efficient and cheaper technology.

Since technology is such an extensive and prominent subject, we will discuss its role, with an emphasis on computers, throughout the remainder of the chapter.

How Innovative Is Your Industry? Knowing the rates at which new developments occur is essential to keeping abreast of trends in your industry. For example, the computer industry is so innovative that you must be equally innovative just to survive. Less innovative fields, however, bestow upon you the opportunity to take control by setting the standard and developing new techniques and fresh ideas (Allen, p. 149).

How Will the Supply and Distribution of Your Good Proceed? When considering how your product or service will be transferred to the consumer, you must take into account both the supply and distribution channels of your good.

For instance, while the distribution channels for your good may be abundant and cheap, this does not necessarily suggest that it will be readily available to your customers. Why? Because there may be few suppliers of inputs for your good, making production costly. And even if suppliers are readily accessible, distributors may be few in number, making it too costly for distributors to carry your product at all since prices will be pushed upward by limited availability (Abrams, p. 67).

At What Stage in Its Life Cycle Is Your Prospective Industry? Every industry goes through a four-stage industry life cycle: (1) the developing period, (2) the stage of proliferation, (3) the stable phase, and (4) the stage of decline.

THE DEVELOPING PERIOD   The rudimentary stages of the industry compose the developing period. Upon the introduction of your industry to the marketplace, there are many opportunities for entrepreneurs to take advantage of. However, since the ideas are so foreign to consumers, there is a limit to what the producers can experiment with. People are always hesitant to test new things until others have already tested and approved of the products. Thus, while a new industry offers many openings and opportunities for entrepreneurs, the extent to which the new businesses can expand is confined by consumer reluctance.

THE STAGE OF PROLIFERATION   The stage of proliferation features rapid growth in the industry and is the most opportune time to introduce a new company into the market. The stage of proliferation itself features three primary phases: beginning, middle, and end. The middle stage is the easiest to recognize because the industry experiences a noticeable influx of new businesses. However, those who can discern the beginning phase of this stage have the opportunity to enjoy the greatest profits.

This brings us to a fundamental rule for all entrepreneurs: Those who learn to identify and exploit new trends before everyone else jumps on the bandwagon are the ones who will survive and succeed in their industries (Allen, p. 12).

NOTE: *The Unpredictability of Your Industry*

Industries that are especially unstable offer even better opportunities to strike it big. For example, the telecommunications industry is still very capricious, allowing for rapid growth and potentially immense success through change and development.

THE STABLE PHASE   The stable stage of the industry life cycle is the stage where the industry's growth levels off. At this point, it is very difficult for new businesses to enter the industry successfully. The greatest barriers to entry are the solid ties that have developed between consumers and established businesses. After providing service for a long period, brand-name companies earn the trust of their customers, and competitors may find it difficult to contend with these long-lived, experienced companies.

THE STAGE OF DECLINE   The final stage of the industry life cycle is just that: the stage of decline. For some reason, be it consumer tastes or resource depletion, the industry declines as companies either leave or declare bankruptcy. As one would expect, aspiring businessmen should not even consider entering dwindling industries, as they are losses waiting to occur. But not all industries necessarily suffer this last stage of the life cycle, so don't worry about a forced exit from an established and sound industry (Abrams, 1993; Dent, 1993).

As you can clearly see, the stage at which you enter an industry can affect the prosperity of your business immensely. Being a new businessperson, your industry will probably be in one of the first two stages during your enrollment.

So, how did your business idea stand up against these questions? If you had an answer for every single question, then consider yourself an ideally prepared entrepreneur. Now take yourself to the level of the intuitive entrepreneur by blending the different questions together to evaluate the situations that result from the myriad of combinations. If you already have some doubts as to the performance of your business, you may want to rethink your idea in light of your industry climate. While all of the answers may not be clear right now, you should be able to answer them before you get started. This background of knowledge is a stronger tool than you may realize at first.

If you are still confident about your idea, you have already planted a firm root of knowledge in your industry, an essential step for successful entrepreneurs. The rest of the chapter is devoted to strengthening that foundation by converting your industry knowledge into advantageous tools for your business.

Follow the Leader

You can learn a lot from your competitors, predecessors, and fellow industry members. While your regional competitors will probably never directly feed you information and advice, you can always follow their example when they experience good times. Sometimes it is even necessary to follow the leader to survive. Take the pizza industry, for example. When most pizza companies were worrying about alterations in conventional ideas such as new toppings, different crust styles, and extra side orders, Domino's Pizza decided to revolutionize the industry. How? Home delivery in 30 minutes or less. This strategy paid great dividends for Domino's, and other pizza companies soon followed suit. Now you can scarcely find a pizza place that doesn't deliver.

Some of the larger and more established businesses in your industry may offer words of wisdom if you seek them out. Of course, it is left to their discretion whether or not to help you, but it is harmless to ask for guidance. Established national companies are usually secure enough that they should not have to worry about smaller competitors. Another valuable source of counsel stems from fellow industry members who do not conduct business in your region. With different target markets, businesses in different regions can share tips and offer suggestions to each other without any fear of losing customers. You should seek out the advice of businesses similar to your proposed one that have already established themselves in areas outside your target region.

Always remember that when you seek help from other companies, they are performing a favor. Thus, you must play by their rules. In addition, whenever researching competitors' strategies, beware of using immoral practices. For example, your contract with them may give them the right to view your full financial files at any time up to five years after the termination date of your relationship. Failure to willingly provide such documents in such a case would be very difficult to justify. Not only does an immoral practice violate the entrepreneurial spirit, but you could also find yourself in a heap of legal trouble.

NOTE: *Giant Competition*

Someone once said, "There are no small roles, only small actors." The economic equivalent of this statement might be, "There are no small businesses, only small entrepreneurs." But while there are both big and small businesses in virtually every industry, the industry climate is the same for everyone.

When you are faced with direct competition from industry giants—the Wal-Marts, Microsofts, and Nikes of the corporate world—learning from your predecessors becomes that much more important. Use the example of successful small companies who have already weathered the competition and succeeded in the presence of these giants.

Perhaps most importantly, don't panic. In any industry—with or without giants—a sound strategy with the ability to make adjustments when needed is essential. So when larger corporations are present in your industry, make the proper adjustments and stick to your plan. New businesses, often intimidated by the presence of giants, commonly panic at the first sign of trouble. They stray away from their original game plan and constantly make unnecessary changes. This in turn leads to an early exit from the industry. Be prudent. Seek knowledgeable advice from experienced sources before making major changes in your original game plan (Adams, p. 111).

If Everyone Else Jumped off a Bridge . . .

You've probably already heard this phrase so many times that you often ignore it entirely. But the question remains, Would you jump off, too? Of course not. Even your most successful competitors make mistakes. There is no excuse for not learning from other companies' previous misfortunes. The lesson is right there in front of you. Thus, following the leader may not always be the best idea. Remember that you can learn from others' success as well as from their failures.

Competitive Intelligence

In his book *Competitive Intelligence*, Larry Kahaner discusses the role of competitive intelligence among large-scale companies and even national organizations. In this section we explain the practice of competitive intelligence more specifically for the beginning entrepreneur. Kahaner's four-step process is thus slightly modified; while the basics of the competitive intelligence technique as presented by Kahaner are preserved.

Competitive intelligence is the primary tool used by successful businesses to study their competitors. Originally, competitive intelligence wasn't even intended for economic purposes (at least not directly). During the Cold War era, countries used innovative political and military intelligence techniques to plot against their rivals. Many major business companies have gradually adapted and molded these methods into the technique now described as competitive intelligence in order to study their primary competitors. Competitive intelligence is a strategic and systematic plan for collecting and analyzing information about competitors and the overall industry climate. So how does intelligence differ from information?

Information versus Intelligence

Information can be thought of as the sum total of all the statistics, facts, and data related to your industry and business. Basically, information is just the numbers; it has no meaning without any context. However, after all of the information is collected, it can be converted into intelligence through detailed analysis. By filtering through all of the peices to obtain the necessary information to obtain the relevant pieces, you can facilitate the information's metamorphosis into intelligence.

The process of discerning competitive intelligence includes three main stages: planning, collection of information, and analysis. Planning involves your decision of which facet of the industry or of your competition to focus on. It can be thought of as the most important step in the process because it provides for the direction of your enterprise. After planning, data can be collected and then analyzed. Critical thinking converts it into intelligence.

Some also recognize a fourth step to the competitive intelligence process: dissemination. However, this step is primarily acknowledged by the organizations whose primary purpose is to conduct competitive intelligence research for other companies. In other words, competitive intelligence agencies should always know who needs their service and the most effective means to relay their analysis to these companies.

Why Competitive Intelligence?

A serious, formalized competitive intelligence program can perform multiple functions. Perhaps the most important is to provide an increased understanding of the workings of the marketplace. You can anticipate trends in the marketplace more effectively with competitive intelligence.

Take a look back at the 1970s, a period when competitive intelligence techniques were still foreign to many American companies. However, the companies of many other countries, such as Japan, had already discovered the utility of the process. Two of the major trends during the decade were rapidly increasing gas prices and a shift in the American family structure from more to fewer family members. This example is simplified so you can clearly derive from these two important trends that members of the automobile industry were seriously affected during this time. How did these trends affect them?

Through competitive intelligence, Japanese car companies recognized that smaller and more numerous households would result in a higher demand for smaller cars. In addition, because of escalating gas prices, they also assumed correctly that consumers would favor higher-caliber cars. More specifically, they wanted cars with better gas mileage. On the other hand, Detroit's myopic view of car industry trends resulted in a lack of response to consumer needs. The bottom line: Detroit didn't respond, Japan did. The trends affected automobile companies in both countries, but in opposite directions.

Competitive intelligence also allows you to study how your competitors perform in order for you to improve your own business. You have just seen how companies can use competitive intelligence to predict industry trends, but you can also anticipate the actions of your competitors. In addition, you can learn about the most innovative technologies that could improve your productivity, along with the political and regulatory news that affects your industry. Perhaps most importantly, you can examine your own business in light of your industry and competition trends, using knowledge of your environment to effectively manage your own business.

Competitive intelligence techniques are fast becoming essential in these changing times. The computer revolution has spurred an information overload, and a means to filter and organize this information is indispensable. Competition has expanded immensely, causing existing competitors to become more aggressive and a flood of new entrepreneurs, many of whom are home-based, to flood the economy. In addition, this fierce competition has gone global. With the changing business, political, and social trends in today's society, a fresh brand of intelligence is ready to expand into new arenas worldwide.

Collecting the Information

When beginning to collect information concerning your industry and competitors, keep in mind that there are two different types of sources: primary sources and secondary sources. As the name suggests, primary sources of information are usually preferred. They contain the original facts directly from the source. Some examples include the annual reports of companies, government documents, and financial information concerning industries or individual businesses.

Speeches and other events such as live television or radio interviews are also considered primary sources. And of course, your personal observations are primary sources because they are your own unadulterated views of certain subjects. For example, you could visit fellow competitors' workplaces or distribution outlets and observe their atmospheres to see how they run their operations.

Secondary sources offer information that is often relatively skewed. Magazine articles and television programs providing commentary on certain issues often contain information that has already been interpreted in a certain fashion. Thus, to utilize secondary sources effectively, you must know the biases and opinions of the authors or suppliers of the information.

Yet another type of information is public domain information. This type of data is available largely through the Freedom of Information Act (FOIA), which allows you to request federal information about specific companies. For example, you can view 10-K reports and the SEC forms for all publicly traded companies. Keep in mind, however, that many federal filings are industry-specific. For example, for information concerning many media-related industries such as radio and television, you will want to consult the Federal Communications Commission. The Interstate Commerce Commission carries information pertaining to the trucking industry, and the Food and Drug Administration has information on the food, pharmaceuticals, cosmetics, and medical devices industries. Remember that primary sources are more accurate than secondary sources, but both are useful and worth considering. But you can still use secondary sources to your advantage if you remember to factor in their biases before attempting to interpret the information.

NOTE: *Always Go to the Source*

Whenever you read newspapers or magazines to find information, don't just view the stories and headlines as such—view them as if they are classified advertisements. If the editors of a magazine favor one stance over others, they might exclude any information against their beliefs and exaggerate information promoting them. In addition, sometimes newspapers edit Associated Press articles, but you can retrieve the original AP story. (To retrieve an original AP story, contact your local newspaper's press room.) So when in doubt, go to the original source!

Interpreting the Information

When analyzing information, remember these basic rules:

- *Use the most recent information*. Times are changing fast, and so is information. Don't miss a beat.
- *Observe your data for anomalies*. Compare your figures with other companies during the same time period and look for any trends in the data. This ensures the consistency of your information.
- *Convert all units into a common unit of account*. Besides accounting for inflation, this also facilitates the comparison of sets of numbers.
- *Play it safe*. Use the most conservative figures for your analysis. It is a common mistake to consciously use exaggerated numbers as a confidence booster. However, you don't want to be overconfident and risk overestimating a given project. Nor do you want to set unrealistic goals (Abrams, p. 24).

By analyzing the pertinent information you have collected, you can convert the data into usable intelligence. Now that the numbers have meaning, ask questions about the results. Do you spot any trends? Can you notice any surprises? After you establish a good understanding of your results, respond accordingly.

Remember that competitive intelligence is a process. It is not just a fragmented series of unrelated steps. If you ever participated in a science fair when you were in grade school, you know that the scientific method was a process composed of many steps itself, with each step playing an integral role in the project. Likewise, every step of the competitive intelligence process is crucial—from the gathering of certain statistics to a resulting strategic move.

After analyzing your data, you should have a firm comprehension of your industry, including its latest trends. But remember, trends continually change. Therefore, competitive intelligence should be a continual process. You need to stay abreast of industry trends and painstakingly monitor technological and social tendencies as well.

By doing so, you will also become better suited to distinguish fads from trends. The discernment of short-term fads from longer-term trends is an essential characteristic of successful entrepreneurs. You want to exploit lasting trends before everyone else does, but you don't want to overreact to transient fads.

Competitive Intelligence at Work

Do competitive intelligence techniques actually work? Coors beer certainly believes in them. If you're familiar with Coors, you know that its home territory is the Rocky Mountain region. You can probably imagine Coors's anxiety when Anheuser-Busch, a larger competitor in the beer industry, threatened to begin a massive marketing campaign targeting the Rocky Mountain area. Such an advance by Anheuser-Busch would certainly prove detrimental to Coors's enterprise.

Coors's natural response would have been to counteract with a massive marketing movement. However, before Coors's directors devoted millions of dollars to this advertising campaign, they decided to examine the situation more closely. One angle they took involved closer inspection of Anheuser-Busch's perspective. By using public records available from the Environmental Protection Agency, Coors discovered some extremely valuable information.

The researchers gathered data concerning the limits on wastewater discharge in the Rocky Mountain area. They also determined Anheuser-Busch's current output and wastewater levels. Putting the facts together, they concluded that Anheuser-Busch's maximum beer-producing capacity was not even high enough to sustain an expensive and successful marketing campaign—their wastewater levels would have exceeded the allotted limit. Thus, by researching many different facets of the situation, Coors saved a great deal of time and money by thinking before acting (Kahaner, p. 57).

What's in a Name?

You already know that magazines are secondary sources of information. However, magazines also provide another means for quick and easy recognition of the most popular trends. By simply looking at the titles of new magazines and publications, you can spot some of the hottest current growth industries. You've probably noticed at newsstands that there are increasing numbers of magazines related to fields such as biotechnology, robotics, and of course, computers. Just as every action causes a reaction, these new magazines are reactions to some of the fastest-growing industries.

Entrepreneur Joseph R. Mancuso (1996) believes that if you can recognize when new titles and subjects are becoming popular via magazine titles, then you can capture a four-year head start over other companies. This lead could allow you to enjoy nice profits until the industry peaks, and everyone else tries to grab a piece of the pie. Obviously, newsstands cannot subscribe to every single magazine and publication, but Samir Husni, an associate professor of journalism at the University of Mississippi, has compiled a resource titled *Guide to New Magazines*, which lists the titles of young magazines. To order a copy send $50 to the following address:

University of Mississippi
Department of Journalism
University, MS 38677

Another popular source of new magazine titles is *Folio*, a publication for magazine management. Here is the contact information:

Folio
6 River Bend Center
P.O. Box 4949
911 Hope Street
Stanford, CT 06907-0949
(203) 358-9900

Whereas magazine titles give you a four-year lead over the competition, another type of title doubles this lead period: newsletter titles. Newsletters are usually designed for specific audiences and are not commonly found on newsstands or in bookstores. However, some sources keep tabs on the newest newsletters so you don't have to. Their contact information follows:

The Newsletter on Newsletters
The Newsletter Clearinghouse
P.O. Box 311
Rhinebeck, NY 12572
(914) 876-2081

Newsletter Publishers Association
Patricia Wysocki
1401 Wilson Blvd., Suite 207
Arlington, VA 22209
(703) 527-2333

If you're not just looking for the latest newsletters, you can try these newsletter directories:

The Oxbridge *Directory of* Newsletters
Customer Service
150 Fifth Avenue, Suite 302
New York, NY 10011
(212) 741-0231

Newsletters-In-Print
Gale Research Company
835 Penobscot Building
Detroit, MI 48226-4013

Joseph R. Mancuso's *Mancuso's Small Business Resource Guide* (1996) provides a comprehensive list of contacts, addresses, and phone numbers for associations, organizations, and government agencies as well.

Some Things Never Change

One of the first places you should look for information is your local library. The most helpful libraries will be the ones that also serve as depositories of government documents. Most large cities contain such libraries, as do many universities. You can find valuable information in the form of government statistics and documents, not to mention any other books or articles concerning your idea. However, most libraries won't carry everything you need. Contact trade associations and other organizations devoted to your industry to obtain extra information.

If you find your library research is getting off to a slow start, don't get discouraged. It often takes an entire day just to become acquainted with the library itself—to discover its wealth of relevant information and the most effective research techniques. Expect to make multiple visits to the library, perhaps using the first day to acquaint yourself with its resources. After all, research is serious business and should be given serious attention.

The government also provides many profitable resources. The American Statistics Index (ASI) offers useful numbers and figures. One segment of ASI, ASI *Abstracts*, often facilitates and speeds up searches. The U.S. Census Bureau also contains much valuable data. (You can also access the online database Cendata.) The Census Bureau regularly releases "Current Industrial Reports" which detail the financial figures of specific industries and "County Business Patterns" for specific regions. The U.S. Department of Commerce publishes the U.S. *Industrial Outlook*, a report on the preceding year's productivity rates and a general economic forecast of growth rates for the upcoming year as well.

Another valuable resource is the Small Business Administration. You can visit you local Small Business Development Center, a college-based center with free resources, or contact the national SBA office at 1-800-827-5722.

You should also look into trade and industry sources specific to your idea. Gale Research Company (listed earlier in the newsletter section) supplies many useful types of these tools. If you're looking into retail trade, the *Small Business Sourcebook* would fit your needs nicely. Although it does not pertain to many businesses, it does provide a fantastic tool for those businesses discussed. For a broader resource, use the *Encyclopedia of Business Information Sources*. While it may not be as incisive as the *Small Business Sourcebook*, it does encompass a greater variety of industries. Another comprehensive resource is *Gale's Encyclopedia of Associations*.

Another quality resource you may want to explore is *Standard & Poor's Industry Surveys*. These provide a solid overview of the entire industry, including a closer look at the larger competition. Another publication, *Predicasts F & S Forecasts* compiles a listing of articles from over 750 business and trade magazines, newspapers, and financial reports. Like the Standard & Poor's guide, *Predicasts* offers insight into the industry itself and its companies. It is divided into two sections. The first, titled "Industries and Products," offers a general overview of the economy, including news of the latest developments and trends. Not only does it cover the newest technological advances, it also offers some analysis of current political and sociological issues, as well as the latest news of the business world, such as recent mergers and acquisitions. The second section, "Companies," offers background information on both competitors and consumers.

Becoming a member of a group could also provide many insights into your potential enterprise. Joining associations concentrating on your industry will introduce you to the players of the field and give you easier access to industry news. Whenever possible, you should also attend industry conventions and trade shows. You can exchange valuable information with your colleagues and competitors, as well as observe the latest technological advances and marketing strategies. You can find your appropriate trade association by visiting your local library and searching the *Encyclopedia of Associations* (Abrams, p. 15).

You can also join other groups via the Internet. There are numerous news and discussion groups with which you can trade ideas through computers. You may want to try some of the following and see which suits you the best:

- alt.business.misc
- alt.business.import-export
- misc.entrepreneurs
- misc.invest

Without joining any organization or club, you can still garner valuable knowledge from other people. Always keep in contact with members of your industry, people involved in government, and academic figures. Remember, members of your industry don't just include your competitors, they also include the manufacturers, wholesalers, and distributors of the product or service. You can learn valuable information about worker and consumer response to the goods by interviewing these less recognized members.

Other contacts involved in the interactions of your industry include lawyers, accountants, and bankers. Lawyers can often offer insight into many of the legal issues concerning business interactions and regulations. Accountants deal directly with the financial figures flowing through the industry. And bankers, who are responsible for the loans that give many businesses a chance, often have a good understanding of the general economic atmosphere surrounding the industry.

People in higher positions at the Departments of Commerce and Labor and the Census Bureau, among other government agencies, are also good sources for learning about trends and deciphering figures. And of course, don't discount your college professors and other staff members. They possess a keen and fundamental knowledge of economic trends which others, such as the media, may misinterpret. Research-oriented universities often boast the most knowledgeable and useful staffs (Allen & Price, 1998, p. 29).

Perhaps the most comprehensive resources are computer databases. (One example of a database, Cendata, was briefly alluded to above.) Computer databases offer a plethora of information. Some databases appropriate for aspiring entrepreneurs follow:

- NEXIS (1-800-227-4908) includes an index of most newspapers and many magazines, and also lists trademarks and patents. One popular outgrowth of NEXIS, LEXIS, also includes an index of legal documents. Industry reports for hundreds of brokerage houses can be found under the subgroup of NEXIS known as "Investext." Another valuable feature of NEXIS is its index of corporate filings with the Securities and Exchange Commission.
- NEXIS EXPRESS (1-800-843-6476) is another feature of NEXIS. It provides the service of performing the search for you, but it does cost money.
- The Maxwell Online Information on Demand database (1-800-999-4-IOD) is similar to NEXIS EXPRESS, but there is a charge.
- The Dow Jones News Retrieval Service (1-800-522-3567) is another service that also provides pertinent information, but is more expensive to run.

Of course, if you have the money, you can always pay someone else to do the research for you. Remember to always consult your industry trade associations before taking such measures. They can recommend suitable research firms and warn against others. Some of the more prominent research companies covering many industries are Dun & Bradstreet and Robert Morris and Associates.

Remember, consider paid research as the spender of last resorts. If you are like most new businesspeople, you must be thrifty with your expenditures. Paid research is usually very expensive, so try doing your own research first.

Additional Resources

The following are additional resources concentrating on current events and trends (including category in parentheses):

The American Forecaster Newsletter
25465 Broadway
Denver, CO 80210
(newsletter)

The H.S. Dent Forecast
(415) 572-2879
(newsletter)

American Demographics Magazine
Ithaca, NY
www.marketingtools.com
(magazine)

The World Future Society
7910 Woodmont Avenue, Suite 450
Bethesda, MD 20814
1-800-989-8274
(organization)

Surf's Up: The Industry Climate

Databases are not the only thing computers are good for. The Internet has increased the flow of information exponentially, and surfing the World Wide Web is becoming increasingly popular every year. Simply knowing that the Internet was originally a classified tool of the military gives you a hint of its vast power and capabilities. Now that its informative power has been unleashed upon the world, knowing your way around the Internet is virtually essential for today's entrepreneur just to survive.

If you're already experienced in using the Internet, congratulations, but there is always more to learn because its potential increases day by day. If you consider yourself computer-illiterate, you must familiarize yourself immediately. The Internet's basic ingredients are web sites, hypertext links, and search engines. Search engines such as Yahoo! and Excite can be used to find web sites relevant to your inquiry. Meanwhile, hypertext links, allow you to delve deeper into web sites, helping you to gather more knowledge with every link.

Some useful web sites we have come across include the following:

- *www.cenacenter.com* This is a nice resource for aspiring businessmen. CENA (Center for Entrepreneurial Activities) offers tips concerning everything from funding to advertising, with some helpful hints concerning industry research.

- *www.edgeonline.com* This is the web site for *Entrepreneurial Edge* magazine. It offers some nice links and a searchable database containing information from over 5,000 documents and book chapters in addition to financial data from Dun & Bradstreet. You can also subscribe to *Entrepreneurial Edge*'s e-mail list, which includes the latest industry-specific information.

- *www.dismal.com* This web site provides annual and quarterly forecasts for a variety of economic indicators, including GDP (gross domestic product), incomes, and interest rates. It also lists financial data and projections for broad industries, as well as information specific to certain states and zip codes.

- *www.dnb.com* This is the official web site for Dun & Bradstreet Corporation. In addition to offering and promoting their services, this web site provides a free index of articles discussing specific industries and trends. Another useful feature is a search engine for other companies in virtually every industry—from media and publishing to health and legal services.

- *www.yahoo.com* This search engine lists many interesting subjects to choose from. Click on the Business & Economy link to obtain an index of pertinent choices, then keep going until you find your desired category and web site. (You may find the Small Business Information link after the Business & Economy link to be very useful.)

Also keep on the lookout for informative postings on electronic bulletin boards, and every once in a while, browse through some cybermalls. You may discover some valuable marketing tools or new products on the market. As Thomas Edison once suggested: "Make it a practice to keep on the lookout for novel and interesting ideas that others have used successfully. Your idea must be original only in its adaptation to the problem you are working on" (Allen, p. 25).

Now that you know where to look for the hottest trends and industry information, let's take a closer look at some of the current trends that will be of significance in the new millennium. If necessary, you can adjust your idea to complement one of these trends or perhaps even develop an entirely new idea. Feel free to use these ideas as a springboard and come up with your own twist for success. Do you think you can name any of the trends before we proceed?

You probably have it engraved in your mind by now that technology will affect your enterprise. Now let's see how you can benefit from all the hoopla. The following are but a few of the primary fields technology has impacted (Celente, 1997; Dent, 1993; and Allen, 1998).

Biotechnology: Biotechnology is an exciting field with many opportunities in a variety of subcategories, including the agriculture, environmental science, genetics, and food-related industries. One of the most prominent international trends is the escalating world population. As food resources are becoming depleted, new techniques are being sought to stimulate crop growth and optimize the limited food supply. Opportunities are also available in preventive medicine and the newly arising field of artificial organs.

Training and Development: Training is important at all levels of the economic ladder, especially with the changing corporate infrastructure. However, there is a special need for training and development in the computer industry. Services that train programming consultants or teach people how to use videoconferencing tools will be in high demand. As new technologies bombard the market daily, training and development services will be essential in teaching the new techniques to the labor force.

Virtual Shopping: Computer technology is even changing the way we shop. Easily accessible computer services will facilitate the sale and consumption of goods. This will allow mass-produced goods to be cheaper and more readily available to consumers, resulting in an increase for their demand.

Home Business: Technological advances are also allowing a growing number of entrepreneurs to work from the comfort of their own homes. New home-based businesses are established all the time. This isn't surprising given the continual introduction of new and improved telecommunications products and services. As a result, home office products and services will be in greater demand in the future.

Telecommunications: Just as the telephone revolutionized the way people communicated in the 1870s, the videophone will revolutionize communications in the twenty-first century by providing another dimension to long-distance sound: vision. Although some people may be slow to greet videophones (or whatever other name will be assigned to them), once they become a component of every household they will decrease business travel costs immensely and promote home-based business development.

The Future of the Digital Revolution: Computers will provide many opportunities for businesspeople in the coming generation, but in the long run, the digital revolution will mean nothing in itself. Think about it. When Henry Ford developed the first car, it certainly revolutionized how people thought about transportation. However, cars gradually became more popular throughout the century, and now they are so ubiquitous that no one even thinks about the transportation revolution that occurred decades ago.

Likewise, the computer technology that has many in awe today will eventually become so entrenched in our everyday lives that we won't remember these times of discovery. The point is this: Technology doesn't change the world, people do. Of course, this doesn't mean you can't prosper from the nation's technological revolution. It is still in its developing stages.

Predictability and the Baby Boom

Many people believe the economy can't be predicted—they are the ones taken aback by every new trend that comes along. The truth is that the economy is far more predictable than you may think. One rather simple indicator of the general state of the economy relies on the relationship between spending patterns and year-to-year birthrates.

Consumer spending accounts for roughly two-thirds of the nation's GDP. As a result, spending patterns closely parallel the well-being of our economy. All we need to foretell the fate of the economy is a means to predict people's spending patterns. That means is the life cycle hypothesis, which basically assumes that most people spend more money during the middle period of their lifetime—the 40s to early 50s range—than during their youth and senior years. As a matter of fact, a 1989 survey conducted by the U.S. Bureau of Labor Statistics, which conducts annual surveys of consumer expenditures, found that the peak spending years of most Americans are between the ages of 45 and 49.

Logically, the greater the number of people in a generation, the greater the spending figures. The United States experienced the creation of its largest generation in history during the middle of the twentieth century: from the 1940s to the early 1960s. The spending peaks of that generation of baby boomers (as predicted by the life cycle hypothesis) are occurring now. It isn't by pure chance that our economy is enjoying such good times as of late. As a matter of fact, the nation's population at its peak spending years has closely paralleled the S&P 500 market indicator for the past four decades (Dent, p. 26).

Quality, Too, Not Just Quantity

It's not just the sheer quantity of baby boomers that has affected and will continue to influence our economy, it's also their qualities and characteristics. The generation of baby boomers is unique in many aspects, primarily its entrepreneurial spirit, which is mirrored by the tremendous technological success of the information revolution. This entrepreneurial spirit has also contributed to an extreme sense of individualism. Baby boomers seek products that promote self improvement, convenience, and leisure. Because they compose about three-quarters of the current workforce, it is crucial to know the trends in their needs and desires. The following are some of those trends (Dent, p. 145):

Health and Fitness. The importance of the health and fitness industries can already be seen by the influx of infomercials promoting exercise equipment and special weight loss pills and diets for the past two decades. Health and longevity statistics showed that during the 1980s, the general health of Americans was actually declining. Thus, the health and fitness trend seemingly started as a fad. However, the trend has matured in recent years, perhaps due to a sense of urgency among the aging baby boomer generation. Furthermore, the turn of the century has ushered forth an era where opportunities in the health and fitness industries are almost endless.

How Convenient! Many companies have already taken advantage of the convenience craze, including home-delivery businesses that have spread from the pizza industry to other fast-food businesses, groceries, and even furniture companies. Baby boomers value their time and will reward businesses that can save them time and trouble. However, keep in mind that while baby boomers want to enhance their standards of living, businesses that can save them money as well will profit even more.

The Great Outdoors: As baby boomers grow tired of the workplace, suffocated by nine-to-five jobs, the great outdoors will offer the ideal retreat from the stress of working. The popularity of activities such as blading, biking, and hiking will reach unknown heights. In fact, a study by the Institute of Medicine showed that during the mid-1990s, people spent ninety-three percent of their lives indoors. A trend toward the outdoors is clearly the next stage, and will provide nice profits to those who respond for at least the early decades of the twenty-first century.

Real Estate: The baby boom generation's shopping spree will have one of its most profound impacts on the real estate industry. The most important idea to remember is the location of these new homes—small-town, exurban (even farther out than the suburbs), and country markets are the primary targets. Baby boomers are tired of the problems—from taxes to pollution to overcrowding—associated with living in big cities. Besides, big cities are running out of space, and the available real estate is becoming more and more expensive. You may want to consider targeting your business idea at these newly evolving "pioneer" communities. Keep in mind, however, that there are about 76 million baby boomers and only 44 million generation Xers—who's going to buy the overabundance of real estate when the baby boomers die off?

Indulge Yourself: After working those long hours every week, why not indulge yourself? This is what many baby boomers have on their minds as well. Indulgence goods are becoming increasingly popular as baby boomers seek to reward themselves. These small luxuries can range from indulgence desserts like Haagen-Daz ice cream to the latest set of golf clubs or bowling balls.

NOTE: *Watch Boomer Industries Shift*

As the baby boom generation ages, you can also estimate when other industries will take off. For example, the roofing repair industry will probably be in greater demand after the baby boomers have lived in their houses for some years. Meanwhile, college tuition, books, and related services will probably be more popular as the baby boomers' children reach their late teens (right about now).

Here are some additional hot industries:

■ Entertainment
■ Children's goods
■ Upscale men's fashion
■ Smart appliances (fax machines, cellular phones, pocket organizers)
■ Ethnic goods

Economics 101

A basic understanding of the economic foundations of our economy will also allow you to better identify trends. Often, the media and sometimes even political figures misinterpret economic concepts and as a result mislead the general public with falsified trends. The following are some basic economic indicators that everyone should know about—especially aspiring businesspeople.

GDP: The gross domestic product (GDP) is a basic measure of the well-being of our country. It possesses four primary components: consumer spending, government spending, investments, and net exports (exports minus imports). As mentioned earlier, consumer spending represents the largest fraction of the GDP, while net exports has been a negative number for some time now (more on this later)

Unemployment: Unemployment has plummeted in the 1990s. The natural rate of unemployment is the rate of unemployment below which the economy could not sustain itself and would collapse. Many economists feel that the current rate of unemployment is very near to the natural rate, implying that the economy is at its peak performance level. We'll see what the rest of the baby boomers have to say about that. Conversely, when unemployment rises, consumer confidence often falls because of lower wages

Inflation: The public views inflation extremely negatively. However, declining inflation rates come at a great price: rising unemployment, which is perhaps even more loathed by the public. Inflation affects everybody in a different way. As expected, the overall effect balances out, but you would much rather be on the end that benefits. For example, borrowers benefit from inflation because the money they repay their lenders is not as valuable as their original loans.

Trade: Exports and imports have been a controversial topic in recent years. As you may know, the United States has had trade deficits for the past few years. In other words, we have imported more than we have exported. However, this is not necessarily an unfavorable situation. Many media representatives and politicians have mistakenly depicted these trade deficits as harmful to the U.S. economy.

In reality, trade deficits are actually a reflection of the growth of an economy. A weak dollar is commonly mistakenly associated with trade deficits, whereas the truth is that strong dollars cause trade deficits. The reason? A stronger dollar (with higher interest rates) means that Americans can buy more of foreigners' goods because they are relatively cheaper. In other words, we import more foreign goods and export less of our own, resulting in the trade deficit.

Biz Quiz

So, do you think you're ready to start your research? Try taking this brief quiz first. Remember, this is only a quiz. Answer yes or no for each statement.

1. I am willing to devote multiple days at the library.
2. I will factor in the biases of writers and commentators when using secondary sources.
3. I will make necessary adaptations to the changing times.
4. I won't panic at the first sign of problems.
5. I can become more knowledgeable in my industry by discussing ideas through group settings.
6. I know what stage of its life cycle my industry is in.
7. I can identify the most common misconceptions of economic indicators.
8. I can predict the economy to a certain extent.
9. I will capitalize on the Internet's research capabilities.
10. I am the master of my domain.

Hopefully, you responded affirmatively to each statement. If not, you may find yourself at a disadvantage to entrepreneurs prepared for knowing their industries. These statements can be seen as mantras. Use the contacts and resources presented in this chapter to begin the collection of your research, and constantly ask questions when interpreting your data. Keeping abreast of the trends in your industry and keeping ahead of your competition could result in an extremely fruitful business career.

Conclusion

Now that you have the necessary tools to begin your research, it's time to put them together. Remember, you are the person behind the idea—you will be the maker or breaker of your business. Thus, you must design the plan of research that will best suit your own needs and foster the most growth for knowledge and intelligence. Researching your industry—its trends, infrastructure, and overall climate—and studying your competitors will keep you in the game. Taking it a step further—identifying trends before the masses do, getting into the minds of your competition, and developing close ties with members of your industry at all levels—will allow you to define the standards for success within your industry.

Now it is time to put the pieces together. While doing so, be sure to constantly shower yourself with questions. Which resources will you use?

How will you evaluate your information? Who will you look to for help? Which organizations will you join? Remember, if your original plan of attack is initially unsuccessful, you can always adapt your research methods to the evolving industry climate.

It's a big sea out there. The only way to survive is to make it your sea. By mastering your domain, you can be in control of your industry instead of being controlled by it. You can react to trends just as they begin to happen instead of being surprised by them. Most importantly, you can be aware of your business environment. So, put on your wet suit and dive in.

Chapter 6
❧❧ ❧❧ ❧❧ ❧❧

Protecting Yourself

As you probably know, protecting yourself and your business is a very difficult task. The legal issues surrounding the establishment of a small business are complex, and many factors may influence your decision to seek a given form of protection. Large companies have legal departments focused entirely on one task: protecting the company and its owners. When you start your business, it is likely that you will be doing the vast majority, if not all, of your business's legal decision making. When faced with this daunting task, it is easy to become discouraged or beset by details. Wise legal decision making always boils down to one criterion: information.

In order to make a legal decision that will be advantageous to your business not only throughout its first few years but far into the future, you must be familiar with the legal and practical implications that your decisions have. You have already chosen to study this book to gain an initial understanding of legal issues facing entrepreneurs like you. Nevertheless, business structures, copyrights, and patents are dynamic and extremely complex legal issues. There are many 700-page books published by lawyers and other experts dissecting each of these topics in overwhelming detail. It is impossible to cover any of these subjects in great depth in this chapter. The aim of this chapter is to present these complex topics in a clear and manageable format that will allow you to gain a solid understanding of each of these issues. Recommendations and references to more detailed information will be included throughout the chapter. It will be up to you, however, to read more specific information about the topics that pertain to your business and are introduced here.

Another point to bear in mind when making legal decisions is that there are no secrets in American corporate law. Corporate law is public information by nature, and it is up to you to take advantage of it by gathering as much information as you can.

Also bear in mind that this chapter is in no way intended to replace a lawyer or expert advice. The book is intended to provide young entrepreneurs like you with enough information to avoid situations that would require the expensive counsel of a lawyer, because legal help is often too expensive for a business in its first stages. One purpose of this chapter is to allow you to do most of your initial legal work without a lawyer, but it is likely that the day will come when you will truly need expert legal advice and will have to work with a lawyer to protect your rights, prepare contracts, or defend yourself in a lawsuit.

In this chapter, you will be introduced to legal business structures, copyrights, and patents. You will be warned of the most common pitfalls inexperienced businesspeople encounter while making early legal decisions. Figures are provided to summarize dense information and make it easier for you to determine what is important to your goals. Unless you are only looking for bits of information regarding a particular topic, it is recommended that you read this chapter completely so that you gain the general understanding needed to make informed legal decisions.

Choosing a Legal Structure for Your Business

There are numerous ways to set up and operate a company, and entrepreneurs are often overwhelmed by the fundamental decision that every person starting a business must make: What should the legal structure of my business be? Businesspeople rightfully worry about this decision, because it is the first step in laying a solid foundation upon which a successful company can be built. A poor decision early in the game may backfire and ruin you financially. In the United States, however, there are a number of ways to set up and protect a business. This section will focus on six common types of legal forms today's businesses take: sole proprietorship, general partnership, limited partnership, limited liability company, corporation, and S corporation. The particulars of nonprofit corporations are not discussed in this chapter, but many books whose scope is limited to just this type of company are available.

Deciding which legal structure your business will take is one of the first decisions you will make. Registering your company as a certain type of business gives both you and your business varying rights and liabilities in the eyes of the law. While choosing a legal structure for your business, you will have to balance advantages and disadvantages to both you personally and your business. The most significant differences between the six business forms we will discuss in this chapter are the manner in which you and your business will be viewed in matters of ownership, liability, and taxation. Another issue you may consider in your decision is manageability. Maintaining a sole proprietorship, for instance, is much easier and requires much less paperwork than maintaining a corporation. A simpler business structure also means less potential of running into legal pitfalls throughout your operation.

There is no correct business form that will fit everybody's needs, and there is no rigid formula that will make your decision easy or obvious. The nature, number of people involved, and projected size of your business will initially narrow the number of legal structure choices. As the founder of your enterprise, it is your task to study those legal structures and choose the one that best suits your needs. The legal structures differ primarily in matters of ownership, liability, and taxation. Consider the following questions as they apply to your proposed business:

1. Are you and your dependents willing and capable of accepting personal liability for all of your business's debts?
2. Will you be the only person involved in handling the daily affairs of the business, or will others be routinely involved in the management of daily operations?
3. How easy would it be for you to liquidate your business if you were suddenly unable to work?
4. How difficult would it be to transfer ownership of your share of the new business to your heirs if you died?
5. Does the nature of your business allow you to shut it down quickly if it is no longer capable of generating a profit?
6. How much time are you willing to invest in researching legal aspects of running a certain type of business and filing the appropriate forms to do so?
7. How much of your business's earnings do you expect to spend exclusively on developing your business further?
8. How many people, if any, will be employed by the business?
9. Does the nature of your business entail a high likelihood of being sued?
10. Do you plan on giving your employees any form of compensation other than a salary or wage, such as fringe benefits?

This chapter will help you use these questions to determine which structure will give your business the most protection in its primary stages. But bear in mind that it is usually possible to modify the structure as your business begins to grow or change.

Sole Proprietorship

Sole proprietorship is the oldest, simplest, and most common legal structure for a small business. If you choose to run your business as a sole proprietorship, you are the only owner, and there are no shareholders or partners involved in your business. Furthermore, you and your business are a single entity in the eyes of the law. Your business's profits and losses are combined with your personal income, and you must report them on your individual federal income tax return, the standard Form 1040. Your tax rate will depend on the amount of money you earn and other factors the Internal Revenue Service takes into account on individual tax returns. A sole proprietorship is not eligible, however, for the lower tax rate from which corporations may benefit.

The legal aspects of establishing a sole proprietorship are relatively simple. Depending on the area in which you plan to operate, starting a sole proprietorship may involve as little as filing a form with the state or local government to establish your business in your name. If you plan to name your business anything other than your own legal name, you will also have to file for an assumed name at the local or state level. Assumed names may not resemble the name of any other business that already conducts similar commerce in your area. Although specific regulations and costs may vary from area to area, these two formalities usually suffice to establish your business. You may have to file for additional business licenses in your area depending on local laws applicable to your type of business. Restaurants, liquor stores, and construction companies are examples of businesses that often require special licenses. Nevertheless, the cost and difficulty of processing these forms is negligible, and many entrepreneurs choose to run their new businesses as sole proprietorships before considering more intricate legal structures.

Ownership: Running your business as a sole proprietorship eliminates any ownership questions. Since you are the sole owner, you are the head honcho, and you do not have to worry about partners or shareholders. The law not only views you as the owner of your business, but regards you and your business as the same entity. Besides the taxes you must pay, any profits that your business makes are immediately yours.

If you should die unexpectedly, all of the business's capital and other assets are part of the inheritance you leave behind. Business assets are not treated separately from any of your other possessions, unless you specify them in a will.

Liability: While many entrepreneurs covet the flexibility and control that a sole proprietorship allows, the majority of them also dread the personal liability that accompanies it. Just like all matters regarding sole proprietorship, liability is a simple issue: You have unlimited personal liability for all business debts and obligations. To risk-averse entrepreneurs, unlimited personal liability is a terrifying thought, and it is the most compelling reason even for very small businesses to incorporate or choose a different legal structure. Even though the liability hazard can be tamed by liability insurance, your personal liability begins where the coverage of your purchased insurance ends. This liability issue makes sole proprietorship an appealing option only for businesses that operate with very little debt, few long-term contracts, and within a low-risk environment.

The following hypothetical situation illustrates how easily unlimited personal liability can change from a purely theoretical consideration to a dangerous threat to your personal financial future. Say you are a talented entrepreneur and shrewdly start the full-service computer retail business that you had envisioned only months before. Your first year of selling is stellar, and your expected profit is high. While one of your employees delivers a computer system to a client in the company truck, he loses control of the vehicle, hits a small car, and severely injures the driver. The victim immediately sues your driver and the company for all damages, including pain and suffering, and wins the lawsuit for half a million dollars. Since your employee does not have the money, your company is liable. Since you are the sole proprietor, the victim has the right to go after all of your personal assets, including your house and car.

Since many entrepreneurs dread the liability risks that accompany a sole proprietorship, they opt for other legal forms that may provide limited liability, even though their businesses are unlikely to incur a large liability.

Taxation: As mentioned earlier in this section, you and your business are a single financial entity for income tax purposes. Your business's income is taxed to you along with all other income you receive from miscellaneous sources. The tax rate you pay is based upon the total net income you earn from all of your sources.

Just like a corporation, a sole proprietor can deduct routine costs of doing business from his taxable income. These tax-deductible costs usually include transportation, business-related meals, and other expenditures incidental to your business.

As a sole proprietor you may also allocate some of your income to specific retirement plans without paying taxes on this sum.

The major tax disadvantage of a sole proprietorship is the inability to provide fringe benefits and retain earnings at a lower tax rate. While a corporation may enjoy a lower tax rate on earnings it retains to improve its capital, a sole proprietorship is taxed the same amount regardless of whether the earnings are used personally or reinvested.

Figure 6.1 shows at a glance the advantages and disadvantages of sole proprietorships.

Figure 6.1   Advantages and Potential Disadvantages of Sole Proprietorships

Advantages	Potential Disadvantages
■ Establishing your business is relatively easy, and the paperwork is simple.	■ You are burdened with unlimited personal liability for all of your business's debts and obligations.
■ You do not have to prepare a balance sheet for your business, and you can file a single income tax return for both you and your business.	■ The cost of reinvesting some of your income in your business is usually, but not always, higher for a sole proprietorship, because you do not enjoy tax benefits on retained earnings.
■ You make all the decisions regarding your business, and nobody can second-guess you.	

General Partnership

A partnership is defined by the Uniform Partnership Act as "an association of two or more persons to carry on as co-owners of a business for profit." If you are starting a business with two or more owners and are not ready to incorporate, a partnership may be the ideal legal structure for your business.

Creating a small partnership is only slightly more complicated than starting a sole proprietorship, and most of the legal considerations in matters of liability and taxation are the same. The law does not even require a written legal agreement between the partners. Nevertheless, a written partnership agreement provides more protection to the partnership and its owners as individuals, and it lays a solid foundation upon which a successful business can be built.

If you are certain that a partnership is the right legal form for your business, it is advisable to begin by drafting a partnership agreement. Although your partners are going to be friends in whose integrity you have absolute faith, a partnership agreement will allow you to put in writing the common principles by which all partners will abide. At a minimum, the act of writing the agreement will be an opportunity to reflect on potential problems in the partnership's future and to come up with plans of action ahead of time. A good partnership agreement will help you protect the business and the friendship among the partners. The typical components of a partnership agreement are covered in slightly greater depth later under "Partnership Agreements."

Once you have signed a partnership agreement, you may have to register your partnership with your local government, usually the township, county, or state. Since partnerships commonly operate under a fictitious name, you will also have to file for an assumed name at the local or state level. If your partnership plans on conducting business in several states, you may have to apply for a federal license or permit for interstate commerce, as well as register in other states. Information regarding these permits can be obtained from the U.S. Department of Commerce.

Otherwise, starting and operating a partnership is very similar to a sole proprietorship. The crucial difference is the number of owners and people involved in the decision-making process. Since you are no longer operating by yourself, you will have to track the amounts of money, time, and capital each partner contributes to the business. It is also important to keep a written record of how much compensation each partner has received from the business. Unless otherwise specified in the partnership agreement, all partners are equal and receive equal compensation, and the partnership dissolves by default upon the withdrawal of any partner.

Ownership: In a basic partnership, the partners all own equal parts of the business, and they have equal say in the decisions made on behalf of the partnership. However, special types of partnerships or specifications within a partnership agreement can make the issue of ownership slightly more complicated. Special types of partnerships may include secret, dormant, silent, or nominal partners who may own less than an equal share of the business. Except for limited partnerships, which are discussed next, these special types of partnerships are beyond the scope of this chapter.

The partnership agreement allows partners great flexibility in dividing ownership of their business among themselves. The agreement usually states how much capital each partner contributed initially, how profits will be divided, and how much authority each partner has. More information about the actual partnership agreement can be found under "Partnership Agreements."

One final caveat is in order here: Because any partner may act as agent for the partnership as a whole without giving prior notice to the others, one of your partners could act on behalf of the partnership and sign a contract that obligates your business to pay a certain sum of money in return for a service, even though you indirectly own a portion of this money.

Liability: A partnership allows you to combine the talents and resources of several individuals to run a successful business as a team. The low cost and flexibility in setting up a general partnership are persuasive enough to lure some businesspeople into adopting this legal structure. The downside is that a partner in a general partnership faces unlimited personal liability for the business just as a sole proprietor does. As a partner, your own house, car, and savings are at risk in addition to the business itself.

Although the greater combined wealth of all partners may dilute the extent of personal liability risks, the risk is also much less in your control. Remember that any partner can act legally on behalf of the partnership without consulting other partners. Therefore, not only are you responsible for the consequences of your own actions, but you must ensure that your partners don't do anything stupid as well. Any damages or losses incurred by any partner on partnership business is the responsibility of all. The only good safeguard against liability hazards is liability insurance, but your personal liability still begins where the coverage of your insurance ends.

Although liability is an important problem to consider and you should never lose sight of it, you are not left completely alone to fend for yourself. While any partner may conduct business on behalf of the entire partnership, all partners are legally entitled to full information regarding matters that concern the partnership. Partners are legally committed to a fiduciary relationship—each partner owes the others the highest legal duty of good faith, loyalty, and fairness. A partner, for instance, could not sell the partnership's business secrets to a competitor, much less involve himself in the management of a competing business. Nevertheless, it pays to be cautious.

Taxation. Profits or losses must be reported to the government on a partnership return form. The taxable income is then divided among the partners. Each partner also declares his or her share of earnings or losses along with other income on his or her personal income tax return. Much like a sole proprietorship, the applicable tax rate is based upon your total, personal net income.

A partnership, just like a sole proprietorship, can deduct routine costs of doing business from its taxable income. These tax-deductible costs may include transportation, business-related meals, and other expenditures incidental to the partnership's business.

The most significant financial drawbacks of running a partnership instead of a corporation are similar to those of a sole proprietorship. Partnerships cannot provide fringe benefits and retain earnings at a lower tax rate. While a corporation may enjoy a lower tax rate on earnings it retains to improve its capital, partners are taxed the same amount regardless of whether the earnings are used personally or reinvested in the partnership.

Partnership Agreements. If you are starting a partnership, possibly the most important document you will sign is the partnership agreement. As mentioned earlier, the law does not require a written legal agreement between individuals who form a partnership. Nevertheless, a partnership agreement is standard procedure, and it is a method of protecting the partnership and its owners beyond the requirements of the law.

Even if you plan on running a partnership with your best friend of 20 years and you plan to split all costs and profits equally, writing the agreement will be an opportunity to reflect on potential problems in the partnership's future and to come up with principles you will follow to resolve these issues. The purpose of a partnership agreement is not to be an emblem of mutual distrust but to provide an opportunity to put common assumptions on paper for later reference. A meticulously written partnership agreement could save the business at some point in the future.

Let's consider an example. Martin, Niels, and John were three equal partners in a partnership. Since they had been good friends for as long as either of them could remember, they founded their business on a handshake rather than a partnership agreement. The business was wildly successful. John died in an accident three years after starting the partnership. Under the Uniform Partnership Act, the partnership automatically dissolved upon the death of one partner, although Martin and Niels would have liked to continue the business. If the three had written a provision for the withdrawal or death of a partner, the partnership could have continued and avoided either a lot of trouble or a forced liquidation.

This hypothetical situation illustrates that the question should not be whether to write an agreement but what type of information to include within your partnership agreement. Every partnership agreement should contain the name of the business, the purpose of starting the partnership, a list of all capital initially contributed by each partner, the full name and address of each partner, authority of the partners, and the duration of the agreement. The partnership agreement should also contain clauses that provide a procedure for the death of a partner, departure of a partner, disputes among partners, adding a partner, and changing the partnership agreement. Finally, the partnership agreement should contain detailed information regarding the distribution of profits and losses among the partners and the distribution of authority. Some partnership agreements even contain lists of obligatory and prohibited acts to which partners are bound. The bottom line is that the partnership agreement is your opportunity to shape and protect your partnership.

Figure 6.2 shows at a glance the advantages and disadvantages of general partnerships.

Limited Partnership

A limited partnership is a special type of partnership owned by more than one type of partner. Rather than several equal partners, each type of partner has separate rights and responsibilities. Conceptually, limited partnerships are created in nearly the same manner as general partnerships, but

Figure 6.2   Advantages and Potential Disadvantages of General Partnerships

Advantages	Potential Disadvantages
■ Expenses of starting a partnership are relatively low, and the paperwork is easier than for corporations.	■ Partners have unlimited personal liability for all business debts and obligations.
■ Resources, ideas, and workload are shared among the partners.	■ All partners are liable for each other's decisions on behalf of the business.
■ Making decisions on behalf of the partnership is a simple matter, and each partner can do it.	■ The withdrawal or death of one partner poses a serious threat to the survival of the partnership, unless prior arrangements have been made.
■ Taxation is easy: The partners declare their personal shares of the profit on individual tax returns.	

the paperwork and cost are significantly more elaborate. Limited partnerships are strictly regulated by law, and there are restrictions limiting the involvement of certain types of partners in the business's management.

A limited partnership must consist of at least one or more general partners and at least one or more limited partners. The general partners face the same rights and responsibilities as a general partnership (see "General Partnerships" discussed earlier), and they have unlimited personal liability for the business's debts and other obligations. Limited partners invest capital, usually a sum of money, in the partnership and risk losing the amount of their investment. If the partnership becomes insolvent, limited partners could also lose dividend payments received from the partnership after it became insolvent. Limited partners are not, however, subject to unlimited personal liability for business debts.

Another aspect to limited partnerships is the degree to which partners may become involved in running the business. A general partner may act as agent for the partnership at any time and is directly involved with the management and operation of the business. A limited partner, however, may not participate in the administration of the business. If limited partners participate in the decision making for the partnership, they automatically lose their immunity from personal liability for business obligations. Since limited partners are not directly involved in running the business, depending on state laws they may be free to sell their interest in the business at any time. In contrast to a general partner, the death or departure of a limited partner does not legally end the partnership.

Maintaining a limited partnership is a complicated and expensive undertaking for a small business. If you plan on using limited partnership as your business's legal structure, there should be distinct benefits to your business that no other structure can provide. Business's that handle real estate are often limited partnerships for tax reasons.

A limited partnership may also be the ideal solution for a partnership that needs more capital than its general partners are able to contribute. As a general partner, you could raise money by admitting limited partners without having to give up control of your business. Adding limited partners may be more feasible and simpler than borrowing from large financial institutions or issuing stock. Limited partners can be compensated by a percentage of the partnership's profits or in a variety of other ways. General partnerships sometimes turn into limited partnerships to finance expansion.

The bottom line is that limited partnerships are complicated entities to manage, and they are only advantageous in a handful of special cases. Before you endeavor to form such a limited partnership, be sure to take a close look at legislation that governs them in your state.

Figure 6.3 shows at a glance the advantages and potential disadvantages of limited partnerships.

Limited Liability Company (LLC)

A limited liability company (LLC) is a legal structure that combines many of the advantages offered by both partnerships and corporations. In a

Figure 6.3 Advantages and Potential Disadvantages of Limited Partnerships

Advantages	Potential Disadvantages
■ General partners do not have to give up control of the business to the limited partners.	■ General partners have unlimited personal liability for all business debts and obligations.
■ Limited partners can put money into the business without facing unlimited personal liability.	■ The paperwork of running a limited partnership can be horrendous.
■ Allows partnerships to expand and raise money without having to incorporate or issue stock.	■ Laws dealing with limited partnerships may be complicated and vary from state to state.
■ Withdrawal or death of a limited partner does not automatically dissolve the partnership.	

nutshell, an LLC combines the benefits of a corporation's limited liability and a partnership's tax status.

The LLC is a popular legal business structure, because it allows the entrepreneur to run a business free from ever-threatening unlimited personal liability and enjoy partnership tax status. Without having to fear the loss of his house, car, and savings to a business liability, the entrepreneur can focus his energy and money on developing a competitive enterprise that will benefit the economy and society as a whole—and maybe even the business owner! Precisely this view is part of the logic behind the very flexible LLC legislation. Business-friendly legislation encourages the entrepreneurship and commercial activity that drive human progress and national economies.

The large-scale emergence of limited liability companies in the United States is a relatively recent phenomenon, though, and it most recently dates back to 1988 when the IRS granted LLCs the federal income tax status of partnerships. Since the LLC as a legal business structure is so young, laws that regulate LLCs are still evolving very quickly. Most states have not adopted uniform legislation for LLCs, and the regulations that govern the creation, organization, and handling of LLCs vary greatly from state to state. Both rapid change and regional differences make LLC legislation a hard topic to discuss in detail. In this section, we will examine the general structure of LLCs and discuss their main advantages and drawbacks. If you believe that a limited liability company is the legal structure that suits your needs best, you should obtain a copy of LLC legislation affecting your state and purchase the most current book specializing in LLCs that you can find. A copy of your state's LLC legislation may be available on the World Wide Web or from your state's corporate division of the secretary of state. Most public libraries will also carry copies in their business sections. For a comprehensive guide on forming and operating an LLC, we recommend the latest edition of How to Form and Operate a Limited Liability Company by Gregory Damman (Self-Counsel Press, Inc.). Since LLC legislation is still developing rather briskly, the most important consideration in your purchase should be the recency of the information you obtain.

The basic procedure to form an LLC is simple and is comparable to drafting a partnership agreement or articles of incorporation. Forming an LLC usually requires little more than filing articles of organization, sometimes called a certificate of formation, with the secretary of state or other appropriate state agency. The information required within the articles of organization varies between states, and you will either have to order information or fill-in-the-blank forms pertinent to your area of intended operation from the secretary of state. A list with contact addresses for each state can be found at the end of this chapter. Information for your state can also be found in the government section of your local telephone book.

Every state has slightly different requirements for filing articles of organization, and the filing fees vary significantly. For example, after reading through the information that several states require, we are convinced that the Massachusetts version is one of the simplest to file. However, Massachusetts charges a whopping $500 to file articles of organization; this sum is one of the highest around and is shameful compared to the mere $50 it costs in some other states. The articles of organization must contain the name of the company, an address for the company within the state, the name and address of the registered agent for the company, a dissolution date, the names and addresses of managers, the general character of the company's business, and the names of persons authorized to file documents with the secretary of state on behalf of the company.

Ownership: Limited liability companies may be owned by many different types of domestic and international entities. Membership in LLCs is legally possible not only for individuals but entire partnerships, corporations, and other groups. The terms of ownership within the LLC are mutually agreed upon by the owners. Any agreements may be written either in the articles of organization or within an operating agreement drawn up by the owners. The owners of an LLC have tremendous freedom in dividing among themselves the rights and responsibilities of running the company. The owners may distribute the LLC's losses and gains according to any formula they see fit, and the same freedom is true for choosing a management system. While some members may be actively involved in handling the company's daily affairs, others may have virtually no management rights. As long as no laws are ignored or broken, an LLC has a lot of flexibility in shaping its own operating rules.

Members of an LLC may only transfer their interest in the company if all other owners approve the transaction. The withdrawal or death of any member dissolves the LLC, unless all remaining members agree to continue.

Liability: Perhaps every entrepreneur's nightmare is losing his personal assets to a lawsuit, a bad loan, or some other business obligation. No matter how much liability insurance you purchase, you ultimately have unlimited personal liability for a sole proprietorship or general partnership. The limited liability company's greatest attraction is the legal shield with which it guards its owners from unlimited personal liability. When an LLC is in debt or loses a lawsuit, its owners are only liable up to the amount of their initial capital contributions to the company.

In theory creditors and plaintiffs can only go after the LLC's property when they seek the payment of a business debt or obligation and cannot touch the personal assets of its owners. While this liability arrangement of an LLC may sound ideal to you now, the principles do work somewhat differently in real life. Even though the LLC's shield protects your personal assets from business obligations and debts, you must still worry about personal liability and negligence. If a client is hurt or the payment of a debt jeopardized because of your own negligence, the LLC's liability shield cannot protect you, and you are still personally liable for your actions. You also shouldn't kid yourself regarding loans by banks or other large financial institutions. If a bank is not absolutely sure that your LLC will be able to repay a loan on time, it will demand that at least one of the LLC's members guarantee the loan personally. Once you personally guarantee a loan, you are just as vulnerable to liability resulting from this debt as a sole proprietor.

Finally, the absence of unlimited personal liability does not imply the lack of legal responsibilities with which a member of an LLC must comply. It would not be advisable, for instance, to take out a loan on behalf of the LLC, pay the money out to its members as dividends, and claim the creditor is out of luck due to the LLC's insolvency. Most states' LLC statutes contain provisions that specify a limit to the amount of an LLC's capital that can be paid out as dividends.

Overall the LLC's liability shield is a safe and efficient way to protect yourself against financial ruin, although you should be wary of overestimating its power. The LLC is a fantastic way to drastically limit your liability exposure, but you are not completely immune.

Taxation: Besides limited liability, partnership tax status is the second most important selling point for the LLC legal structure. In fact, it was the decision by the IRS in 1988 to give LLCs the same tax benefits from which partnerships had already profited for years that sparked the rise in LLC activity. The LLC has the freedom to divide its profits or losses among its members in any way it deems advantageous, and individual gains or losses by members are calculated and reported each year. Each member then declares his or her share of earnings or losses along with other income on his or her personal income tax return. Since members of an LLC can also be corporations or partnerships, dividends from the LLC are taxed with other earnings the member has.

Figure 6.4 shows at a glance the advantages and potential disadvantages of limited liability companies.

Corporation

Forming a corporation is by far the most complicated alternative of the legal business structures discussed in this chapter. It is also the structure that provides you with the most control and minimizes exposure to risk most effectively. Unless specific advantages for your business can only be attained by choosing another legal form or your business cannot

Figure 6.4   Advantages and Potential Disadvantages of Limited Liability Companies (LLCs)

Advantages	Potential Disadvantages
■ Corporations, partnerships, and individuals can all be members/owners of an LLC.	■ Laws governing the creation, organization, and operation of LLCs are evolving rapidly.
■ Owners have limited personal liability for business debts and obligations, even if they are directly involved in the daily operation of the business.	■ States are not ready yet to unanimously adopt a uniform LLC act, and LLC legislation still varies greatly from state to state.
■ LLCs have tremendous freedom in making ownership and management decisions.	■ Although the IRS has granted LLCs tax status similar to that of partnerships, the tax law is still likely to change as LLC legislation comes of age.
■ Although LLCs are more complicated than general partnerships, they are fairly easy to establish and maintain.	
■ Owners enjoy the same tax structure as a partnership.	

yet absorb the cost of incorporating, you are most likely to incorporate your business. Establishing a corporation means creating a distinct legal entity that is completely independent of its owners in a legal sense. Just like an individual, a corporation has rights and responsibilities in the eyes of the law, and it is liable for its own actions. A corporation must file its own tax return independently of its owners, and it must maintain certain paperwork regarding its activities. Think of a corporation as an individual that comes to life as soon as approval for incorporation is obtained from the secretary of state.

Since forming a corporation is so complex, this section is broken down into six parts that outline the most pertinent information on incorporating. A more detailed look at corporations is certainly beyond the scope of this chapter, but there are many self-help books in print that focus exclusively on incorporating your business, such as *Do It Yourself! Incorporation* (E-Z Legal Books).

Corporation versus Other Legal Business Structures: As briefly mentioned before, the corporation is a unique type of legal structure for a business to take, because a corporation is a separate legal entity from its owners. Unlike a sole proprietorship or a partnership, a corporation must be established by filing articles of incorporation with the secretary of state. A corporation is a much more formal business form than the sole proprietorship or partnership, and a corporation must keep accurate records of nearly all its activities. Starting a sole proprietorship or a partnership can be done with as little as a verbal agreement, but a corporation requires many expensive formalities.

Corporations can be divided into two broad categories: public and closely held. Public corporations are the most elaborate to form and are partially owned by stockholders within the general public. Since this book focuses on starting small businesses, we will concentrate on closely held corporations, which are held by only a few people.

Reasons for Starting a Corporation: Any legal business structure serves to protect a business and its owners, but the corporation is a particularly powerful and effective way to obtain a potent set of legal benefits. The advantages of running a corporation include limited liability for the owners, easy transfer of ownership, a corporate tax rate, ability to retain earnings for expansion, and use of fringe benefits at a marginally lower cost.

Since a corporation is a separate entity from its owners, any business obligations or debts must be paid off using only the business's assets. The owners don't have any personal liability for the corporation. In theory creditors and plaintiffs can only go after the corporation's property when they seek the payment of a business debt or obligation and cannot touch the personal assets of its owners. While this may sound like a perfect solution to all your liability problems, you are still vulnerable to some extent. Even though the corporation's liability shield protects your personal assets from business obligations and debts, you must still worry about personal liability and negligence. If a client wins a suit for damages you have incurred or a creditor sues for payment you neglected to make, the corporation's liability shield is of little use to you. You are still personally liable for your own actions.

Ownership in a corporation is easily transferred between people, unless the stockholder's agreement restricts a transfer since the value of each owner's share is known. Unlike a partnership or limited liability company, however, the transfer of a share of a corporation from one person to another does not affect the term of the corporation's existence. The corporation is still an independent entity with a life span of its own, and the dissociation of one of its owners does not change that.

Another reason for choosing to incorporate is the possibility to retain earnings at a lower tax rate for expanding the business. Profits made by a sole proprietorship, a partnership, or a limited liability company must be distributed in the same year in which they were earned. Once the profits are distributed, the individual recipients are required to declare them on their individual income tax returns. The partnership itself is not a separate entity and cannot retain some of the earnings. Since a corporation is a separate entity from its owners and files its own tax return, a corporation has the ability to retain some of its earnings for expansion or other uses.

Taxation: Reading over all of the benefits incorporation brings to your company, you must have been wondering about the drawbacks. A punishing tax rate is one of the most significant problems owners of a corporation face. By forming a corporation, you are creating a separate entity resembling an artificial person. As such, the corporation must file its own tax return and pay taxes on all of its income. Once the corporation has paid its taxes, the remaining profits are distributed among the owners, who pay taxes on the same money again. This double taxation takes a tremendous toll on the net figure you see in your personal savings account at the end of a fiscal year. There are ways to minimize the effect of double taxation. One possibility is declaring your corporation an S corporation. Another option is paying salaries, rather than dividend distributions, to the owner-employees. Spend a little money on an accountant to help with this. The return on that money, in the form of tax savings, will likely be large.

Figure 6.5 shows at a glance the advantages and potential disadvantages of corporations.

S Corporation

A regular corporation is seen by the law and the IRS as a separate entity. As such, a corporation must file its own tax return and pay corporate taxes on all of its income. Once the corporation has paid its taxes, the remaining profits are distributed among the owners, who pay taxes on the same money again. This is a synopsis of the double taxation problem we briefly considered in the previous section. There are ways to minimize the effect of double taxation. One way is to sit down with an accountant or tax lawyer to figure out a clever way to drastically reduce the amount of money that is being taxed twice. While this option may work well for some businesses, it may be too costly for others. Furthermore, if you get too tricky, you may get yourself into some trouble with the IRS! The perfect solution for some businesses is electing S corporation status.

S corporations are viewed by the IRS as corporations but with partnership-type flow-through of most types of income to stockholders. As such a vehicle, an S corporation does not have to pay taxes, and all profit flows directly into the hands of the owners. The owners then file their personal income tax returns and declare their profits with the rest of their income.

Figure 6.5 Advantages and Potential Disadvantages of Corporations

Advantages	Potential Disadvantages
■ The corporate shield protects the corporation's owners from unlimited personal liability.	■ Federal, state, and local governments require corporations to keep and file many types of financial statements and forms.
■ Depending on how your corporation spends its money, you may be able to benefit from lower tax rates.	■ As its own entity, a corporation must pay corporate tax on its earnings. When earnings are distributed to owners, they have to pay personal income taxes on top of the corporate tax—double taxation.
■ Raising capital by selling stock is always an option for a corporation that wants to expand.	
■ The dissociation by death or sale of a corporation's owner does not dissolve the business.	
■ Interest in a corporation is inherited or transferred from one person to another with relative ease.	

When and How to File for S *Corporation Status:* If your normal corporation consists of less than 75 shareholders, you simply have to file Form 2553 at the appropriate time with the IRS to be considered an S corporation. Form 2553 can be obtained from the IRS web site (www.irs.ustreas.gov) or via regular mail. Your local IRS office is listed in the government section of your telephone book.

Who Should File for S *Corporation Status:* Generally speaking, a corporation that spends a proportionately large amount of its profits on paying its owners and spends very little on corporate capital is the ideal candidate for S corporation status. Becoming an S corporation eliminates double taxation of all money distributed as dividends to the owners. The opportunity cost of becoming an S corporation is limited to the taxes paid on the amount of money the owners reinvest in the corporation to purchase capital or expand. Therefore, a corporation with high expenditures on dividends and low expenditure on capital is likely to want S corporation status.

Copyrights

A copyright protects the original thought put into a creative work. The author who holds the copyright to his or her work owns the exclusive right to reproduce, sell, license, display, perform, and distribute that work. Works that can be copyrighted include but are not limited to books, plays, articles, journals, newspapers, e-mail, letters, instructions, poetry, translations, databases, works of art, drawings, ad copy, and speeches.

While all those forms of expression can be copyrighted, an actual idea cannot be protected by a copyright. The actual content of an author's copyrighted work, such as information or ideas, can be reproduced by anybody.

Let us consider this book as an example to illustrate the difference. You may freely write about and publish any of the information or ideas contained within this book. If you copy this book verbatim—even a small portion of it without the publishers permission—and publish it, then you'll violate the copyright of this book.

Who Can Register a Copyright

Authors need not apply explicitly to obtain the copyrights to their work. A copyright automatically exists when a person creates unique material that is subject to copyright laws. The minute an author writes a book, for instance, he of she automatically owns the copyright to that work. Legally there is no requirement to register a copyright.

The only catch to this seemingly convenient legislation is the fact that the owner of a copyright cannot file a copyright infringement suit within the United States unless the copyright is registered with the Copyright Office. Therefore, your copyright's protective value is very limited until you actually register it.

Rights a Copyright Gives Its Owner and How Long These Rights Last

A copyright gives you the exclusive right to reproduce, sell, license, display, perform, and distribute your work. A copyright is an asset, and you can sell your copyright to someone, you may license certain people to use or publish your work in return for regular payments, or you may choose to limit the use of your work to yourself. If another person or entity reproduces or sells your work without your consent, you have the right to file a lawsuit for copyright infringement.

How to Register a Copyright on Your Own

For detailed information on registering copyrights, we recommend *The Copyright Handbook* by Stephen Fishman (Nolo Press). The book provides detailed information on making copyrights work for you and is tailored to those who do not have extensive experience in working with them. Extensive information can also be found at the U.S. Copyright Office Home Page on the World Wide Web (lcweb.loc.gov/copyright). The Copyright Office web site, like all web sites, is a fantastic resource for information, because it is updated often and contains the most up-to-date news available.

Patents

Inventors are often the most successful entrepreneurs of all. Rather than sell just another version of a common product or readily available service, they invent a unique good or find a new and improved application or style for an old good. If you plan on marketing a good you invented yourself, you must be extremely careful to adequately protect your invention with the legal means available to you. Just like legal business structures, the law is in your own hands, and it is up to you to make it work toward protecting your interests.

A patent is one form of legal protection you should seek if you have invented something unique that fulfills a certain purpose or have come up with a unique ornamental design for an object. A U.S. patent is a legal right granted by the government to a person or entity to keep others from making, using, and selling the owner's patented invention for 20 years, or 14 years in the case of design patents. After a patent expires, it cannot be renewed. However, a new improvement of a previously or currently patented invention may be patented.

Who Can Apply for a Patent

There are no limitations on who can apply for a U.S. patent. The applicant must be the true inventor of the invention, and application for the patent must be filed and approved by the Patent and Trademark Office of the United States Department of Commerce.

Rights a Patent Gives the Inventor

As mentioned earlier, a patent gives you the right to keep others from making, using, and selling your patented invention for 20 years, or 14 years in the case of design patents. A patent is just like any other assets you hold. You can sell your patent to someone, you may license certain people to use your invention in return for regular payments, or you may choose to produce and market your invention yourself. If another person or entity reproduces or sells your invention without your prior authorization, you have the right to file a lawsuit in federal court against the violator for patent infringement. However, it is primarily up to you to take action against those who infringe upon your patent.

What Can Be Patented and How Long Patents Last

There are three distinct types of patents for which you may apply: utility patents, design patents, and plant patents. Each protects a different type of invention. Figure 6.6 describes the three types of patents and how long they last. Be forewarned that it is extremely important to file for the type of patent appropriate to your invention. Also realize that the patent's duration is a maximum and assumes that the inventor pays all applicable maintenance fees for the patent.

How to File for a Patent and What It Will Cost

If you are an inventor and seek a patent on your invention, it is advisable to file a provisional patent application (PPA) with the Patent and Trademark Office (PTO) of the United States Department of Commerce as soon as practicable. Legally, however, you have an entire year to file a patent application from the time you first publicize your invention in any manner. The law does not even require you to file a PPA in the meantime, although it is highly advisable.

The cost of filing a patent application without the use of a lawyer or other professional advice may amount to several hundred dollars. Filing a

Figure 6.6   Types of Patents and Their Duration

Type	Description	Duration
Utility Patents	A utility patent covers inventions that serve a specific purpose in a unique manner. A utility patent must have some pragmatic value instead of purely aesthetic value. Examples include microchips, computer parts, appliances, special tools, and anything else that is both unique and useful.	20 years
Design Patents	A design patent covers the unique design or ornamental value of an invention. An inventor could not apply for a utility patent for designing a desk, but he could apply for a design patent if his desk had a truly original shape. If the desk's unique shape had any type of practical value, however, the inventor would have to apply for a utility patent instead of a design patent.	14 years
Plant Patents	A plant patent specifically allows an inventor to secure the rights to a unique type of asexually reproducing plant.	20 years

PPA, however, will not cost more than $150. The most expensive fee is for the maintenance of a patent, which could cost you several thousand dollars depending on the amount of time you wish to keep your patent. A fee schedule is available from the Patent and Trademark Office.

How to File a Patent without Consulting a Lawyer

Filing a patent without professional help or prior experience is not an impossibility. There are many published books that specialize in taking the reader through the process. Since we can devote only a section of a chapter to patents, we recommend that you read *Patent It Yourself* by David Pressman (Nolo Press). Pressman is a patent attorney, and his book is packed with excellent advice for the first-time patent applicant.

Conclusion

Although every entrepreneur will undoubtedly face innumerable risks and pitfalls throughout his career, most potentially disastrous situations can be eliminated or avoided before they interfere with your business. The key to successfully protecting yourself and your business lies in gathering all pertinent information regarding your circumstances and efficiently using it to make sound legal decisions. If you know the law well enough, it can be your key to maximizing your control over your business and minimizing the liability and taxation involved. As you must have noticed throughout this chapter, there is a trade-off among the different legal structures you might choose.

Some legal structures, such as partnerships and sole proprietorships, are early to run and have simple tax structures, and other legal structures, such as the LLCs and corporations, provide better protection from business liabilities but are tough to manage.

The success of your business is heavily influenced by your ability to take advantage of todays corporate law. The informed entrepreneur will gain a tremendous competitive edge by making the corporate laws work on his behalf. The savvy businessman will use the right business structure to protect himself to the maximum extent, and he will take advantage of his legal rights to prevent others from competing with him. It is my hope that this chapter provided you with useful information regarding the primary legal issues that every entrepreneur and new business will face.

For more information on limited liability companies, corporations, and business legislation, contact your secretary of state or equivalent regulating body.

Alabama

Secretary of State
Business Division
P.O. Box 5616
Montgomery, AL 36103
(205) 242-5324

Alaska

The State of Alaska
Division of Banking, Securities,
    and Corporations
P.O. Box 110808
Juneau, AK 99811-0808
(907) 465-2530

Arizona

Arizona Corporation
    Commission
1300 West Washington Street
Phoenix, AZ 85007-2929
(602) 542-3135

Arkansas

Secretary of State
State Capitol
Little Rock, AR 72201-1094
(501) 682-1010

California

Secretary of State
1500 Eleventh Street
P.O. Box 944228
Sacramento, CA 94244-2280
(916) 653-3795

Colorado

Secretary of State
Corporations Section
1560 Broadway, Suite 200
Denver, CO 80202
(303) 894-2251

Connecticut

Secretary of State
30 Trinity Street
P.O. Box 150470
Hartford, CT 06115-0470
(860) 509-6000

Delaware

Department of State
Division of Corporations
P.O. Box 898
Dover, DE 19903
(302) 739-3073

Florida

Division of Corporations
Florida Department of State
P.O. Box 6327
Tallahassee, FL 32314
(904) 487-6052

Georgia

Secretary of State
Business Services and Regulation
2 Martin Luther King Jr. Drive
Suite 306, West Tower
Atlanta, GA 30334
(404) 656-2817

Hawaii

Department of Commerce
Business Registration Division
1010 Richards Street
P.O. Box 40
Honolulu, HI 96810
(808) 586-2727

Idaho

Secretary of State
Statehouse, Room 203
P.O. Box 83720
Boise, ID 83720-0080
(208) 334-2301

Illinois

Secretary of State
Department of Business Services
Howlett Building, Room 359
Springfield, IL 62756
(217) 782-7880

Indiana

Secretary of State
302 West Washington Street,
Room E018
Indianapolis, IN 46204
(317) 232-6576

Iowa

Secretary of State
Business Services Division
Hoover Building
Des Moines, IA 50319
(515) 281-5204

Kansas

Secretary of State
State Capitol, 2nd Floor
300 SW Tenth Avenue
Topeka, KS 66612-1594
(913) 296-4564

Kentucky

Secretary of State
P.O. Box 718
Frankfort, KY 40602-0718
(502) 564-3490

Louisiana

Secretary of State
P.O. Box 94125
Baton Rouge, LA 70804-9125
(504) 925-4704

Maine

Secretary of State
Bureau of Corporations, Elections,
and Commissions
Statehouse, Station 101
Augusta, ME 04333-0101
(207) 287-4195

Maryland

State of Maryland
Department of Assessments and
Taxation
Businesses Services and Finance
Division
301 West Preston Street, Room 809
Baltimore, MD 21201
(410) 767-1350

Massachusetts

Corporations Division
Secretary of State
One Ashburton Place
Boston, MA 02108
(617) 727-2850

Michigan

State of Michigan
Department of Commerce
Corporation and Securities Bureau
P.O. Box 30054
Lansing, MI 48909
(517) 334-6302

Minnesota

Secretary of State
100 Constitution Avenue
State Office Building, Suite 180
Saint Paul, MN 55155-1299
(612) 297-1455

Mississippi
Secretary of State
P.O. Box 136
Jackson, MS 39205-0136
(601) 359-1333

Missouri
Secretary of State
P.O. Box 778
Jefferson City, MO 65102
(314) 751-1310

Montana
Secretary of State
P.O. Box 202801
Helena, MT 59620-2801
(406) 444-3665

Nebraska
Nebraska Department of State
Secretary of State
1301 State Capitol
Lincoln, NE 68509-4608
(402) 471-4079

Nevada
Secretary of State
State Capitol
Carson City, NV 89710
(702) 687-5203

New Hampshire
Department of State
107 North Main Street
Statehouse, Room 204
Concord, NH 03301-4989
(603) 271-3244

New Jersey
Department of State
Division of Commercial Recording
CN 308
Trenton, NJ 08625
(609) 984-1900

New Mexico
State Corporation Commission
P.O. Drawer 1269
Santa Fe, NM 87504-1269
(505) 827-4511

New York
Department of State
Division of Corporations
41 State Street
Albany, NY 12231
(518) 473-2492

North Carolina
Corporations Division
Secretary of State
300 North Salisbury Street
Raleigh, NC 27603-5909
(919) 733-4201

North Dakota
Secretary of State
600 East Boulevard Avenue
Bismarck, ND 58505-0500
(701) 328-4284

Ohio
Secretary of State
30 East Broad Street, 14th Floor
Columbus, OH 43266-0418
(614) 466-3251

Oklahoma
Secretary of State
101 State Capitol
Oklahoma City, OK 73105-4897
(405) 521-3911

Oregon
Secretary of State
Corporation Division
Public Service Building
255 Capitol Street NE, Suite 151
Salem, OR 97310-1327
(503) 986-2200

Pennsylvania
Secretary of Commonwealth
Department of State
P.O. Box 8722
Harrisburg, PA 17105-8722
(717) 787-1057

Rhode Island
Secretary of State
Corporations Division
100 North Main Street
Providence, RI 02903-1335
(401) 277-3040

South Carolina
Secretary of State
P.O. Box 11350
Columbia, SC 29211
(803) 734-2155

South Dakota
Secretary of State
State Capitol, Suite 204
500 East Capitol Street
Pierre, SD 57501-5070
(605) 773-4845

Tennessee
Secretary of State
Corporations Section
James K. Polk Building, 18th Floor
Nashville, TN 37243-0306
(615) 741-0537

Texas
Secretary of State
Corporations Section
P.O. Box 13697
Austin, TX 78711-3697
1-800-735-2989

Utah
Department of Commerce
Division of Corporations and
    Commercial Code
Heber M. Wells Building
160 East 300 South
P.O. Box 146705
Salt Lake City, UT 84114-6705
(801) 530-4849

Vermont
Secretary of State
109 State Street
Montpelier, VT 05609-1104
(802) 828-2366

Virginia
State Corporation Commission
P.O. Box 1197
Richmond, VA 23209-1197
(804) 371-9733

Washington

Secretary of State
Corporations Division
505 East Union Avenue
Republic Building, 2nd Floor
P.O. Box 40234
Olympia, WA 98504-0234
(306) 753-7115

West Virginia

Secretary of State
State Capitol
1900 Kanawha Boulevard East
Charleston, WV 25305-0770
(304) 342-8000

Wisconsin

Secretary of State
Corporations Division
P.O. Box 7846
Madison, WI 53707-7846
(608) 266-3590

Wyoming

Secretary of State
Corporation Division
State Capitol
Cheyenne, WY 82002-0020
(307) 777-7311

Chapter 7

──── 乢 乢 乢 乢 ────

The Faces of Success

After reading about the many different aspects of starting your business—cultivating an entrepreneurial outlook, identifying the market for your product or service, financing your start-up, putting together a business plan, understanding economic trends, and protecting yourself—you're probably feeling the strain of information overload. You may even be wondering whether anyone has actually ever mastered the fine art of entrepreneurship and launched a successful business at your age. What you need now is a little inspiration and encouragement to assure you that it can be done. In fact, what you need is proof.

In this chapter we present you with the stories of 10 people from all over the United States who have succeeded in starting their own businesses while still in college or shortly after graduation. Their businesses run the gamut from computer consulting to 3-D display technology to painting services, but every undertaking was a success for its young entrepreneur. Their stories are inspirational and interesting, and attach real people and real businesses to the ideas and techniques discussed in the previous chapters.

The 10 stories are but a small sampling of the world of possibilities, but they demonstrate that there certainly are many different industries and markets out there—and that entrepreneurs come in many different flavors. As explained in Chapter 1, there isn't any one type of person who makes a good entrepreneur. And you certainly do not need to be superhuman. The people profiled in this chapter are ordinary people like you and your partners. They share one unique quality that allowed them to pursue an independent venture: the entrepreneurial spirit, the drive to successfully carry an idea to its fulfillment.

Like these 10 young entrepreneurs, you can develop the capacity to tackle an industry and take your idea to market. As you read their stories, we hope their voices carry through and inspire you with the entrepreneurial spirit.

Kevin Carlson

Founder, Paradigm Medical Information Solutions (PMIS) *and Paradigm Business Solutions* (PBS)
Northeastern University '98 (Computer Science)
Founded PBS during third year at Northeastern

A few years ago, Kevin Carlson made a decision that largely influenced his life's direction: "I am never going to work for corporate America." Kevin was an undergraduate at Northeastern University then. Having recently graduated, Kevin has already started three business ventures and plans to start more.

With his charming smile and angelic face, Kevin looks like the type of guy you'd want to take home to your parents—even if he weren't your friend. Being independent by nature, he was sure that he would be his own boss for the rest of his life. Ironically, Kevin enrolled in Northeastern University in the fall of 1993 because he was interested in their co-op program. Through this program, he attended school for six months and worked in corporate America for six months each year. He had a technical job at Draper Labs, where he worked on nuclear guidance systems.

In 1995, after a couple of years with the co-op program, Kevin decided he wasn't fully satisfied with the education he was receiving and started doing independent computer consulting. The extra money allowed him to move into an apartment off campus and become more independent. Running the business taught him skills that he could not have learned by taking classes at college. Says Kevin, "You don't learn about the real world in college. . . . The only thing you can get out of school is to learn how to learn." It was through this venture that he realized he would much rather work for himself than for corporate America.

Not long after, he took his independent consulting venture one step further and formed with a friend a partnership called Paradigm Business Solutions (PBS). This consulting partnership provided services to companies that needed assistance with technical or computer-related issues, primarily in database work. Kevin consulted for about 20 hours a week and was doing pretty well for himself, but was looking to start yet another company. His passion for entrepreneurship had now firmly taken hold. Interestingly, it was through consulting for this partnership that Kevin discovered his next idea—and founded his next business.

In 1997, Kevin founded Paradigm Medical Information Solutions (PMIS), a company that develops medical database technology and provides other services for cardiologists. Since he came up with the idea while consulting, Kevin refers to the relationship between his partnership and his new company as a synergy He gets ideas from his consulting jobs, and provided that there exists a nice niche with a large enough market, he will develop more of these ideas by starting companies based on them

Currently, PMIS has six employees: Kevin, his partner, two transcriptionists, a cardiologist, and a computer assistant. He and his partner are currently developing their patented database software called PatientWorks. Besides the software, they also provide a transcription service in which, for a small fee, the transcriptionists take down evaluations from doctors by dictation over the phone. The cardiologist in the company gives advice, acts as their venture capitalist, and gives them free office space in return for a share of the company. This is truly a mutually beneficial relationship. Having formed the company only recently, Kevin is very excited to grow the business and tap into the currently neglected market for cardiology database technology. According to the company's analysis, the market for PatientWorks is around $70 million.

Kevin's foresight, business talent, and modesty are impressive. Like many other successful entrepreneurs, he has some thoughts to offer on entrepreneurship: "Entrepreneurship is an instinct. Not everyone's cut out for it. Entrepreneurs have an instinct, a drive to work for themselves." However, he says, this does not preclude you from learning how to become an entrepreneur, or how to think like one. "You can major in entrepreneurship, [but ultimately] it's a drive. It's like being an introvert or an extrovert. You can't fake it." Along with having this drive, Kevin also thinks entrepreneurs should possess other qualities, such as common sense, knowing your limits, and independence.

Kevin's story definitely demonstrates these qualities, and he has an interesting personal anecdote about one in particular: drive. When he started his businesses, he had a girlfriend. Now, he doesn't have one anymore. Because of his drive, Kevin made his businesses the first thing on his priority list and everything else came second. He doesn't believe it is possible for people to juggle a heavy school workload, a business, an active social life, and a relationship, and succeed in all those areas. Kevin's goals for his business demanded certain sacrifices. However, that's not to say that he doesn't have a social life. In fact, he has a pretty active social life in Boston, but he does focus on what was, and still is, his main priority: business.

Kevin is definitely focused. In fact, he is so focused, he doesn't need an alarm clock. That might seem strange in the fast-paced life of a businessperson, but it actually makes sense. Without an alarm clock, Kevin gets up to work when he wants to. He says there's no point in forcing himself to work. Working on his businesses must be something he wants to do, not something he has to make himself do.

However, though Kevin is very focused on carrying his businesses forward and on starting up new ventures, he realizes that there is more to life than his career. He says, "To be successful is to be able to do what you want. . . . The goal in life is to be happy and to be happy is to be successful." After starting up more ventures, he would like to pull back, get married "around twenty-six or twenty-eight," start a family, and enjoy life. Though his businesses constitute the major focus of his life right now, he says he can pull back once the businesses are out of the start-up phase and are financially independent—when they can pay for themselves and he can make executive decisions without having to concern himself with the details.

With all of this focus, it is refreshing that Kevin isn't entirely focused on himself. He is a true advocate of entrepreneurship and tries to help out people who are trying to start up successful businesses of their own. After being known as "the entrepreneur" on campus, Kevin was asked to be president of Northeastern's Entrepreneurs Club. He accepted and basically started the club from scratch. Now the club has a membership of 30 to 40 budding entrepreneurs who arrange to have speakers and workshops. In addition, Kevin plays a major role in Northeastern's annual business plan competition, which awards $60,000 to those students with the best business plans. The entrants range from undergraduates to faculty members and are judged by professionals, including Kevin himself.

Though he has successfully molded himself into a business professional, Kevin still enjoys many "nonbusiness" activities—hanging out with friends, playing sports, and so forth. But having now received from Northeastern his "piece of paper," as he calls it, he is able to focus even more on what to him is the most fun of all: his companies. Kevin is finally living his dream: to be an entrepreneur exclusively.

Wellie Chao

Founder, Crimson Solutions, Inc. (www.crimson-solutions.com)
Harvard College '98 (Economics)
Founded company during second year at Harvard

When Wellie Chao was only eight years old, his dad bought him his first computer. He started playing games, but soon that wasn't enough to satisfy his curiosity—he wanted to learn how to create those games. So he did. For one of his first programs, the user would enter his or her name—say, Jack—and the computer would respond by displaying "Hello, Jack!" He showed everybody he knew and was treated like "the coolest kid on the block" for the day.

Many years after his first playful experiments with computers, Wellie left Tampa, Florida, for Harvard College to study economics and computer science. A few years into his undergraduate career, Wellie wanted to find a summer job as many college students do. So he went to Harvard's Office of Career Services (OCS) and waded through the sea of binders full of job opportunities. It was near closing time when he found the perfect job for himself. He wanted to make a photocopy but discovered he didn't have any change. So he went back to his dorm to get some change, but by the time he returned to OCS it was locked. He went back the next day and the page describing his perfect job was missing. Someone must have taken it. As a last resort, he called up OCS and asked them if these pages describing job opportunities were accessible over the World Wide Web. To his dismay, they said no. However, they also said that it would be a great idea. What may have seemed like an unfortunate loss of an employment opportunity turned out to be a blessing in disguise for Wellie. The experience led him to come up with the idea of creating an online database of jobs. He spoke with the people at OCS and they agreed to support his development of this online database. And that was the birth of Crimson Solutions. Wellie simply recognized a problem, and decided to develop a solution. According to him, many businesses are started this way.

After Wellie decided to form a company to target this problem, his first task was to develop an online recruiting system that career centers at other schools could use. He views this technology as being very necessary and only recently possible owing to the advent of the web. The web allows career centers to put many of their paper-intensive processes on the web and makes research for potential employees much easier. With a searchable database of jobs, a student seeking employment can find his or her "perfect job" much more quickly and easily. Previously, frustrated unemployed students had to dig through all of the pages in the hundreds of often disorganized binders. Now, they simply enter some personal information and preferences and sit back as the system produces a list of jobs matching these specifications. Additionally, this makes the career center location irrelevant. Instead of having to walk to the career center, users can access it from anywhere they have web access. It is even possible to access it during vacations when the student is not even on campus. Companies can also enter their job information online instead of having to send out descriptions in paper format to the career office. Storing information in an electronic format makes it convenient and accessible, so this database simplifies the process for both students and companies.

Because this software makes the entire job search process easier, many career centers were eager to pay the annual licensing fee that goes with the software. The business is very stable because, as Wellie puts it, "your revenue only grows each year. . . . Once a career center decides to switch to this method, they are basically locked in." Since everything is stored in this format and accessed using the technology Wellie's company developed, there are high costs associated with switching systems. Not only does the career center have to pay for another system, it has to train employees to adapt to the new system. The high switching costs, coupled with the fact that Crimson Solutions has created a very effective product, induce their clients to stay with them.

In the future, Crimson Solutions is looking toward a bigger and better idea with the potential to make the revenues from annual licensing fees seem almost insignificant. Once they have, say, 150 to 200 schools using their system, they want to build a large network of potential employees which can be accessed by employers, advertisers, and anyone else willing to pay a fee. In this way, they will have a large source of students to recruit for jobs or anything else. The employer's task of finding an appropriate candidate is made easier because the system allows the employer to narrow the applicant pool down based on the student's career interests, year in school, and other specifications. This network will be no harder to use than a search engine, and extremely useful for large companies.

Due to the success of his venture and his ideas for further growth, Wellie and three of his colleagues (all of whom have recently graduated) have decided to skip the job market entirely and continue developing Crimson Solutions. They make enough money to support themselves, and Wellie says that he would definitely rather work for himself than for someone else. However, at least right now, he doesn't believe this company will become his lifetime career, even though signs suggest that it could be a quite lucrative one since there is a lot of room for growth. He plans to continue with Crimson Solutions for however long it takes for the company to be "successful." He will leave after that because once the company matures, Wellie says he won't feel challenged anymore. He would have an intact company and a lot of power, but the excitement wouldn't be there anymore. He believes that many entrepreneurs start businesses because they thrive on the challenges.

Looking back on his college years, Wellie definitely thinks he has benefited from his education and experiences. Being in college has allowed him to find great people to work with and to gain critical skills from both economics and computer science courses which have helped him in running his business. College has also "taught him how to learn." Not knowing how to learn could be a serious disadvantage, according to Wellie. He says, "Especially in the high-tech industries, if you don't know how to learn, you will have a static set of skills which will grow outdated."

Moving from his business to the broader notion of entrepreneurship, Wellie offers the idea that entrepreneurs have to be risk takers in order to get the rewards of entrepreneurship. He believes that many people would love the success but are afraid to take the risks. These people feel that they must have a steady income—a paycheck once or twice a month—to feel comfortable. But when someone starts a company, he or she might not get paid for six months. However, though Wellie does take risks, he is confident that he can always support himself since his computer skills are extremely marketable. In order to decrease risks, Wellie thinks everyone should have some marketable skill to fall back on. Aside from business, Wellie likes to row crew, read, and play chess. He is thankful that his parents have provided him with the opportunity to go to college and to start his own company. If they hadn't bought him that computer when he was only eight years old, who knows how different he would be today?

For the developing entrepreneurs out there, Wellie's best advice is to "keep your eyes open," because "there are lots of opportunities out there, but it's really a lot of work, so you have to be really dedicated to your idea." Wellie was uncertain for the first six months whether his idea was going to work, but he stuck with it and now his company is a success.

John Chuang

Cofounder, MacTemps, Inc. (*www.mactemps.com*)
Harvard College '87 (Economics)
Founded company during third year at Harvard

As an undergraduate economics major at Harvard College, John Chuang worked on a student publication called the *Harvard Political Review.* He and two other people were given the task of cutting typesetting costs. To do this, they decided to use desktop publishing instead of having *the review* typeset the old-fashioned way. This was during the mid-1980s in the very early days of the first Macintosh computers, so most people hadn't yet tried desktop publishing. However, it really worked for John and fellow collaborators Steve Kapner and Mia Wenjen when they saved the *Harvard Political Review* lots of money. Since this idea was so successful, they decided to bring it to businesses in Harvard Square. So, in 1986, they started a desktop publishing business, which they called Laser Design, and served various Harvard Square businesses in need of such services. After winning a contract to publish the Harvard Business School's weekly newspaper, they finally had the income to buy computers for the company. For most of the day, however, while they were in class, the computers stood idle and unused. In order to fully utilize those assets, they decided to rent the computers out to students during the day and publish at night.

They ran their company from rented office space in Harvard Square because there are rules at Harvard against running a business from your dorm room. After John and his colleagues had been in desktop publishing for a while, local businesses began to recognize their expertise and wanted them to do some work on-site. This gave them the idea to offer a temporary help service on Macintosh computers. At the time, this was really needed because most companies were IBM- and DOS-oriented. John reasoned that the differences between DOS and Macintosh computers were so great that if there was only one Macintosh computer temporary help company, it would get lots of business. He was right. They ran an ad in the Boston Computer Society's magazine, and in no time their phones started to ring off the hook. John and his collaborators had really tapped into an underserved niche. So they took advantage of this and quickly opened more offices in different areas.

The fact that Macintosh is now losing market share to PCs in the computer industry just makes John's company more relevant. But what's interesting is that they don't view their business as being Mac-oriented; rather they see it as being creative content–oriented. The company is called MacTemps, but John says that the name will probably change. They specialize in creative content personnel with both Macs and IBMs and also have the brand names Portfolio for creative content art and graphics, and Web-staff for World Wide Web work. Although Macintosh's market share is shrinking, 2 to 3 million Macintosh computers are still being sold each year. As a result, the Macintosh-based portion of MacTemps's revenue has grown about 25 percent each of the past three years.

Even with the steady growth of this +$100 million company, John has another vision for the future of his 10-year-old company. In the past, they've viewed themselves as a staffing company. In the future, they will view themselves as a company that helps independent workers develop their careers. This would be another big step for them from the days of desktop publishing and temporary help. To do this, they are molding their company from one that helps companies find people to one that helps people develop their careers. According to John, more and more people these days are working as independent contractors. When people work on their own, they need what are called the four C's in order to be successful: Contacts, to find work; Capital, to finance work; Capabilities, because as an independent worker, the more you learn the more you earn; and Community, to interact with people. John would like to mold MacTemps into a place where they can train independent workers in the four C's: MacTemps has no problem finding people jobs, but they are working on financial and training services for independent workers, and on fostering a sense of community that will bond their entire operation together. What seems like a vision right now may soon become yet another one of MacTemps's successful innovations.

John hasn't forgotten where all of this success originated. Remembering his own journey along the path of entrepreneurship, he knows that entrepreneurs have to be very resourceful. Often entrepreneurs have to work with unbelievable amounts of constraints, lacking experience, money, networks, contacts, and other resources. Entrepreneurs might have a great idea, but in order to overcome the constraints, they have to be very resourceful in solving problems. It is also very important that entrepreneurs target and address a specific market need. Without a proper product, they are not going to be able to buy or market their way to success. For example, when Coca-Cola wanted to enter the orange juice market, it bought Minute Maid, plowed millions of dollars into advertising, and made itself a player. But an entrepreneur can't do that. To enter the orange juice market, an entreprencur has to create a better orange juice, make it in a better way, package it in a better way, or find some other way to deliver it that really answers a market need. The entrepreneur has to contribute something that society needs or wants, according to John.

John also believes that entrepreneurs might sometimes feel impatient or unwilling to work through a system since "they have a vision of how things could be and want to bring the world to that vision faster." Entrepreneurs also tend to have a can-do attitude where they feel that they're always operating in the realm of what's possible, how things can get done, not why they can't be done. Entrepreneurs encounter obstacles every day, but to solve them, entrepreneurs just have to tackle them one at a time and be confident that they can overcome them one way or another. Finally, John says, entrepreneurs constantly have to be learning. They have to know what they don't know and constantly strive to learn it.

This was certainly true for John himself because it was college that opened up the world of business for him. If he hadn't worked for the *Harvard Political Review*, it is likely that MacTemps would not be in existence today. John believes that college really opens up your eyes to see the world. College also enabled him to meet interesting people and create a network of friends, and many of them work with him now. Finally, college allowed him to gain a formal education. According to John, it doesn't even matter what you major in. He has employees who majored in philosophy, biochemistry, and all sorts of other fields. "The thing is, these are smart people who know analysis, can be very thoughtful, know how to look at issues, and have the discipline and logic to know how to think about them. These are basic skills even for life in general and are learned in school. It's how to think—how to learn how to learn."

John was so keen on education that he went to Harvard Business School while still in the process of growing his company. He decided to go to business school as a substitute for the typical postgraduate experience.

Because John had never worked at any other companies besides summer jobs, in order to be able to experience the world of business he would either have to neglect his company and work for a number of years elsewhere or just go straight to school. He chose the latter and felt that going to business school allowed him to go faster up the learning curve than if he had learned it all by himself. He learned a lot about business in a very rapid and structured way, and it paid off. Previously, John had no exposure to high-level finance, manufacturing, sophisticated marketing, international issues, or any of a number of other topics covered in business school. Although John truly believes "it was a great experience," he is aware that "you still have to keep on learning even after. You have to learn continuously, never stop."

Now, as a successful entrepreneur who has had lots of exposure to business, John is able to give advice to would-be entrepreneurs. For those who would really like to start their own companies, John has one piece of advice: "Follow your dreams." He would encourage college students to start companies because "the best time to learn and start a business is when you're young and don't have so many risks and dependents. That's the time when you can explore many creative and crazy things." Additionally, he believes the naïveté of inexperienced college students is important because "experience may give you a sense of realism and that may sometimes be damaging. If you are hardened by bureaucracy, you might not do all the kinds of crazy things that turn out to work. [But] if you really have a burning desire to do it, then do what you love. There's no reason to torture yourself saying you have to do this and that. And you'll struggle to start your own business but that will teach you a lot. An entrepreneur wants to do it, loves to do it, wakes up every day feeling challenged, and has lots of fun."

As for people who start businesses not for the love, but for the money, John still encourages them to try. However, to John, "profits are like oxygen. You need it for life, but you need much more than that." At least for John, just earning profits would not be satisfying enough. He views his company as having a mission: to contribute to the world in a meaningful way by helping people develop their careers. He believes that a company's ultimate mission should be to enhance people's lives, help solve a problem, or help do something better. Ultimately, John predicts, people who do it just for the money won't have the commitment and are likely to sell out.

John certainly has come a long way. He had a "pretty middle class" upbringing in New York City and attended public schools. His parents had money, but not enough to throw around or fund a start-up company. Also, his parents didn't have connections. What is refreshing is that all of his partners have similar backgrounds and are living proof that people can be successful in business without "parents this, parents that," as John puts it. Business is something he has always wanted to do, so he just pursued his dreams. Every so often, though, he does get away from business to play "all kinds of sports" or hang out with people, but his mind is never far from his company. Even if he is not physically there, his thoughts are still on business, because that's what he loves. "You have to love what you do and be good at it. Then just work and it'll be great."

Ian Eslick

Cofounder, Silicon Spice, Inc. (www.silicon-spice.com)
Massachusetts Institute of Technology '96 (Computer Science/Electrical Engineering)
Founded company during fifth year of five-year undergraduate/master's program at MIT

Growing up on a farm with cows, pigs, and chickens in a small town in Washington State, Ian Eslick was a very shy child. He attended a typical high school and didn't really believe that he understood people. However, somewhere along the way, he started meeting "real" people and consequently gained more confidence in everything that he did. He became an A student, and became interested in music, history, liberal arts, and computer science. To Ian, "CS [computer science] problems are like an obsession—they totally eat up your life." So, when it came to deciding where to go to college, he chose the Massachusetts Institute of Technology and pursued his interests in computer science through a variety of different avenues. He worked at MIT's Artificial Intelligence lab all five years. Sometime during his junior year, he was doing some supercomputer work and found lots of things done "wrong," not to his satisfaction. He felt a need to correct them, and found that this type of work was his forte. He had a friend at MIT who told him, "You should go start businesses," and Ian took that advice to heart.

Deciding that working in a big company would be "no fun," he sought to test his entrepreneurial talents by entering the MIT $50K Entrepreneurial Competition in 1995. After succeeding in the competition, his team decided to try and start up the company. So, in October 1995, Ian and fellow collaborators Ethan Mirsky and Robert French decided to start Silicon Spice, Inc. Looking back, Ian is still amazed that he had the "gall" to do it because there were lots of barriers facing them.

Since they are still in the start-up phase, the specifics of their core technology are still confidential. However, the information they have released bodes well for their venture. According to the company's web site, they are "a semiconductor start-up developing a completely new technology that will dramatically alter the telecommunications industry. We're not using the same approach as a hundred other communications companies. We're designing a revolutionary new signal processing architecture to create unprecedented performance in telecommunications applications. In short, we're making some basic changes in the way people communicate."

The company has made great strides in the past year or two. In 1996, they met with Rob Ryan, founder of Ascend Communications, a $7 billion company. Ian describes him as "the guy who is committed to making things work." After receiving $3.3 million in venture capital in March 1997, they finished their core technology and in April 1998, they raised another $7 million. The company now has blossomed from 3 people to 35, and they are hoping to get a product out pretty soon. Also in April, they named Vinod Dham their President and CEO. Dham was previously Vice President and General Manager of Intel and Advanced Micro Devices (AMD), overseeing Intel's 486 and Pentium developments and AMD's K6 development. Some people describe Dham as the "father of the Pentium."

With the success of the company so far, Ian is at a very exciting point in his life. He owes the success of his company to the team. He makes the point that the team should be a close-knit bunch of hardworking and passionate people. Teamwork is essential. In fact, he was previously involved in start-up ventures that failed or broke up because of personality differences, not problems with technology. In Ian's mind, it all starts with a team.

But what made Ian even want to start a company? He attributes it to his desire to create something, to engineer and build things. He is very interested in inventing and building something that's tangible. He says that one of the most important things (especially in high-tech) is "to do things not because they've been done before but because they're the right things to do." Ian constantly asks himself "Why do this?" in order to question his own work. He strongly believes in doing what one feels is important, not what everybody else is doing.

Ian wasn't born with the conviction that what is important to him is "right." In fact, he was a very shy child, but his experiences at MIT changed some things about him. He felt that the attitude at MIT was to convince people to break through traditional models and "do it for yourself" or "solve the problem the way you think it should be solved." MIT, a school Ian believes focuses on teaching students how to think, taught him how to learn. Additionally, for Ian, college was an opportunity to learn how to deal with the world and with people. Thus, he also owes a great deal of his success and who he is today to his college experience.

But who is he today? Ian believes he has through his experiences and hard lessons "inherited" some qualities that entrepreneurs should have.

He is the first to recognize that entering the world of business, especially through start-ups, is a brutal process. There is not a single start-up that doesn't go wrong somewhere along the line. Because of that, entrepreneurs need to be determined and persevering. Entrepreneurs also need to possess what Ian calls a "skeptical faith." He explains that one must have faith that he or she is going to get there, but at the same time, one cannot be blind or complacent—one must continually question oneself. And finally, he believes that entrepreneurs need charisma, because in the beginning they must convince people to invest in them.

Having been involved in this start-up company for many years, Ian has gained some experience from which he can advise those just entering the world of entrepreneurship. His first piece of advice is to "ask yourself why" because one needs to commit and make sure one knows what one is getting into. The second is to think and rethink the idea to see if it is compelling enough to base a company on. He suggests that new entrepreneurs talk to people who have been there before. His final piece of advice is to "just go do it" because "you can't sit and think forever. At some point, you have to commit."

Ian certainly has committed and it has done wonders for him. However, he does not forget the influences of many people close to him. His parents encouraged him to see the world and always told Ian to "be who you want to be." Ian also learned some audacity from a history teacher in high school who told his class, "You be the historian. History is interpretation, not fact. You decide." A geometry teacher in high school told Ian that he was incredibly bright, but never really applied himself and that unless he did, he wouldn't get into MIT. That is part of what really woke him up and turned him into an A student. After getting to MIT, his first-year physics tutor effectively told him, "Ian, you fooled me the entire first year. You can talk about the physics, but you can't do the math. You need to do as well as understand." This led him to be more applied about the way he did his work.

So although Ian is working very hard on progressing his company, he tries to keep some balance in his life. When not at the office, he loves to be outdoors. In fact, he says that if he can't get away to a mountain at least once a year, he'll go crazy. He loves various outdoor activities such as rafting, canoeing, climbing cliffs, playing with mountain goats, and just "being on the edge." He loves adventures. In fact, it's difficult for Ian to decide whether start-ups are adventures or business opportunities. He thinks adventure is hard to come by and entrepreneurship is one of the most adventuresome undertakings.

Entrepreneurship is something that Ian truly cherishes in life. As a very spiritual person, he believes that "when you die, it's the people you know and the experiences you have that will define your life." One has to do what one loves to do. Every so often, Ian asks himself if he were to die tomorrow, would he still be doing the same thing? He answers a big yes to entrepreneurship.

Jacob Farmer

Founder, Cambridge Computer Services, Inc. (www.camcom.com)
Yale University '89 (History)
Founded company during first year at Yale

"My business started much the same way as Michael Dell's [the billionaire founder of Dell Computers]," laments Jacob, "except his mother let him quit school and pursue his fortune." Jacob is now the president of Cambridge Computer Services of Boston, a business that had its origins in a dorm room at Yale University over 10 years ago. Jacob and his college roommate Ron stumbled into the computer industry while looking for deals on computers to use for their schoolwork. Computers were just then becoming affordable for students to own, and Jacob, through a family friend in the computer industry, had gotten a wholesale deal on a computer that became the envy of his roommate and a few other friends who also wanted to get in on the deal.

Jacob's family friend suggested he contact his company's distributor and pretend to be a computer store looking for a new supplier. When he tried that, Jacob found out that he only needed a few key pieces of information in order to buy wholesale—a company name, a tax resale number, and a street address, not a post office box. Without much hesitation, Jacob and Ron decided to go into business selling computers. So, they made up the company name University Computers and put together the other pieces of the puzzle just as easily. The tax resale number, which cost $20, came by getting a permit from the State Department of Revenue. And as for the street address, they found a store equivalent to the Mailboxes, Etc. chain that agreed to use the word "Suite" instead of "Post Office Box." And University Computers was born. It was just that easy for them to start a "business." Jacob says, "Starting University Computers killed two birds with one stone. First we got our computers cheap, and second, we had a project to call our own despite the fact that we were freshmen on a big campus." As freshmen, they thought they had to "pay their dues" before they could "call the shots."

What is interesting about his story is that after graduating from Yale, Jacob had no intention of going into this business after college. At that time, he thought the best thing for him was to find a nice secure job in corporate America. Like most of his classmates, he pursued on-campus recruiting and landed a job with a computer technology consulting firm in the Boston area. It was there he realized that "once you're self-employed, it's very hard not to be self-employed." In other words, he would always desire to change things, to make things better, and to do things his way. As Jacob tells the story, "I thought I had great ideas and solutions to some of the problems, but my employers were not looking for their new recruits to take over the place. Corporate America likes energy and intellect, but creativity and independence in new recruits are synonymous with unmanageability and recklessness." Jacob lasted with the firm a brief two months before what he describes as being "unceremoniously hurled out the front door."

Having not succeeded at his first job in corporate America, Jacob tried again, interviewing at consulting firms and investment banks. At this point, he still didn't think his buy-and-sell company was going to be his career. In the meantime, he did need to support himself, so he went back to what he knew how to do—buying and selling computer equipment. Near the end of 1990, he put an ad in the classified ads to sell computers. Shortly afterward, he went home for the holidays, and when he came back, his 60-minute answering machine tape was entirely full. He had hundreds of callers around the clock. At that time, the economy was in bad shape. Jacob explains, "When the economy is bad, people look to automate, and when it is really bad, they look to automate cheap." Jacob found that "real companies" and major universities were reading the classifieds looking for deals on computers. Also, he didn't have much of a sense of the value of his time, so he always went for technical support at a customer's beckoning. This won the favor of many because "the happiest customers are the ones who've had a bad experience turned positive" since they feel as though the company really came through. With a partner, Jacob started Cambridge Computer Services and he still has some of his first customers from 1990.

Even though there is an enormous amount of work to do in running your own business, Jacob found that there were only a few basic things required for his business: a company name, answering the phone, and a great amount of energy and enthusiasm. For his service business, this energy needs to go into writing well, thinking on one's feet, and communicating. Some of these skills he learned at college. As a history major at Yale, he learned a form of audacity, a willingness to question authority. For example, when his history professors gave him two experts' conflicting views on an issue and asked Jacob for his take on it, he learned to question the authority of these experts. College also gave him a broad perspective and taught him many life skills. He didn't learn any skills that directly applied to computer technology, but he did learn how to interact with people, how to resolve conflicts, and how to deal with personal politics. In his business, knowing how to interact with customers is of utmost importance, even more important than knowing computers.

Having graduated almost 10 years ago, Jacob stresses that college students, if so inclined, should go out and try to start a business, because the stakes are low. College students have fewer responsibilities than they will have later in life. Because of this, he believes that college is a great time to try out the business world and see what happens. Even if one fails, one doesn't really lose much, so it would be worth the risk. Jacob believes in taking calculated risks and learning via trial and error, something that he tries to teach all his employees. He thinks that one must have a strong ego, not a large one, so that he or she can learn from failure and not make the mistake again. People who are so inclined perhaps possess some of the qualities that Jacob has or thinks entrepreneurs should have.

Jacob was "born with a nose for a dollar." He sold seeds as a five-year-old, greeting cards when he was seven, had a candy business through elementary school, and had a snow-shoveling business in high school, so it is his nature to be entrepreneurial. He believes that "a really good entrepreneur has an idea, looks at the idea, thinks how big could this be, dreams up how big it could be, and then works backwards from there." He says that entrepreneurs are like visionaries. All too often, he hears people say, "If I had known then what I know now, I could've made millions." Well, although nobody has a crystal ball, entrepreneurs see something and have the audacity to think it should work a certain way and then do it. This audacity together with the self-esteem which translates into not fearing failure makes for a very entrepreneurial mix of qualities.

Ten years later, Jacob is still in business with a very successful company of 17 people and growing. The products and services have changed to reflect changes in the industry, but the underlying themes prevail. He believes that he will be self-employed for life even if he doesn't stick with this particular business for the rest of his life. He also tries to help some would-be entrepreneurs. He chooses employees who could go out there and do it for themselves, and provides an environment that allows them all of the challenges without all of the personal risks. Jacob's company provides a cushion. But in his early 30s, Jacob is also looking toward other things in life.

He believes that one of the pitfalls of being self-employed is that there's really no end to it. Jacob explains: "The greatest challenge of the entrepreneur is striking a balance between work and personal life." Because building a business is an entrepreneur's passion, something he or she is self-motivated to do, he or she is constantly thinking about it. One could be on a vacation and still be thinking about it. In this sense, the business isn't a job, it's play. To see this, ask the question, Is a painter working or painting? Jacob views the business as a big project that happens to be his source of income as well. Entrepreneurs tend to work very hard and put in very long hours, and other interests can fall by the wayside. "The problem is not that you are working extended hours, because you are doing something you love doing," Jacob says. "The problem is that the business consumes your creative energies, and if you are not careful, it can take over your life." Jacob does not regret the time he put into the business, but believes that the rules change as you get older. He certainly couldn't imagine starting a business like his at age 30, which is why he strongly believes that college and the years immediately after graduation are the best times to start entrepreneurial ventures.

Jacob has much more advice for people who want to undertake their own entrepreneurial ventures. According to him, a business doesn't have to be glorious or fabulous. One should just set up shop and go to work. People should recognize who they are and where they are in life, because each piece of success is coupled with a risk, so one must make sure the stakes are worth it. One should trust oneself to be the decision maker and one's own boss. "If you try and fail, just dust yourself off and try again," Jacob says. With a smirk, Jacob has two final pieces of advice to offer: "Get yourself a book on accounting, and get a lawyer to do your incorporation." What great advice from this successful entrepreneur!

Gregg Favalora

Founder, Actuality Systems, Inc. (www.actuality-systems.com)
Yale University '96 (Electrical Engineering)
Founded company immediately after graduation from Yale

"We provide true three-dimensional display devices," proclaims Gregg Favalora, founder of Actuality Systems, Inc. Gregg (the inventor) and some other technologists have worked on these devices for a number of years and are very excited about the potential of this technology. What they do is make a display box that hooks up to a computer, but instead of having a flat screen they have a volumetric one—the images float inside it and occupy a volume. The user does not need any accessories such as goggles or other gadgets to view the three-dimensional display. It is kind of like a hologram. Furthermore, multiple people can walk around to view the floating imagery from anywhere in the room all at the same time. This technology can be used in any of a number of applications. It can be used in designing pharmaceuticals and automobiles, playing shoot-'em-up games, diagnosing ailments, building houses, and any other application in which three-dimensional display would be beneficial.

In 1988, the summer after eighth grade, Gregg saw the movie *Real Genius* in which there was scene where lasers were used to draw a girl in a bikini. "Well, instead of noticing the women in bikinis, I was noticing the lasers," remarks Gregg, with a grin. At the time, his father owned a laser, so Gregg started playing with it to come up with ideas for making his own three-dimensional display. This fit right into Gregg's hobbies and interests. Gregg's grandfather, an electrical engineer, had taught him how to solder when he was only five years old. Ever since Gregg was young, his hobby has been to take things apart and put things together. In fact, he was an amateur radio operator and used to make small electronic gadgets in high school. Once, he and a friend challenged each other to see who could make the "coolest" thing to fit inside a Tic Tac box. Gregg made a radio that had a plug for headphones, but his friend made a full stereo amplifier. Gregg gave up on this challenge, but ever since he noticed the lasers (not the bikinis) in the movie, 3-D display technology became his project. Whenever he had free time, he would spend it researching and testing his own ideas.

He continued to work on this idea through high school, though at times he felt discouraged. At Yale, he presented the idea to a professor by the name of Peter Kindlmann, the inventor of Indiglo, and he encouraged Gregg to keep working on his idea and even funded him to do this as his senior project. Gregg's hard work proved successful and he was able to build a working prototype of his 3-D display system. In fact, it was such a great innovation that the summer after he graduated from Yale, Gregg was a winner of the BFGoodrich Collegiate Inventors Program.

After Gregg invented and built a successful prototype, he decided he wanted to sell his technology. He got his chance when he ran into one of the organizers of what is now the MIT $50K Entrepreneurship Competition. He entered the 1997 competition, teamed up with some partners, and the seven of them put together a business plan for what they called Eastern Delta Corporation. Their invention, business plan, and presentation were so impressive that the judges named them runners-up in this prestigious competition. This distinction got them a $10,000 prize, a lot of time with lawyers, and much publicity.

After the $50K competition they all went their separate ways and Gregg worked alone for four months to get his company going. He then met up with Rob Ryan, founder of Ascend Communications, and got him to serve as chairman of the board of the company, now called Actuality Systems, Inc. With the wisdom he has gained from many years of experience, Rob said to Gregg: "Go get people and get the technical aspects of this thing done." So Gregg interviewed many people, and by word of mouth brought into the company two very good technologists—Mike Giovinco and Shawn Samuel, both recent Harvard graduates. Ever since then, they have been working very closely and very hard to get all the technical aspects done. They have also been showing their core technology to many potential customers to get a sense of the market. Soon enough, they will have everything lined up and be ready to seek venture capital. Once they get funding, they hope to bring in more people, get some office space, and very rapidly move into formal product design.

Although Gregg is currently pursuing his business, he is also a Ph.D. student on leave from Harvard. If he gets funding, he will pursue his company. If not, then he will consider going back to graduate school. But how does he know when to stop seeking funding? He doesn't know for sure but says there will come a time when he will have to leave. Although he's spent over 10 years on this and it would be very hard, Gregg has enough foresight to know that such a time could come. One important aspect of entrepreneurship is to know when to let go.

But he is very hopeful for the future of this business venture and has certainly benefited from the support of many people close to him. In fact, Gregg believes that support from people is very key to starting a successful business. To him, it is somewhat strange being an entrepreneur. Gregg says, "There are sort of no rules. You don't wake up and do assigned problem sets anymore. You have to decide."

In this game with no rules called entrepreneurship, Gregg believes that the players have certain qualities that make them entrepreneurs. He says, "They probably come from a supportive family. They are not afraid to think differently. They're usually bright though you don't have to be all that smart to make money. You have to be very passionate about what you do. You have to care very little about what other people think. You have to have a strong desire and hopefully want to do good with your technology. . . . You have to be imaginative, and willing to hire people smarter than yourself." But Gregg is not so sure when the question of ego comes up. Does an entrepreneur want a big ego or not? Gregg sees both sides of the coin. A big ego would get in the way of thinking rationally. On the other hand, a strong ego would give one self-confidence and the guts to disregard discouragement from others.

At this point in his life, Gregg is very excited and encouraged, though he admits it's a bit scary. For one thing, he has to wrestle with the fact that his technology could be used for a lot of military applications. Also, he has to spend an enormous amount of time on his company. He recalls once when he was up until 4 A.M. working on his invention. "I [woke up] and a resistor fell out of my bed!" Along with all the time he spends, he has to deal with the constant uncertainty that goes along with starting up a business. At least to him, this is fun. He is doing something that has been his hobby for 10 years and is what he loves to do.

Amar Goel

Founder, Chip Shot Golf (www.chipshotgolf.com)
Harvard College '98 (Computer Science)
Founded company during second year at Harvard

Hailing from the entrepreneurial mecca that is the Silicon Valley, Amar Goel is no stranger to business. From a young age, he has had many ideas and a business-oriented mind-set. As a child, he wanted to sell chicken eggs. In high school, he wanted to start an SAT class. And in college, he wanted to start an entertainment magazine for college students during the summer after his freshman year. Unfortunately, the required start-up capital (about $100,000) was too great and it kept him from realizing his dream. So Amar started looking for another idea. Perhaps influenced by his parents, who both work in the Silicon Valley, Amar found a love of computers. In his first couple of years at Harvard, he had been doing some computer consulting jobs with friends. He found it difficult to expand in consulting because one can only do so much work. He wanted a business in which he could really leverage himself. So he thought of software. With software, one can program a copy and sell as many copies as there are new customers. The cost of producing one additional unit is virtually nil. Amar decided to look into a derivative of software: electronic commerce. Selling things over the Internet via a web site is, says Amar, "pretty much like [selling] software. If you do it right, you can serve a million."

Having played on the Harvard golf team for two years, Amar noticed in 1995 that the demographics of the people who had access to the web and those who played golf were very similar. So in August of that year, he started Chip Shot Golf, a company on the Internet that sells golf equipment—both brand-name (25 percent of sales) and custom-made (75 percent of sales). His company has contracted with manufacturers and tailors, and has made a proprietary piece of technology called PerfectFit which fits people to golf equipment based on their measurements and specifications—entirely online. Other sites don't have competing technology, so Chip Shot Golf has many customers looking to buy custom-made golf equipment. Additionally, each summer they have completely revamped the web site to move the business forward. During the year, Amar mainly deals with customers and doesn't get a chance to redo the site.

But as the company has grown, from sales of $5,000 in 1995 to $120,000 in 1997, the company has been hiring additional employees. Amar brought in one person to take over technology, one to focus on marketing, and now the business grows 30 to 50 percent per month. Amar expects Chip Shot Golf to have about $1 million in sales in 1998. They are even entering into lots of deals with various golf and e-commerce sites on the Internet to expand their business further. They've established themselves as the leading seller of custom-made golf equipment on the Internet.

Having recently graduated, Amar and a few of his colleagues have passed up the job market and are going to continue with this growing business instead. Their next step is to try to get $0.5 to $2 million in venture capital. Amar thinks it's pretty interesting that their business has expanded so much because they haven't been doing that much marketing until recently. They simply listed with search engines and the customers came rolling in. According to Amar, "It just tells you how big the market is out there."

Although he has been extremely successful, Amar has had to make some sacrifices in college—most notably sleep. With the combination of this successful business, playing on the golf team for two years, his classes, and his social life, Amar was often very busy and had to sacrifice some sleep. But he thinks it was worth it because being busy is what he loves and thrives on. His parents have also been very supportive of his entrepreneurial ventures and support his decision to keep up this business after college. They understand that Amar would rather work for himself because he wants a lot of responsibility. Unless he's the CEO, he can't do a lot of things working for a big company in corporate America.

Looking back, Amar definitely thinks he gained a lot from his college experience. He says that it depends on what one does, but in general nothing one learns in college is going to be directly applicable to his or her future career. However, college has taught him how to think and has also allowed him to meet lots of people. Also, getting a degree gives a person instant credibility. Amar says, "College is like a chance to mature socially and academically. It's probably true that while some courses might not be applicable to your business life, they may be in your personal life. It's not useless."

As for his thoughts on entrepreneurship, Amar thinks entrepreneurs have to be creative, learn quickly, be decisive, and never give up. In the business world, there is inevitably a series of doubts. In the beginning, Amar didn't even think this company was that great of an idea. Now he is realizing that it's a pretty good idea even though it is not necessarily a complicated one. He didn't give up in the face of hardship. Of course, one must know when to cut one's losses, but most people probably quit too early, according to Amar. A piece of advice he would give budding entrepreneurs is "Just do it." Amar is certain that there are many resources out there that aren't hard to acquire, such as books on starting a corporation. Also, one doesn't necessarily have to write a business plan to start a business. Amar says, "One has to start a business to start a business. It's a matter of getting out there and doing it. You make mistakes along the way, but you don't want to sit there saying you don't have a plan because you won't start it that way. If you can't adapt to change, then you can't be an entrepreneur."

Being the entrepreneur that he is, Amar will want to move on from Chip Shot Golf eventually. They are indeed successful, but he only wants to run this company for maybe four or five more years. He doesn't view the product to be intellectually challenging enough and he wants to move on to bigger and better things—to start up a billion-dollar company. His life's goal is to start several large companies. Also, sometime in the near future, he would like to work for an investment banking firm like Goldman Sachs or a management consulting firm like McKinsey. His reason for desiring this experience shows a lot of planning on his part. He says, "The reason I want to work there is so that when I start my $100 million company, I don't get removed from the CEO position when the venture capital guys come."

Always looking for bigger and better things, Amar is driven and loves business because it's a lot of fun. It is very appealing to him because he gets to do what he wants. To Amar, it is very satisfying to create a company that provides enough value to society that people want to work for it. "It's like a game."

Krisztina Holly

Cofounder, Stylus Innovation, Inc. (www.stylus.com)
Massachusetts Institute of Technology '89 (Mechanical Engineering)
Founded company while in graduate school at MIT

Ever since she was a young girl, Krisztina Holly always thought she would start a company because her father had started one. However, she didn't think she would start one in college—it just sort of happened. She and a group of classmates were assigned a project in a class at MIT to create a computer-based product to help the elderly stay independent longer. And what they came up with eventually became their company's first product.

Stylus Innovation originally started with a product that was a bar code wand that could be used to order items or communicate over the telephone. For example, someone could take a catalog of groceries with bar codes on them and order them over the phone line by scanning the wand over the bar codes. This information would be transferred using touch tones to a computer at the store, which could take that information and feed back, for example, "Peaches 59 cents." It turned out that this device was more applicable to people ordering groceries or companies that might have a closed system for the sales representatives than to the elderly, but it was the first project that got them going. So they (Krisztina, Mike Cassidy, and John Barrus) decided to start a company based on this product. Their first step was to enter and win in 1991 what is now the MIT $50K Entrepreneurship Competition. At this time, the company was using the name Dial-A-Fish. Entering and winning the competition was a very good experience because it really made them focus on presenting their ideas and also led them to many good contacts.

After incorporating the company a year later, they decided to license this original idea to a company called Direct Data, which gave them enough capital to change directions and turn into a software company. In fact, they were even more successful with the computer telephone software products they developed and, in 1996, Stylus Innovation, Inc. was sold to Artisoft, Inc. for $12.8 million.

Krisztina left a few months after the company was sold and she made sure everything was in place. She "retired" for nine months to figure out what to do with her life. Now she does video and television documentary production and editing and really enjoys it. She enjoys teaching people and hopes to change people's attitudes about science, math, and technology. That's a pretty huge goal and she doesn't know if she'll ever get there, but she hopes her work will at least make technology more accessible to people.

Another thing she is doing right now is serving as president of the New England Mountain Biking Association which has over 1,000 members and runs lots of special programs. Because this association gets its work done through volunteers, she's thought a lot about motivating volunteers and also her motivating factors. She is a great example of the well-roundedness seen in many entrepreneurs. Krisztina discovered that she likes challenges and to make things happen. When she sees an opportunity, she gets excited about it.

She has seen lots of fellow students start companies and noticed that the more successful ones are started by people who have an idea and start a company because they feel passionate about it. This is in contrast to the people whose entire goal is to start a company and who are looking around for ideas, according to her. In her experience, it was her team's passion that made the company successful.

Of course, she also had to have the business and technological skills to make her business successful. She learned some business skills through the MIT $50K competition, advice from people, and design courses at MIT that stressed marketing. Technically, Krisztina specialized in mechanical engineering and product design. Though she did pick up some useful skills in college, Krisztina doesn't think that people necessarily have to come into something with a specific set of skills in order to be successful. She feels that people who are smart, have a broad view, and are willing to work hard are the best players. "You just have to roll with the punches," says Krisztina.

But though she was able to pick up some useful skills in college, Krisztina believes that "the key to school is to learn how to learn, [because] you're never going to be able to learn, in school, the exact skills and knowledge that you're going to need for the exact thing." Moreover, school is not only a learning experience, but a social one. "You just can't beat it—the kinds of experiences you get and the socializing with people who have the same passions and aspirations as you. The most important things you learn are social."

A lot of people believe that all entrepreneurs are risk takers, but Krisztina doesn't see it that way. In fact, she doesn't consider herself to be a risk taker as much as people looking at her from the outside might. She admits that she sticks her neck out a lot, but she doesn't take risks for risk's sake, she takes calculated risks. She goes out on a limb because she's confident about the strength of that limb. Especially with experience, one realizes how he or she can get out of a jam so one doesn't take unnecessary risks.

Also through her experience, Krisztina discovered that "absolutely, hands down, the biggest quality of entrepreneurs is passion. That can manifest itself in different ways. Volunteers can be entrepreneurial. People working for larger companies can be entrepreneurial. And some people decide to show that by starting their own company. It's just passion, you have to believe in what you're doing." One must have passion, but one also can't be stubborn. "You have to have an open mind, be open to criticism, and not be so insecure that you take things personally," she says. In addition, she would caution entrepreneurs who have invented something new against being paranoid about people stealing their ideas. According to Krisztina, "It's hard enough to try to sell your idea to somebody, but to convince them that not only should they buy one, they should make one themselves and try to market it is a lot more difficult. So sometimes people are a lot more paranoid than they should be about that." But her strongest advice is still passion. She says, "If you're passionate about something, follow your dreams. [Don't] listen to people who tell you it's too difficult, but do listen to people who have suggestions and ideas."

She would also advise people starting up companies to "keep a balance in your life." Because there can be a lot of work involved in starting a company, there may be a point at which the founders just work and do little else. That is to be expected, but she would advise such founders to "fit in some sort of social life, be happy." One last piece of advice: "Don't do it for the money because if you do, you're in the wrong business." Krisztina considers herself lucky, but she certainly didn't do it for the money. If she did, she might have made the wrong choices by being motivated by the money. "Very few companies actually survive, but that doesn't mean you don't get something out of it other than money," says Krisztina. "If at any point you start doubting that what you've gone through so far is valuable, you shouldn't do it anymore. At any point, you should be able to say, 'If everything fails at this point, it was worth it.'"

Krisztina has certainly kept that attitude throughout her entire life—she has always been very passionate about something. Krisztina was born in Boston but grew up in Los Angeles. In high school, she was serious about scuba diving and underwater photography to the extent that she became a scuba instructor as soon as she turned 18. Later in high school, she got into bass guitar and played in a couple of bands at MIT, one of which won the "battle of the bands" contest one year. In graduate school, her passion was the company. Now she is very much into mountain biking and her job producing and editing educational videos.

Krisztina has been influenced greatly by a number of people close to her. Both of her parents courageously escaped from Hungary and she respects that very much. She had a coach in high school who showed her that she could do anything she really wanted to. Krisztina is the first to admit that she "was not athletic back then." But still, she "went from fourth- to first-string basketball the first year," which she owes at least partially to the encouragement of her coach. He simply had an attitude that gave her lots of confidence. She strongly believes that "it's really important to have that feeling that you can do it if you really want to." She hopes that all budding entrepreneurs have such a feeling.

Mike Itagaki

Founder, Kimberlyte, Inc. (www.kimberlyte.com)
Harvard College '98 (Chemistry)
Founded company between first and second years at Harvard

Ever since his high school years in Honolulu, Hawaii, Mike Itagaki has been a chemistry buff. In between the tennis team, rifle club, scuba diving, and sailing, Mike was introduced to advanced chemistry in tenth grade and has been in love with the subject ever since. So naturally, when he came to Harvard College to major in chemistry, he took organic chemistry in his freshman year. A very challenging class which covers an enormous amount of material, organic chemistry forced many people to find ways to study other than reading the book—note cards, modeling sets, using recommended (but not required) textbooks. Mike noticed this phenomenon and was himself a part of it. After his first year at Harvard, he decided to take a semester off from school. While reflecting about his organic chemistry class, he found no reason why he couldn't design (and start a business with) a piece of software that would encapsulate all of the information found in the various study aids that students used. Because first-year organic chemistry is pretty standard throughout the country, many students could use this software and avoid burdening themselves with making less detailed note cards and study aids on their own.

He started on this venture during the fall of 1994 and quickly found out that to be successful he had to wear many hats. At that point, Mike was a chemistry student, not a computer programmer or businessman. Starting from scratch, he first used books to teach himself C and programmed a Macintosh version of organic chemistry tutorial software. He found learning a computer language on his own to be difficult but very intellectually challenging and he was certainly up to the task. After finishing the first version, he put it up on a web site and the response was modest. Professors thought it was a decent piece of software and some people started to use it. However, it wasn't enormously successful, so Mike decided to be more serious about this venture. He incorporated Kimberlyte in the spring of 1995 and programmed a more sophisticated version which included professional-looking illustrations he drew using a program called ChemDraw. However, at that time, he also came back to Harvard for the spring semester, so he was faced with the challenge of balancing his business with school. His solution was to sacrifice the possibility of rapid expansion for the security of low overhead. Because his company was entirely Internet-oriented, he faced very low costs—for the most part, just the cost of running a web site and spending his time. The Internet also allowed him to run his company from many places. His company was incorporated in Hawaii, but he runs his business from Massachusetts or anywhere else he happens to be.

Along the lines of taking this business more seriously, Mike decided to expand his product line by programming a Windows version for the PC. During the summer of 1995, he again taught himself another computer programming language—C++—and worked full-time to program a Windows version during the summer. This version really sold and taught Mike a lesson in market share. Because Windows machines have a much larger share of the computer market, there are many more potential customers for a Windows version than a Macintosh version. Not long after the Windows version was released, it was recommended to a class at the University of Ohio, which ordered $7,000 worth of product. But he still wanted to "capture" the entire market, so he decided to program an improved Macintosh version during the summer of 1996. He did a much better job on this version because he was much more experienced at computer programming. But even so, the Macintosh version has since sold only two copies whereas the Windows version has sold hundreds.

Having pretty much achieved his goal with the organic chemistry tutorial software—programming a working piece of software that sold hundreds of copies—Mike decided in the summer of 1997 to take his company in a new direction through an idea he had discovered while promoting his chemistry tutorial software. To promote his software on the Internet, Mike visited many chemistry-related web sites to find the e-mail addresses of potential customers. He cut and pasted these addresses to send out e-mail advertising his product. However, this got to be a very tedious task, so he sought to make it more efficient. This is where his next idea came in. Mike taught himself the Java programming language to program a web browser that could find targeted e-mail addresses. For example, Mike could use this program to compile a list of 10,000 e-mail addresses of people who are interested in biochemistry.

Such a program definitely could have broad implications in the area of marketing, but unfortunately, his quest in legitimizing this novel form of marketing has been hindered by the many irresponsible uses of e-mail advertising—pornography, get-rich-quick schemes, and other illegitimate services sent to millions of e-mail addresses. Mike believes that everything could be much more legitimate and responsible if, for example, instead of sending 40 million e-mails to everyone offering, say, auto parts in Chicago, one could send 7,000 to Chicago mechanics. He believes this form of advertising can work really well because the Internet has offered an unprecedented opportunity to market. It must be further legitimized, but Mike believes he has positioned himself very well to capitalize on this technology if it expands. Though this idea goes into uncharted territory, it has been met with some support. In February, Mike was awarded the first-place award in the Harvard Student Agencies Entrepreneurial Contest.

In the future, Mike would like to continue to develop more ideas and grow his company. He is also starting an M.D./M.B.A. program at the University of Illinois at Urbana-Champaign in the fall to get a joint medical and business degree. Having always been a chemist and now a businessman, the program seems to match Mike's interests very well. He hopes that his self-acquired computer skills and knowledge in medicine may help him develop ideas in medical informatics, a field that has recently sparked his interest.

For people interested in starting their own businesses while in college, Mike would advise them to be aware that to be a successful businessperson, one has to wear many hats. In Mike's case, he had to develop products and market them at the same time. One also has to be willing to learn all the time to expand his or her base of knowledge. This must be done not only by reading books, but also by gaining experiences, because there are things one can only gain through experience. One also must be passionate and self-motivated. One must have that feeling inside oneself that just gives the entrepreneur the drive and energy to undertake this venture. Mike remembers times when he coded until 3 A.M. before finally going to sleep and then popping out of his bed at 7 A.M. and going right back to his computer even before he ate breakfast. This passion provides more energy than anything else. One also needs to be observant and realistic. This somewhat contradicts believing in one's idea, because to be realistic, one must think skeptically. However, it is necessary because one must know the existence of an ideal and the reality and be able to see the differences.

And at the same time, one must have some balance in life. It is true that starting a company takes a lot of time, but Mike finds a way to balance it with the rest of his life. He graduated from Harvard in February 1998 and makes it a point to get away from school and from his company every so often. He studies the martial arts, sails, and has recently been involved with kendo, a form of Japanese fencing. He believes that suiting up with armor and pounding your best friend with sticks is one of the best ways to relieve stress after a long week. Mike's life has been rather stressful balancing a growing company and schoolwork at Harvard and now the University of Illinois, but he is doing what he loves and that is the single largest motivating factor for him. Mike simply views his company and the whole business world as an adventure and he's in it for the chase.

Joshua Kanter

Founder, Joshua D. Kanter Painting
Harvard College '98 (Psychology)
Founded company during first year at Harvard

Joshua Kanter came home for winter break during his freshman year at Harvard and found in a stack of junk mail a letter with a message on the envelope proclaiming "How would you like to start your own business? Earn $8,000 to $10,000." Coming from an average household in Princeton township, this was an opportunity that Josh could not afford to ignore. He proceeded to call and find out that this involved starting up his own professional house-painting franchise under the company University Painters. Josh had never thought about painting a house, and never looked at a paintbrush, but the money was enticing.

So he decided to give it a try and went through the application process. He found it interesting that though it seemed like he was applying to be hired, he was actually applying to be his own boss. Even though he was part of a franchise, his experience was entrepreneurial in nature. To start this business, he would pay University Painters for training and ongoing support, but it would be Josh, not University Painters, who made all the decisions. Josh himself would carry the responsibilities of hiring, training, and firing employees, marketing, finances, sales, and everything else that came with running one's own business. Essentially he would pay the company for the benefit of their experience. Everything seemed reasonable, so he decided to enter into a franchise with University Painters and, as a freshman, he created Joshua D. Kanter Painting, a business he ran during the summers after his freshman and sophomore years.

Starting in February of his freshman year, he went into training. During spring break, he started marketing in Princeton by knocking on doors and saying, "Hi, my name is Joshua Kanter. I'm a manager with University Painters this summer and I was wondering if I could offer you a free estimate for any painting you might need on your house." He continued to do this the rest of his freshman year. Every other weekend, he commuted from Massachusetts to New Jersey to knock on more doors. He also advertised with door hangers, signs, and other marketing materials. By the time exams had ended in May, he had booked about 15 jobs with an average job size of $1,500 to $2,000.

When summer came along, he had to go about the second part of his venture—finding, training, and managing employees. According to University Painters, he should've worked about 60 to 70 hours a week during the summer but he ended up spending over 90 hours a week. For Josh, it was definitely harder than his classwork at Harvard. To find employees, he first made the mistake of hiring his friends but later ran an ad throughout the summer in the local newspaper. In his first summer, he did not want too many employees because he did not want to run out of work. He later discovered that if this happened, his 15 or so employees could just go out and drum up more work themselves. Thus, his sales increased from $50,000 the first year to over $100,000 the second year.

Though he enjoyed the challenge and the experience of running this successful business, Josh decided to give it up after two years because he wanted to branch out into the nonprofit sector working at the Princeton Center for Leadership Training. He gave the business to his brother, who ran it successfully for another year. But his two summers paid off. Not only did he earn lots of money, he learned the value of hard work and the love of painting.

Being a successful entrepreneur himself and meeting others both successful and not, Josh learned to appreciate certain qualities in those who were successful. For him, his business was a sink-or-swim situation and there was no way to prepare for some of the nightmares that came up. A successful entrepreneur has to improvise and make things happen through a results-oriented mind-set. They are tireless, motivated, extremely dedicated and focused, and have an undying optimism.

Josh certainly must have been dedicated and optimistic because he received lots of discouragement from family, friends, and even his girlfriend along the way. The people closest to him were afraid that he may get himself into a situation in which he would lose lots of money. But Josh felt that he was able to work smart and gain the experience that would make him successful. He was certainly overworked during his first summer, working almost 100 hours per week, but it was this experience that taught him how to work smart. Because he had already made all the mistakes and learned many lessons, he was able to work more efficiently and effectively the second year. In his second summer, he worked only 50 hours a week while doubling his sales. So even in the face of discouragement and doubt, a successful entrepreneur has perseverance, creativity, problem-solving skills, and unwavering motivation, focus, and desire.

Those are some things that Josh believes one can gain from an education. Josh believes very strongly that education is the most valuable thing in his life. Because he never took any economics or business classes, his education had no direct influence on his business. However, in college he learned how to articulate himself, to be expressive with words, to think clearly, and to spell out an argument from start to finish. For Josh, these skills were very helpful while running his business, but they are also life skills which he values very highly. His studies in social psychology have also helped him to win the favor of customers and pick up business skills more quickly. He also believes in asking questions, something that some students may shy away from in college.

While running his business, Josh asked many questions to people who were more experienced than he was. These included questions he probably should have known the answers to—so-called dumb questions. But the trick was that he only had to ask the questions once. By asking many questions, he was able to learn that much faster and make his business more efficient. He went from being a kid who didn't know anything about painting to being a very knowledgeable professional painter. This took him from being one of Princeton's least expensive painters the first summer to one of the most expensive the second summer. Thus, a piece of advice he would give is that one should always ask questions. Josh also believes that entrepreneurs need to have a willingness to be humbled. "There is real strength and real power in knowing what you don't know," he says. "You don't have to know the answer, but you have to be aware that you don't know the answer."

As for budding entrepreneurs, Josh would advise them to question their motives and be aware of what they are willing to sacrifice. According to Josh, if you're doing it just to make money, chances are it won't be enough incentive to keep you into it. "You must love what you're doing, be passionate about it, and find a serious reason why it is worth 100 hours of your time each week," he says. This is interesting, because he first got into business for the money. However, though that was his initial motivation, he grew to love it. He saw the business as a challenge and it became his life, something that really mattered to him. He thinks that entrepreneurs start businesses not so much for the money but more to see if they can do it, to succeed, and because it's their vision. Doing it for the money won't be as fulfilling as doing it for higher goals.

These goals may depend on personality, and Josh believes that some of his success comes from his personality. He describes himself as a flirt, very outgoing, loves people, and enjoys group activities. He plays jazz trumpet and was a local track hero at home. His success as a hurdler in high school gave him some name recognition when he first started offering painting jobs. Josh has overcome many hurdles to start and grow his business and hopes his story and experiences can benefit budding entrepreneurs.

Conclusion

We hope these stories of successful college entrepreneurs have given you insight into starting businesses and that you see how the topics we discussed in earlier chapters can be applied. We also hope you recognize that there is no one definition of success. Success can mean different things to different people. For some, the monetary profits (whether it's $10,000 or $10 million) outweigh all others. For others, it is the learning experience that is most valuable. Still, for others, conquering the challenges and overcoming the obstacles involved in starting a company provide the ultimate reward.

As is also clear from these profiles, one does not have to be Michael Dell to be a successful entrepreneur—many people of all sorts can succeed at starting a company. However, at least in terms of the people we profiled, they all had something in common: a passion, a drive for starting their own business. To them, in a larger sense, their entrepreneurial ventures are not jobs because it's what they love to do. They possess an entrepreneurial spirit that provides energy, motivation, and excitement in starting and growing their own businesses. Several of these young entrepreneurs have echoed again and again that if their company fails tomorrow then everything still would have been worth it.

The actress Jennifer Love Hewitt once formulated the motto "Always follow your heart" for a scholarship she was promoting. In the world of entrepreneurship, that is the best advice a budding entrepreneur can receive. We hope that many of you have found an entrepreneurial spirit within yourselves, are listening to what your heart is telling you, and are eager to begin what may amount to your single largest project in life.

Chapter 8

————— ❧❧ ❧❧ ❧❧ ❧❧ —————

The Business Ethic

We have taken you on a quick tour through the issues facing you as a start-up college entrepreneur. At this point we have to conclude our manual, and give you a chance to get started. Although there is much more advice we could offer, and many more suggestions we could make, we realize that experience truly is the best teacher.

Before we finish, however, we would like to leave you with some thoughts on the major components of a winning business ethic. In an attempt to draw all of what you have read so far together into a cohesive way of thinking, we must acknowledge the fact that there is no one right way to go about entering the business world. Every person's experience is different. But it isn't enough to have an idea and a goal. One thing every entrepreneur needs is a solid business ethic.

What Is a Business Ethic?

A *business ethic* is an overall frame of mind with which you approach the tasks of starting and running your business. It is sometimes difficult to switch between your college suit and your work suit so many times in a day. (Speaking metaphorically, of course. You have clearly got your business suit hidden away neatly beneath your jeans and sweater—in the style of Superman, or more recently, Arnold Schwarzenegger in *True Lies*.) Between meeting with a study group and making dinner reservations for a date, you may get a phone call from a crucial business contact. It is imperative that you be prepared and know how to switch into and out of business mode easily.

Some would argue that a true entrepreneur is always ready for business. And that is true, to an extent. But we don't believe that you should be an entrepreneur and nothing else. It is far more respectable and impressive when someone can be all things to all people, as need be. So you have to be capable of switching on the business button whenever necessary. At risk of making it sound like a multiple personality thing, you have to be able to jump right into business character—and that means more than just the voice.

This is where the business ethic comes in. There must be some truths which you hold to be self-evident, some ideals you strive to live up to, some set of qualities you believe should characterize your business style—this is your business ethic. Your business ethic is the aura you wish to portray, the qualities you wish to display, and the values you wish to live up to in your business dealings with others. For first-time venturers into the vast world of creative self-employment, we have put together a preliminary list of standard ideals that we believe you should aim to meet. If you believe strongly in the merit of these ideals, and if you train yourself to see successful business as a function of the right mental approach, you will have no problem switching into business mode whenever necessary.

Think of the popular television show *Mr. Rogers' Neighborhood*. Mr. Rogers advocated the use of what he called a thinking cap. A business ethic is sort of like a business cap—but after you use it for a while, it will become instinctive.

Overall, our winning business ethic includes a commitment to building solid relationships, setting feasible goals, being realistic and prudent, and not jumping the gun. Here's our six-point list of the components of a winning business ethic:

1. Patience
2. Integrity
3. Humility
4. Goal setting
5. Realistic expectations
6. Fruitful flexibility

Patience

Whoever coined the proverb "Patience is a virtue" didn't do it just so your parents would have something to say in order to justify putting off buying you a car. He or she had larger, loftier lessons in mind. Patience has gotten a bad rap, as a way to learn to pass the time before things start moving. It has also gained a reputation as a safety blanket under which not-so-motivated/not-so-sure entrepreneurs can hide. Patience should be seen in a positive light, and that is what we hope to instill in you—a true appreciation for the value of patience, and a sense of its merit as a component of your business ethic.

Patience can be defined loosely as the quality of not being hasty or impetuous. Through our definition, patience is seen in a positive light for being the virtue that it is. Patience is about exercising intelligent and informed restraint, not blind and submissive resignation. It is a tolerance for the time required to execute the perfect business transaction. Do not see it as a sign of inner weakness. Nor is it a lack of belief in the inevitability of your own eventual success. Keep in mind that patience is a skill, and that much like the tolerance for spicy food, it can be acquired through practice. The success of even the best entrepreneurial idea depends critically on a healthy dose of patience. Even a so-called overnight success is going to take more than just 24 hours.

Some of the issues you will encounter during the process of starting your own business involve the approval or review of others. For example, when you draft a business plan and send it to potential investors, you will need to wait for them to get back to you. Since your blood, sweat, and tears have gone into getting the proposal just right, you are confident that it is a perfect plan that requires no further explanation or debate. But investors might not immediately see it that way. Just as you have done research in preparing the proposal, they, too, will conduct their own research and implement their own evaluation before coming to a decision. Acting in their own best interests (as everyone does), they cannot take a proposal at the entrepreneur's word. In a case like this, you simply have to be able to wait for a response. The case is the same when waiting for pending patenting, pending acceptance of a contract, and so on.

Waiting for a response can be frustrating if you expect results too quickly. Don't be too hard on yourself. Speak with people in your industry, and get an idea for how quickly you should expect to hear. Ask the investors themselves for an estimated response time. Base your worries on these estimates, and learn to be patient. The world won't stop spinning to attend to your idea, so it helps to be patient.

In a broader sense, be patient for your business to be able to stand on its own two feet. You are taking on the world, you know. Although the task is not impossible, it will take time. And if you believe in patience as a virtue from the start, you will be better off in the process. As a component of your business ethic, patience will help you not to disappoint yourself by expecting too much too soon. While fast and direct success would be ideal, it cannot be expected. Slow and steady will get you there with half the stress.

Integrity

Your reputation is more important than you may realize at first. As the representative of a business enterprise, you must remember that relationships are fragile and depend a lot on trust. Word travels quickly, and even the slightest impropriety will be remembered. Fostering a reputation of integrity from the start is an invaluable component of a strong business ethic. If you play fair from the start, people will notice, and they will be drawn to you.

While we don't want to sound cynical, we hope to convince you of exactly how important your reputation is, and how easily it can be tarnished. People will be much quicker to remember the few mistakes you have made than to sing the praises of your otherwise unblemished career. The good is easier to forget than the bad.

You may think *integrity* is a word that is typically only used in commercials by banks that want to make people feel confident in them. Well, no matter whether you provide flower delivery or outsourced business consulting, you need people to put their faith in you. You develop a solid customer base and assure the loyalty of your consumers by being loyal to them.

Integrity is basically a synonym for honesty. It is a strict and reliable devotion to a code of moral principles. It is about having your word carry weight. If people feel that your honest modus operandi is dependable, they will be more comfortable doing repeat business with you, as well as recommending you to others. Consistency in your method of doing business gains trust and loyalty in business partners, and can be a strategic way to maintain a customer base. When you are good to people, they feel a responsibility toward you. They are less likely to choose competing providers or look elsewhere in the first place.

As a component of your business ethic, integrity has a dual benefit. It gives others faith in your operating style, and it teaches you to live up to their expectations. Take, for example, the idea of reliable consistency in a product. On any given college campus, there are probably a number of coffeehouses. Usually they are situated pretty close together. If you were on the run, and wanted to grab a hazelnut latte to fuel up for a two-hour biochemistry lecture, where would you get it, Starbucks or CafeCaffeine? Clearly, you would opt for the tried-and-true Starbucks over the small-town unknown CafeCaffeine. Why? Because the local place is a gamble. Will they make the hazelnut latte well? Will the cup be burning hot? Do they have convenient sugar packets? Will they have the right kind of hazelnut syrup? Will they be friendly and courteous? All these questions are unnecessary at Starbucks. They have built up a reputation for consistently good hazelnut lattes (according to our standards), and the general public believes that it can rely on the integrity of Starbucks in always offering the same product.

Of course, that is not to imply that only a national chain can develop a reputation for consistency in a product. (But to become a national chain, you must have consistency in your product.) The feeling of integrity demonstrated by a consistently good cup of java can be applied to any business, and includes the reputation for integrity in standards of product, pricing, promptness, friendliness, customer service, and the like.

Please pardon the gratuitously obvious reference to Starbucks, but we are trying to use examples that everyone can relate to. And sadly, coffee is as strong a common ground as can be found among the college population today. But we digress. The point here is that integrity can take many forms. Above all, a reputation for integrity in the way you operate is an important component of your business ethic because it will simultaneously strengthen your client base and establish your name and principles.

Humility

Humility is the quality of being unpretentious, not arrogant or overly proud. Maintaining the appearance of humility convinces everyone around you that you are a real person, conscious of your limits and place. It shows people that you pay them respect and that you do not overstep your boundaries. It also has the added benefit of reminding you of your humble beginnings. When your plans take off, it is tempting to let your ego take off with them. Be wary of this doomed fate. Humility is a good quality to include in your business ethic, because it will keep you from getting so comfortable with your direct route to success that you let go of the steering wheel.

> While you (i.e., your company) are still small, act small. When you get big, still act small.

Maintaining the appearance of humility trains you to see yourself as a small part of something bigger—a cog in the wheel. When the company grows, your arrogance does not grow proportionally. Most CEOs and high-level executives strive not to seem arrogant, since their track records and performance histories speak for themselves. There is no need to sing your own praises; it works much better when you allow people to ask you questions, and let the answers do the impressing.

Take Bill Gates, for example. On any television appearance (and there are few), you will notice that the man is very understated in his demeanor. He is soft-spoken and courteous. He can take a joke and is in no rush to divulge his personal financial information. It is said that he wears jeans to the office. This does not mean that he may not be a shrewd, cutthroat, intelligent businessperson. But he feels no need to prove anything—and neither should you. Humility is not about bowing your head and putting yourself down, it is about being comfortable with yourself and not having anything to prove. If you train yourself to incorporate this virtue into your business ethic, you will be that much better off.

We won't go so far as to say that people want to see you fail, but they will definitely shed fewer tears for a braggart than for a humble guy. You must appreciate the value of people's support and overall interest in your success. Be confident, not cocky. The higher you build your personal pedestal, the less humble you will appear, and the farther you will fall. It is better to have a stool, and friends to help support the legs, than to have a towering pedestal, and no one who cares to catch you if you fall.

Goal Setting

Think about a goal in terms of sports. In a football game, for example, the goal is the terminating point of a play. The team with the most goals wins the game. But in this framework, the goal is more than just where you want to end up, it is a direction to be facing while you are playing the game. It is the finish line toward which your efforts are aimed. But when you ask a pro football player what football is all about, he will not say the touchdown. He will most likely say the game. This is the crucial distinction we believe you should keep in mind when setting goals as an entrepreneur.

It is important to recognize your goal as the intended destination of your efforts. Clearly then, if you fail to set a goal, your efforts will have no direction. Most people are good at setting general goals, and therefore believe they have the necessary skill set. Do not fall into this trap.

Being a successful entrepreneur involves setting concrete and specific goals for yourself. The difference lies between saying generally, "I will expand my marketing tactics," and stating specifically, "I will identify two more local customer pools by next month, and I will advertise in more papers and hand out more flyers until I have doubled my revenues, hopefully by six months from now." If you give yourself specific and reasonable personal due dates and time limits, you are more likely to get things done. You are also likely to set realistic goals, and not stretch yourself. Having only yourself to answer to, you learn how to keep the pressure on yourself. The fear of disappointing yourself can be almost as scary as the fear of disappointing a boss. Being your own boss involves a healthy dose of self-guilt, and setting specific goals gives you concrete measures of your progress.

While setting your goals, it is necessary to recognize the difference between long- and short-term goals, and to address both kinds. Standard economic theory distinguishes between the long- and short-term based on the time it takes a company's level of capital stock to be variable. In the short-term, the level of capital stock is fixed; in the long-term, it is variable. The economics majors among you will be familiar with this idea. But for a start-up entrepreneur, the distinction should be made clear along other lines. Basically, the short-term can be seen as the time before which no formal partnerships or final deals are made. It must be redefined based on each individual project, but intuitively it is the time frame from today to the end of the month.

When you are making plans in the short term, you must concern yourself with near-term events. Short-term goal setting is about organization more than aspirations. Each day should begin with a list of things to achieve, written at bedtime the night before. We cannot emphasize enough the value of lists. It may sound unnecessary, but a to-do list is the best way of getting the most out of your day. Organizing your affairs is quite a task without a secretary, and short-term goal setting is the most efficient way to go about it. Your goal should be to accomplish everything on that list today.

Long-term goal setting is about direction. While you should set specific timelines for the completion of your long-term goals, these should be somewhat flexible. The long-term goal itself is meant as a prize to keep your eyes on. It gives you direction, but it does not mandate your path. It is a finish line to work toward.

Whereas short-term goal setting is about organization, long-term goal setting is more about direction. Both, however, are about accountability. When you are organized and headed in the right direction, and have specific goals to achieve, you generally cannot go wrong.

Realistic Expectations

Whoever said, "Expect the worst, hope for the best," was wrong. It would have been more appropriate to say, "Expect the realistic, hope for the best." We believe there is a fine line between optimism and insanity. Be careful not to cross it. You should aspire to great heights, but not expect too much. Expectation is the beginning of all disappointment—if it is overzealous.

You are not a Bill Gates—yet. You are still in college and have a lot more to think about than just your business. Lacking others' experience, expertise, contacts, and free time does put you at a slight disadvantage. While we have no doubt in your capability to take over the world market eventually, we warn you against expecting it to happen right away.

Take the popular example of daytime cartoon characters Pinky and the Brain. These two cartoon lab mice start out each episode with the same plan. Pinky asks the Brain, "What are we going to do tonight, Brain?" Brain responds, "The same thing we do every night, Pinky—try to take over the world." In each episode these lovable rodents find innovative, creative, sneaky, and sinister ways to take over the world. And each time they fail.

One important difference between these mice and the overzealous entrepreneur is that the mice do not feel the emotional effects. They are cartoons. In the next episode, they simply try again. While we admire their persistence, we must keep in mind that they are insane and are not real. In the real world, they would never have the stamina to try again each night. But in the real world, mice don't speak English and walk upright, either.

We don't want you to have to exercise the same insane persistence as Pinky and the Brain. We want you to succeed, slowly but surely, the first time around. We want you to learn from obstacles as you go along, not from the disappointment of ending up back where you started at the end of each day.

While we understand your excitement and desire to grow your company and have its stock listed on the NYSE overnight, we advocate a more prudent approach. Chances are you will not take over the worldwide pizza delivery market anytime soon. So don't set yourself up for a fall from the height of the unrealistic expectations you are tempted to hold on to. They say that if you aim for the heavens, you will at least land among the stars. We agree that you should aim as high as you can dream. But we hope you don't expect to arrive too quickly.

In trying to train yourself to hold realistic expectations, you must understand that a reality check is essential to your business ethic. For reality training, we advocate the use of the principle of delayed gratification. The idea is basically that if you put off claiming your prize, and work harder to achieve it, instead of pouncing on it instantly, you will appreciate and savor it more when you get it. It isn't that you cannot conquer the world overnight, it is more that you see the merits of a slower, steadier path to success. You choose that path, and thereby limit your expectations by choice to a more manageable level. Your realistic expectations therefore are more like well thought out plans. As a part of your business ethic, the ability to have realistic expectations will not only calm you down, it will also show others that you are an intelligent businessperson, not a money-hungry, naive kid.

Fruitful Flexibility

An entrepreneur is like a chameleon, making its way strategically through the jungle. The chameleon does not automatically change colors to match the environment. Instead, it assesses each situation and decides when it is useful and necessary to change color. This color shift may be in response to a change of background, or it may be in anticipation of a more useful state of color.

Successful entrepreneurs are not simply going to "change colors" for anyone, but are flexible. And when the time is right and the situation calls for it, they are willing to initiate the necessary change. Do not get hung up on a routine, and do not be unwilling to hear new ideas and suggestions. You must change along with the business world you operate in. You must also be able to change the business world for your own good without being pressured by outside forces. Be flexible, not flimsy.

This business ethic of rolling with the punches can also be referred to as productive inconsistency. Successful managers constantly evaluate and reevaluate their own projects, looking for ways to improve them. The saying "If it ain't broke, don't fix it" doesn't carry much weight in the entrepreneurial ethic, because it is up to you to design the perfect product. Realize, however, that you will never have the perfect product. You will always look for ways that it can be improved, refined, and built upon. The end of the process of perfecting a product is like the death of the idea. The excitement of a big project is the challenge of constantly making it better. Call it inconsistency, flexibility, changeability, whatever. The bottom line is that you must be ready, willing, and able to initiate change at the right time.

Questions You Should Ask Yourself

Before you begin your journey, it may be worthwhile to ask yourself a few crucial questions. We have done our best to explain the key business issues to you, and to describe how we feel entrepreneurs would ideally act and see their world. But we can't answer all the questions for you. Take some time to reflect on the following questions before you embark on your journey, in order to get a clearer picture of the path you have chosen:

- How do you measure success?
- Are you prepared to "go it alone"?
- Do your means match your plans?
- What are your priorities?

How Do You Measure Success?

We would all love to make our first $10 million by the time we are 30. Would that figure equal success for you? Would happiness equal success? Do you want to be respected? To make your parents proud? Do you want to pay for your own college education? Do you want to save enough money to Eurorail for six months? Is success a function of receiving a particular award? Of getting into a particular business school? Will you be successful when you sell your thousandth item? Or when your company finally goes public on the stock market? Will you feel successful when there is an article about you in the local newspaper—or in *Money* magazine?

You should figure out exactly what you expect to get out of this business. List all of the components of happiness you hope to derive from this project, and decide if they are good reasons to work so hard, and whether they are strong enough motivators to carry you through the process. Success is a personal feeling of achievement and fulfillment—the idea that your efforts have paid off. Each person has his or her own personal barometer. If what you want is to be famous, your approach to business is going to be quite different than if what you want is to be rich.

Are You Prepared to "Go It Alone"?

❧❧❧❧

> "It is the lone worker who makes the first advance in a subject:
> the details may be worked out by a team, but the prime idea is
> due to the enterprise, thought and perception of an individual."
>
> Sir Alexander Fleming, *Address at Edinburgh University* (1951)

You are a powerful force, and you can move mountains with your determination. We know that one person really can change the world, and we encourage you to give your dream your all. But you must consider very carefully what your life will actually be like in the first few months or even years of your enterprise. When you decide to start a business in college, you will receive the encouragement of your friends and the pride of your parents. But as much as people are interested, you will probably find pretty quickly that they do not have much time to devote to your concerns, or much interest in helping you with the dirty work. Essentially, you will have to go it alone. Are you ready for that?

Visualize yourself working late into the night. Imagine yourself staying in on a Thursday night (or many Thursday nights) so you can wake up in time for an appointment on Friday morning. Picture yourself spending half of your summer working on the business instead of pursuing easier work like friends. How will you feel when you must give up spring break in Cancun with friends for a series of meetings you otherwise don't have time for?

You must be aware that there are many difficulties here. Not only will you be doing the majority of the work by yourself initially, but your lifestyle and mind-set will necessarily change, possibly isolating you from your friends and former interests. We are not trying to imply that you must give up your college life to be an entrepreneur—on the contrary, you can do both. But this substantial undertaking will necessarily have an effect on your interests and personality. Be ready for that change, and for the enormity of the project. Are you prepared to go it alone?

Do Your Means Match Your Plans?

You are obviously ambitious and motivated. Ambition is what this country was founded on. It is the cornerstone of success. But before they built New York City, the pilgrims started a small settlement. And before they went national, the founders of Pepsi tested their product on a smaller market. Like the pilgrims, you should be careful not to overextend yourself. Recognizing your current capacity and limits does not mean you have decided to be small potatoes. It is a sign of your prudence and business acumen. But be careful to have big dreams and realistic plans. Do not confuse the two. You will grow—in time. But Rome wasn't built in a day.

Do your means match your plans financially and emotionally?

■ *Financially.* Do you have the resources to start at the size you are planning? Contemplate your realistic possibilities for funding before making any decisions. Schedule-wise, do you have enough free time to devote to the business? Consider your other time commitments and extracurriculars.

■ *Emotionally.* Do you have the capacity to juggle two lives? Weigh your love of success with your interest in college fun. Be honest with yourself about your capabilities and resources. Do not let your excitement blind you to reality. Be careful and prudent in your decisions. Make sure that your means match your plans.

What Are Your Priorities?

In our efforts to impress upon you the wide ocean of opportunity that is the business world, we have strived to help you understand that you are capable. We hope that you are psyched, and that you are determined to succeed. But in your frenzy to get started we hope that you will be able to take a step back and remind yourself of what is really important. If you are still in college, your grades mean a lot. It is tempting for college entrepreneurs to sacrifice their academics for their businesses. Do not let this happen to you. Before you embark on your entrepreneurial adventure, be sure of where your priorities lie.

If you are still in school, you should remember what you came there for in the first place—to get educated. No matter what becomes of your business, acquiring a fulfilling education is an invaluable rite of passage. By deciding to value your education, you choose to be an educated person. Educated people can be respected, and can respect themselves. And although your business may or may not fail, your education will always be with you—it will be a part of you. Do not lose sight of that.

We encourage you to venture into the business world, but we implore you to keep education as your highest priority. When it begins to call for the sacrifice of your education, a business needs to be put on hold. Your grades should take first priority, and should never suffer on account of business. That way you will have no regrets. If the business fails, you are proud of yourself for having tried, and you haven't lost anything. If your business takes off, you can be even prouder of yourself for having done it all.

You probably cannot answer all of these questions right now. That's okay. You don't have to have all of the answers yet. Otherwise, there would be no exciting journey lying before you, would there? Eventually, however, you will begin formulating answers for these questions and developing systems of operation and motivation that work best for you. The point is that you should always keep mental checks on yourself, to make sure that you are moving in the best direction. These questions will begin to pop up in your own head as you go through the trials and tribulations of the process of starting your own business. And whether you are a college student, a recent college graduate, or a 50-year-old who has had enough of the nine-to-five, you still have a lot to learn about business. There are certain lessons you simply cannot learn except by doing.

We hope you remember these questions, and ask them often. As long as you are honest with yourself, you will probably come out ahead more often than not, and have fun along the way. Being an entrepreneur is serious business, but it should also be fun. Questioning yourself constantly is a surefire way to be ahead of the game. Identifying your own faults before others do is what will keep you evolving toward the successful entrepreneur you want to be.

Conclusion

Well, this is our stop. We seem to have traveled as far as we can with you in our little guide. In our efforts to share what knowledge we have learned about the big bad business world, this guide is a mere token. While the job you have hired us for is essentially over, we hope that our words of advice will linger in your minds and ring true. And your job is only just beginning. We have tried to instill in you the spirit we think defines a successful entrepreneur, and to endow you with the basic business tools we believe you will need. In explaining the intricacies of the financing and marketing issues you will be faced with, we hope we have successfully given you a taste of what is to come. That was our mission.

The book you hold in your hands is the fruit of our own entrepreneurial adventure, and we certainly have learned a lot along the way. We ventured into the publishing world with the vision of showing college students and recent college grads how they, too, could do it. Through the book proposals, the content decisions, the search for the perfect set of contributing writers, the meetings and e-mails, the late-night inspirations, the occasional writer's blocks, the deadline frenzies, the research, the research, and the research, we really did have a blast. Any experience that starts with an idea and ends in an achievement is an exercise in entrepreneurship. We regret that we have but one book to publish right now, and that we have not had the opportunity to go into depth as much as we would have liked.

So as this entrepreneurial exploit of ours draws to a close, it is time to draw that final curtain. Remember that if you can dream it, you can do it. We would not have written this book if we didn't believe in you. Strive for success, however you may define it, and make sure never to look back. Enjoy the ride, because no matter what the outcome,

---

"The reward of a thing well done, is to have done it."

Ralph Waldo Emerson

Good Luck!

Notes

Introduction

Halliday, Lisa (Ed.). (1997). *The Unofficial Guide to Life at Harvard.* (Cambridge, MA: Harvard Student Agencies, Inc.) 62.

Beck, Susan. (1998, March). "Students as Investments: Professors Get their Shares." *Inc. Magazine*, 52.

Stewart, Tracy (Asst. Ed.). (1997). *The Handbook for Students.* (Cambridge, MA: The Office of the Registrar, Harvard Univ.) 294–323, 430–437.

Chapter 2   Marketing Your Product

Kotler, Philip. (1997). *Marketing Management: Analysis, Planning, Implementation, and Control.* (9th ed.). (Upper Saddle River, NJ: Prentice Hall).

Beemer, Britt (with Robert L. Shook). (1998). *Predatory Marketing: What Everyone in Business Needs to Know to Win Today's Consumer.* (New York: Broadway Books).

Small Business Computing & Communications. (June, 1998). Coca-Cola Bottling Co. *Consolidated 1994 Annual Report*, Charlotte, NC.

Levison, Jay, and Seth Gooden. (1993). *Guerrilla Marketing.* (Boston, MA: Houghton Mifflin Co.).

NTC Business Books. (1993). *Putting It All Together and Making It Work.* (Lincolnwood, IL: NTC Business Books). 12–13.

Body Shop Annual Report. (1997).

Starbucks Corporation Annual Report. (1997).

Chapter 3   Financing Your Dream

Benjamin, Gerald A., and Joel Margulis. (1996). *Finding Your Wings: How to Locate Private Investors to Fund Your Venture.* (New York: John Wiley & Sons).

Fraser, Jill Andresky. (1998). "How to Finance Anything." *Inc.* (February). 34–42.

Grover, Mary Beth. (1998). "Go Ahead: Buy the Dream." *Forbes* (June 15). 146–152.

Gladstone, David. (1988). *Venture Capital Handbook.* (Englewood Cliffs, NJ: Prentice Hall).

Gruner, Stephanie. (1998). "The Trouble with Angels." *Inc.* (February). 47–49.

Hise, Phaedra. (1998). "Don't Start a Business without One." *Inc.* (February). 50–53.

Kaufman, Jonathan. (1998). "An Aspiring Game Mogul Finds a Boss's Life 'Weird.' " *Wall Street Journal* (June 18).

Mandell, Mel. (1989). "High-Tech Guru Steven Burill: On High-Tech Start-Ups." *High Technology Business* (November).

Selz, Michael. (1998). "Anyone Need Cash?" *Wall Street Journal* (May 21). R14.

PriceWaterhouse. (1998). "Something Ventured, Something Gained." *Business Week* (June 15). 6.

Wetzel, William E., Jr. (1997). "Venture Capital." *The Portable MBA in Entrepreneurship.* (New York: John Wiley & Sons).

National Association of Small Business Investment Companies (NASBIC). 1156 15th St., Suite 1101, Washington, D.C. 20005. (202) 833-8230.

National Venture Capital Association. 1655 North Fort Meyer Dr., Suite 700, Arlington, VA 22209. (703) 528-4370.

Chapter 5 The Importance of Industry

Abrams, Rhonda M. (1993). *The Successful Business Plan: Secrets and Strategies.* (Great Pass, OR: Oasis Press).

Adams, Bob. (1996). *Adams Streetwise Small Business Start-Up.* (Holbrook, MA: Adams Media Corporation).

Allen, Kathleen, and Courtney Price. (1998). *Tips & Traps for Entrepreneurs.* (New York: McGraw Hill).

Celente, Gerald. (1997). *Trends 2000.* (New York: Warner Books).

Dent, Harry S. (1993). *The Great Boom Ahead.* (New York: Hyperion).

Kahaner, Larry. (1996). *Competitive Intelligence.* (New York: Kane Associates International, Inc.).

Mancuso, Joseph R. (1996). *Mancuso's Small Business Resource Guide.* (Naperville, IL: Small Business Sourcebooks).

Taylor, Don, and Jeanne Smulling Archer. (1994). *Up Against the Wal-Marts.* (Boston, MA: Amacon).

U.S. Bureau of Labor Statistics. (1989). *Annual Surveys.*

Index

ABC TV, 66
Abrams, Rhonda M., 152, 153, 155, 156, 161, 165, 248
Actuality Systems, Inc., 219–221
Adams, Bob, 158
Advanced Micro Devices (AMD), 214
Advice/help, professional, 52, 94, 113, 121, 167
Aikido leadership, 34
ALCAS Corp., 8
Allen, Kathleen, 154, 155, 166, 169
Alliances, 107–108
American Demographics Magazine, 167
American Express Small Business Services, 83
American Forecaster Newsletter, 167
American Health and Beauty Aids Institute, 2
American Statistics Index (ASI), 164
Andreessen, Marc, 91
Angel investors, 84, 99–104
Anheuser-Busch, 162
Arthur Andersen's Enterprise Group, 83
Artisoft, Inc., 225
Ascend Communications, 220
Au Bon Pain, 8, 22

Baby boomers, and economic predictions, 170–172
Bacque, Steve, 8
Balance sheet, 145, 147
Band of Angels, 100
Bank loans, 109–111
Barksdale, James, 91
Barriers to entry, 153–154
Barrus, John, 224
Beemers, Britt, 60
Benjamin, Gerald, 100, 101, 102, 103
Berkus Technology Ventures, 100

BFGoodrich Collegiate Investors Program, 220
Bierce, Ambrose, 23
Bindi, 17
Biochemistry, 227–230
Biotechnology, 169
Birthrates, year-to-year, 170
Bloomberg, Mike, 31
Bloomingdale's, 8
Body Shop, The, 76, 77
Boston Chicken, 8
Boston Federal Reserve Bank, 8
Bourne, Randolphe, 37
Brew Moon, 8
Brodsky, Norm, 72
Brown, Gibbons, Land, and Company, 82
Bunche, Ralph, 20
Burrill, Steven, 81
Business, starting your own:
    entrepreneurial qualities (*see* Entrepreneur(s))
    financing (*see* Financing)
    industry research (*see* Industry research)
    marketing (*see* Marketing)
    planning (*see* Business plan)
    protecting yourself (*see* Legal protection)
Business ethic, 14, 234–246
    components of, 235
    defined, 234
    goal setting, 239–240
    questions to ask yourself, 242
    success, measuring, 242
Business Newsbank, 62
Business plan, 13, 113–149
    and business secrets, 120
    and financial funding, 111, 115–116
    goals of, 115–117

Business plan (*Continued*)
  as map for early years, 116–117
  marketing (*see* Marketing plan)
  need for sound research and
    assumptions, 117
  outside help with, 121
  production quality
    (font/paper/binding), 121
  professional *vs.* academic writing,
    118
  protecting yourself, 120
  software, 119
  statistical evidence for predictions,
    118–119
  technology, 119
  tips on writing, 118–121
  using Internet, 121
Business plan contents/elements
    (descriptions/samples), 122–146
  business identification statement,
    127–129
  competition overview, 142–145
  confidentiality statement, 123–124
  cover letter, 122–123
  description of products and
    services, 135–140
  executive summary, 125–127
  financial projections, 146, 147, 148,
    149
  management and personnel list,
    129–132
  marketing strategy, 140–142
  market research, 132–135
  table of contents, 125
  title page, 124
Business trends, and marketing,
    60–61
Business Week, 61, 92

Cabbage Patch Kids, 17
CafeCaffeine, 237
Caffery, Michael E., 73
California, University of, at Irvine
    (Small Business Development
    Center), 100
Cambridge Computer Services, Inc.,
    216–219

Carey, Pat, 69
Carlson, Kevin, 83, 204–206
Cash flow statement, 145, 149
Cassidy, Mike, 224
Celente, Gerald, 169
CENA. *See* Center for Entrepreneurial
    Activities (CENA)
Cendata, 164, 166
Census Bureau, 164, 166
Center for Entrepreneurial Activities
    (CENA), 168
CG & Associates, 8
Chang, Steven, 13
Chao, Wellie, 206–209
ChemDraw, 228
Chip Shot Golf, 221–224
Chuang, John, 83, 209–213
Coca-Cola, 69, 211
Communication(s), 57–58, 61, 78, 170
Competitors/competitive intelligence,
    158–167. *See also* Industry research
  collecting information, 160–161
  example of competitive intelligence
    at work (Coors/Anheuser-
    Busch), 162
  information *vs.* intelligence,
    158–159
  interpreting information, 161–162
  magazine names, and trends,
    162–163
  in marketing plan, 78
  newsletter titles, 163–164
  overview, in business plan, 142–145
  reasons for, 159–160
  sources, 161, 164–167
  trends, and marketing, 60
Compromise, 25
Computer magazine, 119
Confidentiality statement, in business
    plan, 123–124
Connections, using, 50
Consumer trends, and marketing, 60
Convenience, trend toward, 171
Coolidge, Calvin, 36
Coors beer, 162
Copyrights, 194–195
Corel Paradox, 69

Corporate incubators, 108
Corporation, 189–192, 193
Countercyclical industry, 152
Credit cards, financing business with, 106–107
Crimson Solutions, Inc., 206–209
C's, four. See Four C's
Customer strategy, 56–58, 67–69, 73, 75–76
CyberSource, 71
Cycle, business, 152

Damman, Gregory, 187
Database management software programs, 69
Decline phase, industry, 155, 156
Dell, Michael (Dell Computers), 216, 233
Delta, 71
Dent, Harry S., 156, 169, 171
Design patents, 196
Desktop Data, Inc., 8
Developing phase, industry life cycle, 155
Development stages (business), and venture capital, 87–89
Dham, Vinod, 214
Dial-A-Fish, 224
Digital revolution, future of, 170
Direct Data, 224
Direct marketing, 70–73
Directory of Angel Investors, 101
dismal.com, 168
Distribution, 69–70, 79, 154–155
Do It Yourself Incorporation (E-Z Legal Books), 190
Domino's Pizza, 156–157
Dow Jones News Retrieval Service, 166
Draper Labs, 204
Duckett, Ngina, 5, 12
Due diligence, 97
Duluk, Jerome, Jr., 82
Dun & Bradstreet, 167, 168

Eastern Delta Corporation, 220
e-commerce, 71

Economics, fundamentals of, 172–173
Economist, The, 59
Edison, Thomas, 90, 168
Education as priority, 244
Emerson, Ralph Waldo, 246
Emotional readiness, 244
Employee stock ownership plan (ESOP), 108–109
Employee stock ownership trust (ESOT), 99
Encyclopedia of Associations, Gale's, 165
Encyclopedia of Business Information Sources, 165
Enron, 9
Entrepreneur, 61
Entrepreneur(s), 12, 16–53
  vs. businessperson, 32
  and ideas, 41–47, 49
  qualities of, 12, 16–41
Entrepreneur(s), myths about, 47–49
  age, 47
  family, 49
  gender, 48
  good idea sufficient, 49
  success chances, 47–48
  superhumanness, 48–49
Entrepreneurial dos/don'ts, 50–52
  advice/criticism, 52
  connections, 50
  friendship, 51
  honesty, 51
  partner selection, 50–51
  persistence, 52
  verbal contracts, 51
Entrepreneurial Edge magazine, 168
Environmental Protection Agency, 162
Environmental regulations, 153
Ernst & Young, High Technology Group, 81
Eslick, Ian, 83, 213–216
Ethic, business. See Business ethic
Excite (search engine), 168
Executive summary (in business plan), 125–127
Exit strategies, 92–93, 98–99
Expansion financing, 88
Exports/imports, 173

Fads, 162
Fadule, Jill, 8
Family financing. *See* Angel investors
Farmer, Jacob, 216–219
Favalora, Gregg, 219–221
Federal Communications Commission, 160
Feiner, Eliot, 8
Financial projections (in business plan), 146, 147, 148, 149
Financial Times, The, 59
Financing, 13, 81–112
  alternative, 104–109
  angel investors, 99–104
  bank loans, 109–111
  "beg, borrow, or steal," 104–106
  business plan for, 115–116
  with credit cards, 106–107
  employee stock ownership plan (ESOP), 108–109
  franchising, 108
  incubators, 108
  joint ventures or strategic alliances, 107–108
  lease, 108
  management buyouts, 108–109
  and objectives, 93–94
  R&D arrangements/limited partnerships, 108
  readiness for, 244
  Small Business Administration (SBA) loans, 111–112
  venture capitalists, 83–99 (*see also* Venture capital/capitalists)
Finding Your Wings (Benjamin & Margulis), 100, 103
First, Tom, 8
Fishman, Stephen, 194
Fleming, Sir Alexander, 243
Focus groups, 63
Folio, 163
Food and Drug Administration, 160
Forbes, 61, 101
Fortune, 61
Four C's:
  capabilities/capital/community/contacts, 210

customer/communication/cost/convenience, 57
Four P's (product/promotion/price/place), 57
Franchising, 108
Fraser, Jill Andresky, 82
Freedom of Information Act (FOIA), 160
FreeLoader, 66, 69, 70
French, Robert, 213
Friendship, 50, 51, 105

Galante's Complete Venture Capital and Private Equity Directory, 95
Gale Research Company, 165
Gambling, 23–24
Gap, The (and Gap to Go), 60
Gaston, Robert J., 100
Gates, Bill, 1, 3, 24, 49, 114, 238, 240
Gaugh, Bob, 8
Gender, 48, 101
General Business File, 62
General partnership, 181–184, 185
Generation X'ers (number of), 172
Giovinco, Mike, 220
Gladstone, David, 86, 88, 97
Goel, Amar, 221–224
Gold cards, 75
Goldman Sachs, 223
Goodin, Seth, 70
Grant Thronton LLP, 82
Gross domestic product (GDP), 173
Grover, Mary Beth, 101, 108
Growth financing, 88–89
Growth opportunity, 92
Gruner, Stephanie, 100, 103
Guerrilla marketing, 70, 75
Guide to New Magazines, 163

Haagen-Dazs, 172
Halliday, Lisa, 4
Harrison, Lee Hecht, 8
Hart, Myra, 8
Harvard Entrepreneurs Club (HEC), 4–9
Harvard Pilgrim Health Care, 9
Harvard Political Review, 209, 211

Harvard Student Agencies (HSA), 2,
11–12, 229
Harvard student entrepreneurs
(success stories), 206, 209, 220,
221, 227, 230
Health and fitness industry, 171
Hirshberg, Gary, 8
Hise, Phaedra, 83, 109
Holly, Krisztina, 83, 224–227
Home business, 169
Honesty, 28, 51
Hotwired magazine, 69, 70
H.S. *Dent Forecast*, 167
Hugo, Victor, 41
Husni, Samir, 163

IBM, 71
iCat, 71
ICN Pharmaceuticals, 9
ICR. *See* International Capital
Resources (ICR)
Idea(s):
attachment to (*vs.* potential), 117
hunt for perfect, 41–47
increasing proneness to, 43–44
myth that good idea is enough, 49
tactics (inside-out/outside-in), 42, 43
types of (service/product/
technology), 45–46
Illinois, University of, 229
Imagineering, 39
Imports/exports, 173
Inc. magazine, 2, 8, 58, 61, 72, 82, 103,
107
Incubators, 108
Indiglo, 220
Industry life cycle (four stages),
155–156
Industry research, 13–14, 150–175
barriers to entry, 153–154
competitive intelligence (*see*
Competitors/competitive
intelligence)
cycle-sensitive/countercyclical,
152
definition, 152
innovation, 154

leaders/giants, 156–158
learning from others'
success/failure, 158
predictability (and Baby Boomers),
170–172
readiness quiz, 174
regulations, 153
seasonality, 153
supply/distribution, 154–155
technology, 154
unpredictability, 155–156
Inflation, 173
Information:
collecting, 160–161
vs. intelligence, 158–159
interpreting, 161–162
primary/secondary sources, 160
Initial public offering (IPO), 85, 88, 98
Initiative for a Competitive Inner City,
59
Innovativeness, industry, 154
Inside-out tactic, 42
Intel, 214
Interactive media, 66
International Capital Resources (ICR),
101, 102
Internet, 58, 62–63, 70, 71, 119, 121,
165–166, 167–170
basic ingredients of, 168
competitive information source,
167–170
groups to join, 165–166
market research, 62–63
online commerce/marketing, 58, 70,
71
Interstate Commerce Commission, 160
Interviews, in market research, 63
Int'l Corp. Resources, 101
Investext, 166
Iowa, University of, 2
Itagaki, Mike, 227–230

Jamba Juice, 108
Japanese car companies, 159
Joint ventures or strategic alliances,
107–108
Jordan, Michael, 72

Kahaner, Larry, 158, 162
Kane, Louis, 8, 22
Kanter, Joshua (Kanter Painting),
    230–232
Kapner, Steve, 209
Kimberlyte, Inc., 227–230
Kindlmann, Peter, 220
Kinloch, Cameron, 5
Kmart, 58, 65
Kotler, Philip, 54
Kwestel, Mendy, 82

Laine, Erick J., 8
Laser Design, 209
Lauterborn's Four C's, 57
Lawyers as information sources, 166
Leaders, industry, 156–157
Leadership, 32–35, 41
    aikido, 34
    available/accessible, 33–34
    example, 33
    recognizing coworkers, 34
    team, 33
Lease financing, 108
Legal description, in business plan,
    127
Legal protection, 106, 176–202
    and angel investing, 106
    copyrights, 194–195
    liabiliity (see Legal structure options)
    ownership (see Legal structure
        options)
    patents, 195–197
    registration (state-by-state list,
        contact information,
        Secretaries of State), 198–202
    taxation (see Legal structure
        options)
    with venture capitalists, closing,
        97–98
Legal structure options, 14, 177–193
    corporation, 189–192
    general partnership, 181–184
    limited liability company (LLC),
        186–189
    limited partnership, 108, 184–186

S corporation, 192–193
    sole proprietorship, 178–181
Levinson, Jay, 70
LEXIS, 166
Liability issues, 176–202
    general partnership, 182–183
    limited liability company (LLC),
        188–189
    sole proprietorship, 179–180
Library, local, 164
Life cycle, industry (four stages),
    155–156
Life cycle hypothesis, 171
Limited liability company (LLC),
    186–189
Limited partnership, 108, 184–186
Lippman, Walter, 35
Little Bear Organic Foods, 65
Livelli, Thomas, Sr., 8
Loans, 109–112
Lotus Approach, 69
Loyalty, customer, 57

MacTemps, 209–213
Madonna, 19
Magazines, 74, 160, 161, 162–163
Mailboxes, Etc., 216
Mailing lists, 63
Mail order/marketing, 70, 72
Management buyouts, 108–109
Management team, 90–91, 120,
    129–132
Mancuso, Joseph R., 163, 164
Mandell, Mel, 1989, 81
Margulis, Joel, 100, 101, 102, 103
Mark, Rebecca, 9
Marketing, 12–13, 54–80
    in business plan, 132–135,
        140–142
    customer relationships, 56–58,
        67–69
    distribution plan, 56, 69–70
    networking, 58–59
    segmenting market, 55, 64–65
    strategy, 54–56, 61–70
    and trends, 59–61

unique selling proposition (USP),
    55–56, 65–67
Marketing methods, 67, 70–76
  customer (making feel special),
    73–76
  customer word of mouth, 73–74
  direct, 70–73
  guerrilla, 75
  press release, 74–75
Marketing plan, 76–80
  components of, 76–80
  mission statement, 76–77
  objectives, 78
  overall strategy, 78–80
  situation analysis, 77–78
Market research, 55, 62–64, 132–135
Massachusetts Institute of
    Technology, 213, 220, 224, 225
Mass marketing, shift away from, 66
Maxwell Online Information on
    Demand database, 166
McDonough, William, 8
McKinsey, 224
McLagan, Don, 8
Mencken, H. L., 24
Mentoring programs, 59
Micros Access, 69
Microsoft, 63, 71, 157
Minute Maid, 211
Mirsky, Ethan, 213
Mission statements:
  Body Shop, The, 76, 77
  Harvard Entrepreneurs Club, 4–5
  in marketing plan, 76–77
  Starbucks, 76, 77
Money magazine, 242
Moody's, 62
Morby, Jacqueline, 8
Morse, Allen, 9

Nantucket Allserve/Nantucket
    Nectars, 8, 69
NASDAQ, 98
National Association of Small
    Business Investment Companies
    (NASBIC), 95

National Association of Women
    Business Owners (NAWBO), 59
National Foundation for Women
    Business Owners, 58
National Venture Capital Association
    (NVCA), 95
Nations Business, 61
Negotiation/compromise, 25–27, 41
Netscape Communications, 91
Networking, 58–59
Newsletter(s), 72, 163–164
Newsletter on Newsletters, 163
Newsletter Publishers Association, 163
Newsletters-In-Print, 164
Newspapers, 161
New York Stock Exchange, 98, 241
New York Times, 61
NEXIS/NEXIS EXPRESS, 166
Nguyen, Eric, 5
Nike, 157
No Doubt (band), 17
Northeastern University, 204, 206

Objectives, 78, 93–94
Online information/marketing. See
    Internet
Outdoors, trend toward, 171–172
Outside-in tactic, 43
Ownership issues. See Legal structure
    options
Oxbridge Directory of Newsletters, 164

Painting company, 230–232
Panic, Milan, 9
Paradigm Business Solutions (PBS), 204
Paradigm Medical Information
    Solutions (PMIS), 204–206
Park, David, 5
Partnerships:
  and friendship, 50–51
  general, 181–184, 185
  limited, 108, 184–186
Patent It Yourself (Pressman), 197
Patents, 195–197
Pentium, "father of," 214
Pepsi, 243

Perrault, Anthony, 13
Perron, Kirk, 108
Picasso, Pablo, 32
Place (in 4 Ps), customer convenience
    vs., 58
Plans. See Business plan; Marketing
    plan
Plant patents, 196
Pratt's Guide to Venture Capital Sources, 95
Predicasts S & F Forecasts, 165
Pressman, David, 198
Press releases, 74–75
Price, Courtney, 154, 166, 248
Pricing, 58, 64–65, 79
Problem-solving skills, 22–23, 41
Product(s)/services:
    vs. customer needs, 57
    description of (in business plan),
        135–140
    idea types, 45–46
    venture capitalists looking for
        unique, 91–92
Profit and loss statement, 145, 148
Proliferation phase, industry, 155
Promotion. See Marketing
Protecting yourself. See Legal
    protection
P's, four (product/promotion
    /price/place), 57
Public, going. See Initial public
    offering (IPO)
Public domain information, 160

Questionnaires, in market research,
    63–64

Radcliffe College, 10, 11
Raycer Graphics, 82
R&D arrangements/limited
    partnerships, 108
Real estate, and baby boomers, 172
Regulations, 9–12, 78, 153
Relationship marketing, 57
Research, 152
    companies, 167
    industry (see Industry research)
    market (see Market research)

Resilience, 29–30, 41
Return on investment (ROI), 85
    needed by venture capitalists
        (Table 3.1), 86
Risk taking, calculated, 23–24, 41
Robert Morris and Associates, 167
Rupani, Reena N., 5
Ryan, Rob, 220

Saks Fifth Avenue, 65
Sale of company to another company,
    99
Samuel, Shawn, 220
SBICs. See Small business investment
    companies (SBICs)
Schullen, Robert, 38
Schwarting, Carsten, 5, 14
Schwarzenegger, Arnold, 234
SCORE. See Service Corps of Retired
    Executives (SCORE)
S corporation, 192–193
Scott, Tom, 8
Search engines, 168
Seasonality, 153
Secretaries of State, 187, 198–202
Securities and Exchange Commission
    (SEC), 98, 160
Seed money, 87
Segmenting market, 55, 64–65
Selz, Michael, 1998, 82
Service (type of idea), 45–46
Service Corps of Retired Executives
    (SCORE), 111
Sharma, Poonam, 0.7–0.8, 5, 12, 14
Silicon Spice, 213–216
Situation analysis, in marketing plan,
    77–78
Skytel, 65
Small Business Administration (SBA),
    84, 100, 111–112, 165
Small Business Computing and
    Communications, 69
Small Business Development Centers
    (SBDCs), 59, 111, 165
Small business investment companies
    (SBICs), 84, 95, 112
Small Business Report, 61

Small Business Sourcebook, 165
Software, business, 69, 70, 119
Sole proprietorship, 178 181
Solicitation, university regulations
    about, 10–11
Spreadsheets, 119
Sprint Corporation, 67
Stable phase, industry, 155–156
Standard & Poor's Industry Surveys, 165
Standard & Poor's Register, 62
Staples, 8
Starbucks, 69, 237, 238
    mission statement, 76, 77
State requirements, filing articles of
    organization, 188
    contact information (state-by-state
        list, Secretaries of State),
        198–202
Statistical evidence, basing
    predictions on, 118–119
Stevenson, Burtin, 38
Stock purchase by
    company/entrepreneur, 98–99
Stone, Gregory, 11
Stoneybrook Farms Yogurt, 74
Stonyfield Farm Yogurt, 8
Strategic thinking, 40–41
Strategy, marketing. *See* Marketing,
    strategy
Stress management, 35 36, 41
Stylus Innovation, Inc., 224–227
Success:
    learning from others', 158
    measuring, 242
    personal stories of, 14, 203–233
    rates, 47–48, 117
Supply. *See* Distribution

TA Associates, 8
Taxation:
    corporations, 192
    general partnership, 183
    limited liability company (LLC), 189
    S corporation, 192–193
    sole proprietorship, 180
Team leadership, 33
Technology, 46, 119, 120, 154

Telecom, 65
Telecommunications, 170
Telemarketing, 71–72
Time management, 18–19, 40
Toys "R" Us, 17
Trade (exports/imports), 173
Trademarks, 66
Training/development, 169
Traub, Marvin, 8
Trends, 59–61, 151, 152, 161–162
    business, 60–61
    communication, 61
    competitor, 60
    consumer, 60
    and marketing, 59–61
Troisi, Angelo, 8
Trump, Donald, 29
Tseng, Greg, 5, 14
Turlais, John, 13

Unemployment, 173
Uniform Partnership Act, 181, 184
Unique selling proposition (USP),
    55–56, 65–67
University:
    courses/programs in
        entrepreneurship, 2
    incubators, 108
    regulations, and entrepreneurs,
        9–12
University Computers, 216
University Painters, 230
U.S. Department of Commerce, 164,
    166, 182
U.S. Department of Labor, 166
U.S. Industrial Outlook, 164
Utility patents, 196

Venture capital/capitalists, 83–99
    vs. angel investors, 101–103
    and business plan, 114
    criteria sought by, 89–93
    defined, 83–84
    due diligence, 97
    exit strategies for, 92–93, 98–99
    goals of, 85–87
    and growth opportunity, 92

Venture capital/capitalists (*Continued*)
  and management, 90–91
  process involving, 95–98
  professional advice from, 94
  return on investment needed by
    (Table 3.1), 86
  and stages of development, 87–89
  two forms (leveraged and equity), 84
  and unique product/service, 91–92
Verbal contracts, 28, 51
Virtual shopping, 169
Vision, in the business plan, 116
Vogelgesang, Bill, 82

Wall Street Journal, 61, 81, 102
Wal-Mart, 157

Washington University Hatchery, 2
Web sites. *See* Internet
Wenjen, Mia, 209
"Women on Their Way" program, 71
Women-owned business, 58
Word-of-mouth marketing, 73–74
World Future Society, 167
Writing style, business *vs.* academic,
  118
Wysocki, Patricia, 163

Yahoo!, 168
Yale University, 216, 219